TEXAS
THE BEAUTIFUL
COOKBOOK

AUTHENTIC RECIPES FROM THE REGIONS OF TEXAS

*Left to right: Aguas Frescas (recipe page 45), Summer Green Beans and Tomatoes
(recipe page 195), Shrimp with Pumpkin Seed Sauce (recipe page 122)*

AUTHENTIC RECIPES FROM THE REGIONS OF TEXAS

TEXAS
THE BEAUTIFUL COOKBOOK

RECIPES BY
PATSY SWENDSON

TEXT BY
JUNE HAYES

FOOD PHOTOGRAPHY BY
E. JANE ARMSTRONG

HarperCollinsPublishers

First published in USA 1995
by Collins Publishers San Francisco.
Reprinted 1998.
Produced by Weldon Owen Inc.
814 Montgomery Street
San Francisco, CA 94133 USA
Phone (415) 291-0100   Fax (415) 291-8841

Weldon Owen Inc.:
Chairman: Kevin Weldon
President: John Owen
General Manager: Stuart Laurence
Co-Editions Director: Derek Barton
Associate Publisher: Anne Dickerson
Project Manager: Judith Dunham
Assistant Editor: Jan Hughes
Copy Editor: Sharon Silva
Proofreader: Sharilyn Hovind
Recipe Tester: Peggy Fallon
Production: Stephanie Sherman
Co-Editions Production Manager (US): Tarji Mickelson
Design: Tom Morgan, Blue Design
Design Assistant: Jennifer Petersen
Design Concept: John Bull, The Book Design Company
Map: Kenn Backhaus
Illustrations: Diana Reiss-Koncar
Index: Ken Dellapenta
Food Stylists: Diana Isaiou, Patty Whittmann
Photography Assistants: Greg DeBoer, Matt Pugsley

The Library of Congress has catalogued the hardcover
edition as follows:
Swendson, Patsy.
    Texas, the beautiful cookbook : authentic
    recipes from the regions of Texas / recipes by
    Patsy Swendson ; text by June Hayes ; food
    photography by E. Jane Armstrong.
        p.   cm.
    ISBN 0-00-225035-7
        1. Cookery. American—Southwestern
        style. 2. Cookery—Texas.
    I. Hayes, June. II. Title.
    TX715.2.S69S83   1995
    641.59764—dc20   94-45573
                                       CIP
    ISBN 0-06-757596-X (pbk.)

Printed by Toppan in China

A Weldon Owen Production

*Endpapers: Rodeos, a year-round sport in Texas, began in the
1800s with informal riding and roping contests.*

*Pages 2–3: The moss-laden cypress trees and swampy lakes
of Martin Dies Jr. State Park typify the area known as the
Piney Woods.*

*Right: Horse drives through the Guadalupe Mountains
perpetuate the traditions and myths of the Texas cowboy.*

Pages 8–9: Chicken Fajitas with Guacamole (recipe page 127)

*Pages 10–11: The beaches of South Padre Island gently
sloping to the sea are one of the strongest tourist magnets
of Texas.*

*Pages 14–15: Dallas, which began in 1840 as a single log
cabin, is now a cosmopolitan city sharing with nearby Fort
Worth the third-busiest airport in the world.*

Clockwise from top left: Texas Corn Bread (recipe page 85), Mixed Grilled Vegetables with Chimichurri Sauce (recipe page 126), Texas Rib-eye with Fresh Herb Marinade (recipe page 161)

CONTENTS

The "lone star" proudly displayed on the Texas flag is testimony to the state's nine years as an independent republic in the mid-1800s.

INTRODUCTION

The tastes of Texas are as varied as the people who prepare the dishes associated with the regions of the vast Lone Star State. More than two hundred years of independent thinking have produced a fierce regional pride that is as ingrained as the dust of cattle trails. Today, Texans are as international in their approach to cuisine as they are in their business dealings. Diners may choose a formal restaurant with a national reputation or a tiny two-table barbecue shack. Texas *is* a state apart, and it has inspired the imaginations of everyone who has settled here.

The land draws people from Europe, the Far East and Mexico, just as it did in early times. The only state to have seen six different flags fly in its history, Texas was molded primarily by the Spanish, French, Mexicans and Germans who early on established the soul of the state, a soul that has become a symbol for hospitality. It is no wonder that people from other countries are comfortable here, for pockets of Old World traditions and foods remain strong influences even today.

Some families in the Fredericksburg and New Braunfels areas speak pure High German and keep alive the proud legacy of the Prussian princes who settled the areas in the mid-1800s. Other concentrations of German and Polish descendants exist, as do pockets of French, Italians, Canary Islanders and Czechs. The people of China, Vietnam, Latin America, the Caribbean, Japan, Korea, the Philippines and India are sharing their customs and cuisines as twentieth-century settlers in the "new world" of Texas. Add to this diverse international background the determination of American settlers, the boldness of early heroes and the farsightedness of early ranchers, farmers, politicians and plantation owners, and the result is the Texas of today. Texans embody the spirits of the Native Americans who staunchly defended the land, the armor-clad Spaniards who searched in vain for gold and silver, the Prussian immigrants who sought to establish new kingdoms abroad, and countless other nationalities.

The conquistadors brought with them the horse, which forever changed the way the Plains Indians lived, particularly the way they hunted for food. They came in search of gold; instead they found amethyst, cinnabar, granite, topaz and agate, resources of great beauty that are seen today in the architecture around the state. An astonishing number of prehistoric and Native American artifacts excite contemporary prospectors and provide insight into the cooking utensils and foods that early people used.

The citizens of Texas are proud of the role that their state has played in history and are prone to tell anyone who will listen about the adventures of the last two hundred years. There also is widespread pride in the monumental nature of the state, with its two time zones, three distinct climates, 624 miles (one thousand kilometers) of coastline and ninety mountains more than one mile above sea level. Over three hundred thousand miles

The seemingly endless vista from the Chisos Mountains in Big Bend National Park provides a stunning backdrop for the vibrant flowers of the claret cup cactus.

(five hundred thousand kilometers) of roadway extend from the High Plains of the Panhandle to the heartland, south through the Rio Grande Valley to old Mexico, and across to the Trans-Pecos region, the "Gateway to the West." But Texans are secure in the knowledge that their highly individualized approach to living—their zest for large homes, opulent offices and huge parties—has been influenced by all the people who came before them, especially their neighbor to the south, Mexico.

The menus at Texas gatherings are a celebration of life—past, present and future. Texas cuisine remains true to old-time ranch and Mexican-inspired favorites. Mountains of tortillas, salsa and beans are served with German-based potato or cabbage salads at traditional barbecues in true cattle-baron style, whether on a backyard patio or on one of the many working ranches. But cooks also embrace new influences from the far corners of the globe, and even casual meals may include foods laced with Chinese or Caribbean seasonings alongside the tried-and-true basics. Everything is presented with a casual graciousness that reflects the state's southern plantation connections, and is served with the best of the Lone Star beers and Lone Star wines.

To understand the Texas food trends of today, one must look back to the foods of yesterday. Although some of the recipes in this volume have catchy titles and innovative seasonings, many of the basic ingredients remain the same as in the past. Beef, pork and chicken, potatoes, cabbage, corn, okra, greens and tomatoes, tortillas and rib-sticking breads, and pecans, apples and peaches are just as popular as they were two hundred

Locals enjoy the refreshing water of the Comal River near New Braunfels in Texas's Hill Country.

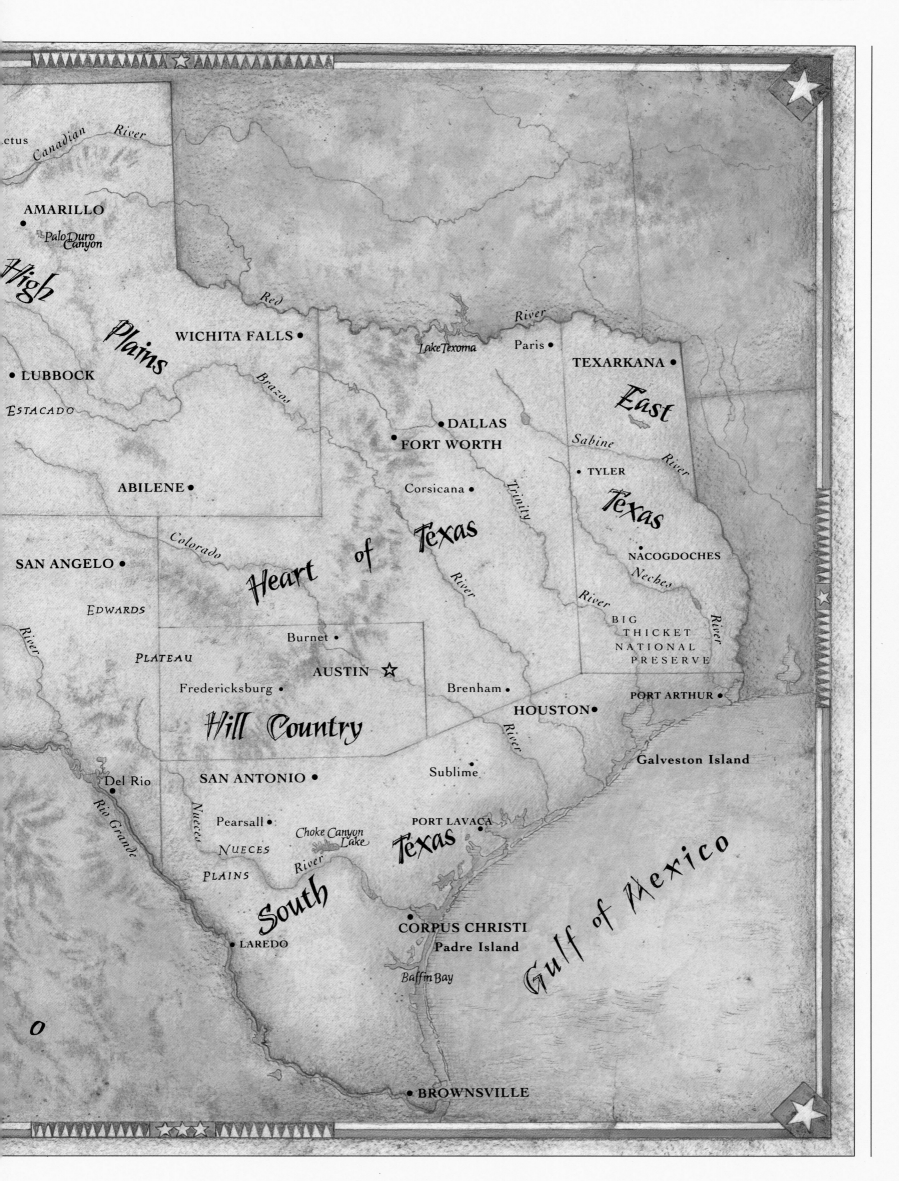

years ago. There are chicken-fried steaks, the cowboy adaptation of the German *wienerschnitzel* and the ever-present barbecue, beans, chili and Tex-Mex dishes, the foundation of traditional Texas eating habits.

Recent Asian immigrants, most of whom have settled in Houston and the Coastal Plains region of the state, provide inspiration for the continued evolution and refinement of Texas cuisine. Bringing with them the culinary methods and influences of their respective homelands, many have opened restaurants or become involved in rice farming and fishing. They arrived in Texas with a taste for seafood, rice and lemon grass and a preference for stir-frying and steaming foods at about the same time that the nation as a whole began to focus on these ingredients and techniques in the quest for heart-healthy menus. Texas chefs quickly incorporated Chinese, Vietnamese, Indian and Thai seasonings into their own styles of southwestern, southern and French cooking, and found the combinations with seafood especially appealing.

The earliest accounts of Texas wine making claim that vintages were produced in the 1600s. A small, but flourishing industry lasted until the days of Prohibition. Most recently, the industry has grown from two wineries in 1975 to more than twenty-five in the mid-1990s, and several more are in the process of maturing. Although the Texas Wine Institute estimates that more than 90 percent of the state's wine is sold within its boundaries, the word is out that Texas wines are competitive with those of California, France and New York.

The Texas spirit of adventure extends to farming and ranching efforts. The many catfish, crayfish and shrimp farms, emu and ostrich ranches, exotic-game ranches, apple orchards and truffle farms would amaze the Texans of the past, who relied on cattle and sheep. Blueberries, Asian vegetables, herbs, spinach, watermelons, peaches and onions are big business in a state that many outsiders envision as expanses of cactus-filled desert. And even the cacti are playing an important commercial role. The fruit of the prickly pear cactus, also known as *tuna,* is being touted as the food of the twenty-first century.

Venison has always been an important part of the diet in areas of the state. Hunters, in quest of the large antlers that can be taken only from older animals, were destined to be left with tough meat. Cooks tried valiantly to prepare leathery meat by dousing it with heavy sauces to conceal its texture and strong flavor. As a result, venison fell from grace until recently, when

The Alamo, used as a fortress in 1836 when rebels attempted to secede from Mexico, became a symbol of the fierce independence of early Texans.

The rodeo, the sport of cowboys, originated with the skills required to master everyday ranch tasks.

21

The Hill Country, with its picturesque valleys and rural charm, is a retreat and resort area for many Texans.

chefs and health-conscious cooks began serving farm-raised, tender meat that is prepared like beef.

More than two centuries separate "down-home grub" from sophisticated cuisine, cauldrons of pinto beans and haunches of meat cooked over an open fire from Thai-spiced catfish with an exotic fruit sauce and mint garnish. But both enjoy a place on the new Texas menus found throughout the state.

In those early days, people roamed the vast plains of North Texas, eked out an existence amid the miles of prickly pear cactus in South Texas, survived in the heat of the West Texas desert and hacked their way through the swamplands and thickets of East Texas. They ate the mammoth bison, the tender doves and quail, and the plentiful venison, nibbled the delicate new leaves of plants and trees, learned the healing properties of bark and gathered unusual seeds and a vast array of herbs. They introduced early cooks to the multiple uses for corn and *chiltepin* (a small, very hot chili also known as the *pequin*), to the ways of preparing the creamy white blooms of the yucca plant and the fruit and leaves of the prickly pear cactus and to the elusive flavor of mesquite honey.

People with the names Hayes, Schreiner, King, Solms, Crockett, Tobin, Driscoll, Taylor and Boone traversed the region in an effort to carve out the new land. They shared the knowledge brought with them from their homelands, their love of the land, their new skills learned from experience and mishap, their foods and basic possessions. This generosity has made its way into the character of present-day Texans, for hospitality and warm friendship are deeply ingrained in the nature of most Texans.

Hot may be *haute,* but yesteryear's simple, unpretentious foods remain the essence of Texas cooking. Even as the new century approaches, traditional German, ranch, plantation and hacienda foods still hold appeal. These styles are the foundation for the new Texas cuisine, which will continue to evolve as it shows off local products and welcomes fresh influences.

The following pages are your key to the spirit, tastes and foods of Texas. They introduce you to the Texas of today and the Texas of the past. They explore the scenic beauty and ethnic richness of the state. And they tempt your palate with traditional and inventive recipes that reflect the hospitality of Texas.

23

Settlers who emigrated from Mexico brought with them a rich tradition of music and dance. Mission San José in San Antonio holds a mariachi Mass every Sunday.

WEST TEXAS

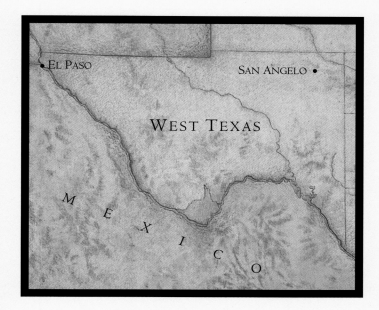

WEST TEXAS

Out here it is impossible to be lonely.
The Land walking beside you is your oldest friend,
pleasantly silent, like already you've told the best stories
and each of you knows how much the other made up.

—Naomi Shihab Nye

The last stanza of "At the Seven-Mile Ranch, Comstock, Texas," a work by award-winning author Naomi Nye, places this stark, beautiful land in the role of friend and confidant. At first glance, strangers appreciate the grand beauty of the landscape, but then their gaze settles on the rugged terrain, the harsh sun, the seemingly barren soil, and they turn away—admiring the land from afar, but reluctant to experience it firsthand, reluctant to become its friend.

But this desert land plays an important role in Texas, and indeed in the Southwest. The harsh, arid Trans-Pecos river basin is the only place in the state to find the peregrine falcon, the fastest bird alive. It is here, in the shadow of the Glass, Barrilla, Delaware, Apache and Guadalupe mountains, that generations of men and

Previous pages: The Chisos Mountains, the Rio Grande River and the surrounding vast desert form the spectacular wilderness known as Big Bend National Park. Left: Rugged terrain and a harsh climate characterize the dramatic landscape of Guadalupe National Park in West Texas.

Gathering storm clouds contrast with the shimmering gypsum dunes near the Guadalupe Mountains.

The rapids of Big Bend National Park, located in the rugged section of far West Texas along the Mexican border, provide the setting for an enjoyable and unusual culinary experience staged by San Antonio chef François Maeder several times each year. He gathers the finest wines and ingredients and leads a select group of gourmets on the trip of a lifetime, shooting the rapids by day and dining in splendor beneath the stars each night. This exciting experience rivals a Hollywood production in planning and, not surprisingly, has a long waiting list.

The land "hereabouts," as local ranchers say with a sweep of the hand, is both cattle country and sheep country. Perched at the base of the Davis Mountains stands Fort Davis, the outpost established in 1854 to protect the mail routes and travelers journeying the six hundred miles between San Antonio and El Paso. Three generations of family members work at the Prude Guest Ranch, located in these mountains. Established in 1897, the ranch began hosting visitors in 1921, when city dwellers became interested in trail rides and campfire cookouts with singing cowboys. In Presidio County, twenty minutes away, the famous Marfa Light sheds its mysterious blue glow in the mountains. No one seems to know why the light appears, but it has done so for as long as anyone can remember.

The remote Trans-Pecos land beyond the Pecos River once boasted the richest source of salt in the state. It was mined with great difficulty, however, and the living conditions were harsh. Many of the early cooks who depended on this source of livelihood subsisted on whatever could be

The area around El Paso is renowned for its bountiful harvest of Mesilla Valley chilies.

women have learned the healing properties of desert plants. This land, sometimes referred to as the "Gateway to the West, where the handshake is firmer, and the smile is friendlier," is the locale of the first sheep shearing of the season, and buyers come from all corners of the world to bid on the fine wool. It is also home to the largest and one of the most successful vineyards in the state, Ste. Genevieve Winery, and to the mammoth McDonald Observatory, where the stars at night are bigger and brighter than anywhere else in the state. The 165-ton Big 107 is the largest telescope in the world open to the public.

The landscape is diverse, the climates various. On the mountains that hover above the Chihuahua Desert, great oak, juniper and piñon pine lift their majestic heads to the seemingly endless sky. Above seven thousand feet (three thousand meters), Douglas fir, ponderosa pine and limber pine sway in the wind. In contrast, the desert never offers more than the most tenacious tufts of grass or stringy mesquite trees, unless there is a rare rainfall. Then, seeds that have lain dormant for years spring into flower and create a carpet of color that rivals the most vivid serape, lasting for only a few days, or sometimes for only a few hours.

28

Right: The towering peaks and autumnal hues of Guadalupe National Park display a rarefied beauty unique to the Trans-Pecos region.

foraged, and they contributed to the evolution of the cuisine that has become a national phenomenon. Southwestern food owes its popularity in part to its ability to evoke this image of the Old West and its link with the land.

Small cafes, some of which look as if they grew straight out of the earth sometime in the distant past, still offer succulent barbecue, the type of local cooking that exists in only one or two locations in each corner of the state, and Mexican food. In El Paso, choices range from the West Texas version of Tex-Mex and barbecue (served with the plantation-style potato and vegetable side orders typical of East Texas instead of beans and slaw, much to many people's surprise and delight) to Italian food to New Mexico cuisine laced with red *mesilla* chilies instead of the jalapeños found elsewhere in the state. Cactus paddles are served in salads or grilled whole, and yucca blooms are sautéed with tomatoes and onions or stuffed with meat or seafood fillings and baked.

In this sparsely populated land, esoteric seeds and pods have become medicinal necessities in areas where physicians are few and far between, and folk medicine is practiced with great accomplishment by *curanderos,* the Mexican folk healers.

Other activities have a pace of their own. West Texas power breakfasts are just as apt to take place around a chuck wagon coffeepot as in the Gage Hotel in Brewster County, the refurbished Outback Hotel in tiny Sanderson or the Westin Paso Del Norte Hotel in El Paso. The latter, with its impressive stained-glass dome, original mahogany carvings, cherrystone wall, European chandeliers and black-and-white serpentine marble, is an unexpected oasis of elegance in this part of the world.

Throughout history, the people who live on this land have had a mind of their own, as evidenced by the two years (1839–40) that they refused to be part of Mexico or the United States. Even today, many of the people of West Texas are far removed from any neighbors. Most are descended from the families who have always lived on this land, and their resources are few. Their faces are creased from the sun and wind, their espadrilles red with dust. Father Mell ministers to a handful of these people at a tiny chapel in Copia Guadalupaña, a village overlooked by the rest of the world but cared for by this one dedicated man. Father Mell had a dream: he wanted to have a Christmas tree for his people, for they had never experienced this holiday tradition. In 1993, Texas Overnight Delivery's Ed Marcelo heard of this need, so he flew a special mission, a mission symbolic of the long tradition of Texas generosity. He brought a beautiful tree the one thousand miles from a tree farm in East Texas to the dollhouse chapel of Copia Guadalupaña.

West Texas is a taste of the American wilderness that once visited is never forgotten. One expects at any moment to experience the mesmerizing Sioux Ghost Dance, to feel the land throb with war chants, to hear the rattle of cavalry swords or at least to wave a sad farewell to a lonesome cowpoke as he rides off into the sunset. This corner of the world is a continuing scene of people and nature coexisting in a beautiful and often unforgiving land.

Situated at a multicultural crossroads, El Paso is an interweaving of historical and modern Texas, New Mexico and Mexico.

FIRST IMPRESSIONS

Preserving food was a necessity for early settlers and is a pleasurable pastime for today's Texans.

FIRST IMPRESSIONS

Seafood, flowers and unusual garnishes abound in salads and appetizers, illustrating just how inventive the state's cooks are. The opening act is likely to be painstakingly prepared with only the freshest and most interesting ingredients, and although the recipe may be simple, the goal is to make the first bites memorable.

The state's seafood industry is thriving, and shrimp is particularly popular. Whether fried, baked, broiled, barbecued, boiled or steamed, or prepared with Cajun, Asian, Italian, Mexican or American seasonings, shrimp is the undisputed favorite. Commercial shrimp farms are being developed or expanded to ensure an adequate supply. Approximately twenty thousand shrimpers work on some forty-five hundred vessels that harvest shrimp in the traditional manner, and new preserving techniques allow trawlers to remain offshore a month or more before returning to dock. Another thirty-five hundred privately owned noncommercial boats harvest shrimp for individual consumption. Shrimping rivals the lumber, petroleum and mineral industries in economic importance, and stringent regulations dictate the shrimping season. Even with all this activity, only 20 to 25 percent of locally consumed seafood is produced within the state.

As popular as shrimp is, nachos are even more ingrained on Texas menus. Nachos are the state's all-time favorite snack food, rivaling popcorn, peanuts and potato chips in sales. Nachos, made of quartered corn tortillas, fried or baked (to lower the fat content), are a Tex-Mex treat that is almost an obsession with Texans of all ages. Potato skins used in place of traditional tortilla chips have gained in popularity. Both may be smothered in melted, calorie-laden cheese, then topped with a chili salsa straight from the jar, with sliced jalapeños, or, more creatively, with a variety of chili pepper slivers, puréed black beans, caramelized onions or mesquite-grilled chicken tidbits. Nachos are the one food most often requested when travelers return home from points beyond the state's borders, and the one food almost all Texans dream about when they move away.

Appetizers and salads frequently include the ever-popular jalapeño pepper or one of its cousins. Honey-mustard dressings are found on many menus; Rio Star grapefruit and the sweet 1015 onions are important as well. Middle Eastern influences are found in the growing popularity of tabbouleh salads and minted cucumber sauces. All of these lighter salads and appetizers are healthful alternatives to foods such as chile con queso, fried nacho chips and guacamole, which contain more fat and calories but will never disappear from the table. Lime juice, garlic, green (spring) onions and cilantro (fresh coriander) are essential ingredients that complement salads and appetizers, as do herbs and flowers.

Flowers play an important role in Texas in general. There are more than five thousand wildflower species, and many miles of Texas highways are adorned with plantings that add to the beauty of the countryside. Fields of bluebonnets flirt with Indian paintbrush, black-eyed

Previous pages, left to right: Mexican May Wine (recipe page 47), Mixed Green Salad with Nasturtiums (recipe page 38)

Women make gorditas, a tortilla of masa harina, *in San Antonio, an area where the Hispanic influence on Texas cuisine is pronounced.*

Onions have always been an essential ingredient of Tex-Mex dishes.

Susans, buttercups, primroses and cacti from border to border. It is natural that some of these flowers have found their way into recipes.

The edible flowers of Texas hold a strong allure for chefs. You will find nasturtiums, violets, pansies, squash blossoms and any number of other edible flowers and herb blooms used as garnishes, lending extra beauty and flavor to salads or adding a special essence to flavored vinegars used in dressings. Although trendy in the early 1980s, flowers were important in early Texas recipes, and they continue their popularity as prominent ingredients in reception menus, spring and summer salads, and south-of-the-border and southwestern recipes. It therefore is not surprising that this affinity for using flowers exists. Whether appreciated in the landscape or enjoyed in a distinctive recipe, flowers provide that essential Texas flamboyance.

Flower-garnished drinks and a wide array of appetizers are thought to be a carryover from plantation days. The women of the time, tightly laced in their stylish corsets, depended on frequent small nibbles of tempting appetizers to eat enough food to survive while dressed in their constricting garments. As a gesture of hospitality, Mexican dons served their guests tempting foods that were mere preludes to the generous hacienda feasts prepared in their honor. The tradition of serving tantalizing openers prevails in Texas today.

Top to bottom: Shrimp Pasta Salad with Cilantro Pesto,
Roasted Multicolored Corn Salad

Shrimp Pasta Salad with Cilantro Pesto

Here, pesto is combined with succulent shrimp from the Gulf in a colorful pasta salad. Grilled chicken breast may be substituted for the shrimp. For a smoother, creamier consistency, add ¼ cup (2 fl oz/60 ml) mayonnaise to the pesto. A crisp, herbal Fumé Blanc is an ideal partner to these flavors.

½–¾ cup (2–3 oz/60–90 g) dried rotelle pasta or pasta of choice
1½ tablespoon olive oil
½ lb (250 g) shrimp (prawns) in the shell
1 large ripe tomato, chopped
1 green bell pepper (capsicum), seeded and chopped
1 red bell pepper (capsicum), seeded and chopped
4 tablespoons chopped fresh cilantro (fresh coriander)
2 green (spring) onions, including tender green tops, minced

¼ cup (2 oz/60 g) cooled and drained, cooked black beans
  (see glossary) or drained canned black beans
¼ cup (2 fl oz/60 ml) cilantro pesto (see glossary)
toasted pine nuts

★ Bring a saucepan three-fourths full of water to a rolling boil, add the pasta and cook until al dente, about 10 minutes, or according to package directions. Drain well and place in a bowl. Add the olive oil and toss to coat evenly. Let cool at room temperature.
★ Refill the saucepan three-fourths full of water and bring to a boil. Add the shrimp and boil until they turn pink and curl slightly, 2–3 minutes. Drain and place under cold running water to cool. Peel and devein the shrimp, then chop.
★ In a bowl, combine the shrimp, tomato, bell peppers, cilantro, green onions, pasta and black beans. Stir to mix. Add the pesto and toss to coat all the ingredients evenly with the sauce.
★ Sprinkle the salad with the pine nuts and serve at once.

SERVES 4

South Texas

ROASTED MULTICOLORED CORN SALAD

San Antonio chef Steve Peterson developed this recipe to reflect the colors of summer—red, yellow and green.

4 ears of corn, husks and silks removed
½ cup (4 fl oz/125 ml) corn oil
1 cup (8 fl oz/240 ml) prepared barbecue sauce
1 red bell pepper (capsicum), seeded and diced
1 green bell pepper (capsicum), seeded and diced
1 red (Spanish) onion, diced
1 cup (8 oz/250 g) julienne-cut canned or cooked fresh cactus paddles (see glossary)
2 tablespoons fresh lime juice
1½ teaspoons chopped garlic
2 tablespoons balsamic vinegar
1 bunch fresh cilantro (fresh coriander), stemmed and chopped

★ Prepare a hot indirect-heat mesquite fire in a charcoal grill and oil the grill rack.
★ Rub the ears of corn with ¼ cup (2 fl oz/60 ml) of the corn oil and place them on the oiled grill rack. Baste the corn with ¼ cup (2 fl oz/60 ml) of the barbecue sauce and turn it continuously to avoid burning. Remove the corn from the grill and let cool.
★ In a bowl, combine the red and green bell peppers, onion, cactus, lime juice and garlic. Using a sharp knife, cut the kernels from the cooled ears of corn. Add the corn to the bowl holding the bell pepper mixture. In a small bowl, stir together the remaining ¼ cup (2 fl oz/60 ml) corn oil, the balsamic vinegar, the cilantro and the remaining ¾ cup (6 fl oz/180 ml) barbecue sauce and mix well. Add the sauce mixture to the corn mixture and toss well. Cover and chill well before serving.
★ Spoon onto a platter to serve.

SERVES 8–10

Texas

TEXAS LANDSCAPE WITH CHILI-LIME VINAIGRETTE

Here, brightly colored regional vegetables are combined to paint a Texas landscape. Most of these ingredients are readily available. The prickly pear (nopal) cactus paddles (leaves) can be purchased fresh or canned. They are breaded, fried, grilled, added to omelets and salads, and even made into candy. The ripe cactus fruit, or tuna, has been described by some adventurous chefs as the kiwifruit of the next decade. If you like, use chipotle mayonnaise (recipe page 117) in place of the vinaigrette. For a dramatic garnish, cut out large arrows from red corn tortillas (see glossary), deep-fry them in vegetable oil until crisp, drain and place them along the periphery of the "landscape."

FOR THE CHILI-LIME VINAIGRETTE:

½ cup (4 fl oz/125 ml) olive oil
2 tablespoons balsamic vinegar
1 tablespoon Dijon-style mustard
1 clove garlic, minced
juice of ½ lime
3 tablespoons minced fresh cilantro (fresh coriander)
3 tablespoons chopped fresh basil
1 tablespoon snipped fresh chives
red pepper flakes
salt and freshly ground pepper

1 lb (500 g) stemmed spinach leaves
1 small jicama (yam bean), peeled and cut into long, narrow strips
2 ripe Haas avocados, pitted, peeled, sliced and dipped in 1 tablespoon fresh lime juice
2 red bell peppers (capsicums), roasted (see glossary), peeled, seeded and cut into long, narrow strips
6 tomatillos, brown husks removed and thinly sliced (see glossary)
6 baby crookneck squashes, cut in half lengthwise and parboiled
corn kernels cut from 3 ears of corn
2 purple potatoes, boiled until tender, drained, peeled and cut into chunks
¾ cup (6 oz/185 g) sliced canned or cooked fresh cactus paddles (see glossary)
fresh cilantro (fresh coriander) leaves for garnish

★ To make the vinaigrette, in a jar with a tight-fitting lid, combine all the ingredients, including salt and pepper to taste. Cover and shake vigorously to mix. Set aside.
★ Arrange the spinach leaves on a large platter. Mound the jicama in the center. Attractively arrange the remaining ingredients, except the cilantro, in separate mounds around the jicama. Garnish with the cilantro leaves. Shake the vinaigrette, then drizzle it evenly over the salad. Serve at once.

SERVES 6

Texas Landscape with Chili-Lime Vinaigrette

37

MIXED GREEN SALAD WITH NASTURTIUMS

Serve this gorgeous salad in a chilled clear crystal salad bowl so all the various colors of the ingredients are visible. You will find the taste of nasturtium flowers a bit peppery and slightly salty, similar to the taste of watercress. Pansies, blue hyssops or borage blossoms can be substituted for the nasturtiums.

½ cup (4 fl oz/125 ml) olive oil
¼ cup (2 fl oz/60 ml) red wine vinegar

1 tablespoon Dijon-style mustard
1 clove garlic, minced
salt and freshly ground pepper
8 cups (8 oz/250 g) assorted greens, such as chicory (curly
    endive), arugula (rocket), and Bibb (butterhead) and red-
    leaf lettuce, torn into bite-sized pieces
2 hard-cooked eggs, quartered
1 cup (1 oz/30 g) fresh basil leaves
1 cup (6 oz/185 g) tiny green beans, boiled 1 minute and drained
½ cup (¾ oz/20 g) chopped fresh parsley
salad burnet
fresh dill feathers

Top to bottom: Jalapeño Potato Salad, German Potato Salad

Fredericksburg

JALAPEÑO POTATO SALAD

A barbecue is not complete without a bowl of this spicy potato salad, a recipe created at the Peach Tree Tea Room in Fredericksburg. The amount of jalapeños can be adjusted to taste.

3 lb (1.5 kg) russet potatoes, peeled
5 celery stalks, diced
5 green (spring) onions, including tender green tops, minced
1 yellow onion, diced
4 hard-cooked eggs, coarsely chopped
2 cups (16 fl oz/500 ml) mayonnaise
¼ cup (1½ oz/45 g) chopped pickled jalapeño chili peppers, plus 1 tablespoon juice (see glossary)
3 tablespoons minced fresh parsley
1 teaspoon ground cumin
salt and freshly ground pepper
fresh cilantro (fresh coriander) leaves for garnish

★ Place the potatoes in a large saucepan and add water to cover generously. Bring to a boil and boil until tender when pierced with a fork, 20–25 minutes. Drain and let cool then cut into ¾–1-in (2–2.5-cm) cubes.
★ Place the potatoes in a large bowl and add the celery and green and yellow onions. In a smaller bowl, combine the eggs, mayonnaise, jalapeños, parsley, cumin and salt and pepper to taste. Add to the potato mixture and mix well. Cover and chill for several hours or overnight before serving.
★ Just before serving, garnish with cilantro.

SERVES 12

New Braunfels

GERMAN POTATO SALAD

German festivals in Texas, such as the Slaton Wurstfest and the Wurstfest in New Braunfels, draw thousands of people every year. The traditional German fare offered includes assorted sausages, sauerkraut, beans, potato salad, homemade breads and pastries. Here is a version of Heisser Kartoffelsalat, *a salad that is served with great pride at these affairs. Although it can be eaten at room temperature, the salad is best when served hot.*

1½ lb (750 g) russet potatoes, unpeeled
8 slices bacon, chopped
1 yellow onion, finely chopped
4 dill pickles, chopped
1 cup (8 fl oz/250 ml) mayonnaise
½ cup (4 fl oz/125 ml) cider vinegar
½ cup (4 fl oz/125 ml) heavy (double) cream
1 teaspoon sugar
2 teaspoons Dijon-style mustard
salt and freshly ground pepper

★ Place the potatoes in a large saucepan and add water to cover generously. Bring to a boil and cook until tender when pierced with a fork, 20–25 minutes. Drain and place in a bowl. Using a wood spoon, break up the potatoes into bite-sized pieces. Keep warm.
★ While the potatoes are cooking, in a frying pan over medium-high heat, fry the bacon until crisp, 3–5 minutes. Using a slotted spoon, transfer to paper towels to drain. Reserve the bacon drippings in the pan.
★ Reheat the drippings over medium heat. Add the onion and sauté until translucent, about 5 minutes. Add the pickles, mayonnaise, vinegar, cream, sugar, mustard and salt and pepper to taste and stir until well mixed. Heat to just under the boiling point; do not allow to boil.
★ Pour the hot mayonnaise mixture over the warm potatoes. Mix lightly and then fold in the reserved bacon. Sprinkle the top with pepper. Serve at once.

SERVES 4

fresh thyme leaves
about 16 pesticide-free nasturtium blossoms

★ In a small bowl, whisk together the olive oil, vinegar, mustard, garlic and salt and pepper to taste until an emulsion forms.
★ In a large salad bowl, combine the assorted greens, eggs, basil, green beans and parsley and the salad burnet, dill and thyme to taste. Drizzle the dressing over the top and toss gently, being careful not to break up the eggs. Add the nasturtiums and again toss gently. Serve at once.

SERVES 8   *Photograph pages 32–33*

APPETIZER CHEESECAKE WITH ANCHO SWIRLS

The interesting combination of flavors present in this spicy dish is nicely partnered with ice-cold margaritas. Offer blue or yellow corn tortilla chips (see glossary) for dipping into the cheesecake.

½ lb (250 g) cream cheese, at room temperature
dash of ground jalapeño chili
2 tablespoons gold tequila
2 cloves garlic, minced
2 green (spring) onions, including tender green tops, minced
2–3 tablespoons Tex's ancho paste or cilantro pesto (see glossary)
pico de gallo (see glossary)
chili powder
toasted pine nuts

★ In a food processor fitted with the metal blade, combine the cream cheese, ground jalapeño, tequila, garlic and green onions. Process until smooth. Line a shallow 2-cup (16–fl oz/500-ml) mold with plastic wrap or cheesecloth (muslin) so that the edges overhang the rim of the mold. Pour the cheese mixture into it. Using a knife blade, swirl the ancho paste or cilantro pesto through the cheese mixture to create an overall pattern. Cover tightly and chill overnight.
★ To serve, invert a flat platter over the mold, hold them together firmly and invert the mold. Lift off the mold and peel off the plastic wrap. Surround the cheesecake with *pico de gallo*. Dust the top with chili powder and then sprinkle with pine nuts. Serve at once.

SERVES 4–6

POTATO NACHOS WITH HAM AND TOMATO CONFETTI

Potatoes grow in abundance around the South Texas town of Pearsall. This variation on traditional nachos made with tortillas can also be served on potato skins or in hollowed-out tiny new potatoes.

12 slices baked unpeeled potatoes, each about ½ in (12 mm) thick
4 green (spring) onions, including tender green tops, minced
½ cup (3 oz/90 g) finely diced ham
1 ripe tomato, seeded and diced
¾ cup (3 oz/90 g) shredded sharp Cheddar cheese
1 or 2 fresh jalapeño chili peppers, seeded (if desired) and minced
½ cup (4 fl oz/125 ml) crème fraîche (see glossary) or sour cream
¼ cup (⅓ oz/10 g) chopped fresh cilantro (fresh coriander)

★ Preheat a broiler (griller).
★ Place the potato slices in a single layer on a lightly greased flameproof serving plate. Sprinkle with the green onions, ham, tomato, Cheddar cheese and jalapeños. Place the plate in the broiler and broil (grill) until bubbly and heated through, 3–4 minutes.
★ Remove from the broiler and spoon dollops of the crème fraîche or sour cream evenly over the top. Sprinkle with the cilantro and serve immediately.

SERVES 3 OR 4

Left to right: Appetizer Cheesecake with Ancho Swirls,
Potato Nachos with Ham and Tomato Confetti

Big Thicket Salad

East Texas

BIG THICKET SALAD

The Big Thicket National Preserve of East Texas protects one of the most biologically diverse wilderness areas in the United States. This salad can boast a range of components almost as diverse as those of the Big Thicket, thus its name. You can omit the cured lemons and quail eggs and in their place use toasted brioche stars that have been cut out with a cookie cutter. A light, crisp but fruity Chardonnay is ideal with this interesting salad.

FOR THE VINAIGRETTE:

⅓ cup (3 fl oz/80 ml) olive oil
1 tablespoon balsamic vinegar
1 large shallot, minced
1 clove garlic, minced
2 teaspoons country-style whole-grain mustard
salt and freshly ground pepper

½ cup (4 fl oz/125 ml) olive oil
1½ lb (750 g) assorted fresh domestic and wild mushrooms, such as shiitake, crimini and oyster
¾ cup (¾ oz/20 g) assorted fresh herb leaves, such as thyme, chives, oregano, basil and flat-leaf (Italian) parsley, in any combination
1½ cups (1½ oz/45 g) arugula (rocket) leaves
1½ cups (1½ oz/45 g) radicchio leaves
1½ cups (1½ oz/45 g) oakleaf lettuce leaves
½ cup (2½ oz/75 g) pine nuts, toasted
2 ripe tomatoes, seeded and diced
slivered zest of cured lemons (see glossary) and hard-cooked quail eggs (optional) for garnish

★ To make the vinaigrette, in a small bowl, using a whisk, mix together the olive oil, vinegar, shallot, garlic, mustard and salt and pepper to taste. Set aside.
★ In a sauté pan over medium heat, warm the olive oil. Add the mushrooms and sauté until tender, 4–5 minutes. Add the herbs and mix well. Keep warm.
★ In a large bowl, toss together the arugula, radicchio and oakleaf lettuce leaves. Add the vinaigrette and toss again. Arrange the mixed leaves on individual plates and top evenly with the hot mushroom mixture. Sprinkle the pine nuts and tomatoes over the top. Garnish with lemon zest and quail eggs (if using). Serve immediately.

SERVES 4–6

El Paso

BLUE CORN NACHOS WITH BACON AND SWEET ONION

This appetizer from cookbook author Park Kerr is part of the mouth-watering borderland food featuring the sweet Texas 1015 onions that El Paso is known for. These nachos are a favorite with margaritas or Texas beer.

½ lb (250 g) sliced bacon, coarsely chopped
36 lightly salted blue corn tortilla chips (see glossary)
1 Texas 1015 onion or other sweet onion, finely diced
6 pickled jalapeño chili peppers, drained, seeded (if desired) and minced (see glossary)
2 cups (8 oz/250 g) shredded Monterey Jack cheese
fresh cilantro (fresh coriander) sprigs for garnish
1 cup (8 fl oz/250 ml) sour cream or crème fraîche (optional; see glossary)
sliced radishes

★ Preheat an oven to 450°F (230°C).
★ In a frying pan over medium-high heat, fry the bacon until crisp, 3–5 minutes. Using a slotted spoon, transfer to paper towels to drain. Arrange the tortilla chips in a single layer on a large ovenproof plate. Scatter the fried bacon, onion, jalapeños and Jack cheese evenly over the tortilla chips. Bake until the cheese melts and the nachos are sizzling, about 5 minutes.
★ Garnish the nachos with cilantro sprigs, dollops of sour cream or crème fraîche, if using, and sliced radishes.

SERVES 4–6

South Texas

CRAB MEAT–STUFFED JALAPEÑOS WITH SOUTH TEXAS CRAB GRASS

Stuffed jalapeños are a specialty of South Texas. One bite and you will be hooked. This recipe calls for filling them with a crab meat mixture, but the variations are endless: cream cheese, minced green (spring) onion, crispy bacon and sour cream; cream cheese, minced hard-cooked egg and garlic; cream cheese and chorizo sausage. The stuffed chilies can also be dipped into a mixture of egg and milk, rolled in flour followed by fine dried bread crumbs and then deep-fried until crispy and brown.

1 can (27 oz/840 g) whole pickled jalapeño chili peppers, drained (see glossary)
ice water, to cover
1 lb (500 g) fresh-cooked blue crab meat, picked over for cartilage and shell fragments and flaked
½ lb (250 g) cream cheese or fresh goat cheese, room temperature
2 green (spring) onions, including tender green tops, minced
2 cloves garlic, minced
2 teaspoons minced fresh cilantro (fresh coriander)
salt
South Texas crab grass for garnish (see glossary)

★ Cut the chilies in half lengthwise. Wearing rubber gloves, remove the seeds and ribs. Rinse the chilies well under cold running water. In a bowl, combine the chilies with ice water to cover, tightly cover and let stand overnight in the refrigerator. (The soaking helps to remove some of the heat of the chilies.)
★ Drain the peppers and set aside. In a bowl, combine the crab meat, cheese, green onions, garlic, cilantro and salt to taste. Mix well. Carefully stuff the chili halves with the crab mixture, mounding slightly, and arrange on a plate. Cover and chill well.
★ Just before serving, garnish with South Texas crab grass.

SERVES 6–8

Top to bottom: Blue Corn Nachos with Bacon and Sweet Onion,
Crab Meat–Stuffed Jalapeños with South Texas Crab Grass

FALL FLORAL SALAD

Innovative San Antonio chef Daniel Block created this simple salad with a unique mosaiclike presentation. It is reminiscent of an autumn walk when the leaves first start to fall and the air is turning cooler. You will need 6 solid-colored 12-inch (30-centimeter) serving plates and 6 clear glass 10-inch (25-centimeter) salad or dessert plates.

oak, maple or other fall leaves, dried oats, corn silks, celery seeds, pumpkin seeds, black sesame seeds, in any combination
¼ cup (2 fl oz/60 ml) balsamic vinegar
4 teaspoons honey
½ cup (4 fl oz/125 ml) olive oil
salt and freshly ground pepper
6 large ripe tomatoes
6–8 oz (185–250 g) bite-sized mixed tender salad greens

★ Decoratively sprinkle the fall leaves and other seasonal ingredients on the 6 solid-colored serving plates. Place a clear glass plate on top of each leaf-covered plate, allowing the fall foliage to show through.
★ In a small saucepan over medium-high heat, stir together the vinegar and honey. Whisk in the olive oil and bring to a rapid boil. Reduce the heat to medium and cook, whisking constantly, until reduced to a syruplike consistency, 15–20 minutes. Let cool. Season to taste with salt and pepper.
★ Cut a ½-in (12-mm) slice off the top of each tomato and scoop out the pulp, leaving a shell ½ in (12 mm) thick. (Reserve the tomato pulp for another use.) Fill the hollowed-out tomatoes with the salad greens. Place on the glass plates. Drizzle the vinegar-honey mixture evenly over the greens and serve.

SERVES 6

HOT CRACKERED TEXAS CRAB WITH PECANS

This traditional crab dish takes on an entirely different character with the addition of pecans. The nuts are native to over 150 counties in Texas and are grown commercially in some 30 additional counties.

4 tablespoons (2 oz/60 g) butter
¼ cup (¾ oz/20 g) minced green (spring) onion, including tender green tops
¼ cup (1½ oz/45 g) minced green bell pepper (capsicum)
¼ cup (1½ oz/45 g) minced celery
2 tablespoons minced jarred pimiento
1 cup (6 oz/85 g) fresh-cooked crab meat, picked over for cartilage and shell fragments and flaked
salt
¼ teaspoon dry mustard
dash of cayenne pepper
½ cup (1½ oz/40 g) soda cracker crumbs
3 tablespoons chopped pecans, toasted
3 tablespoons minced fresh parsley
¼–½ cup (2–4 fl oz/60–120 ml) heavy (double) cream

★ Preheat an oven to 350°F (180°C).
★ In a small sauté pan over medium heat, melt 2 tablespoons of the butter. Add the green onion, bell pepper, celery and pimiento and sauté until they begin to soften, about 1 minute. Add the crab, salt to taste, dry mustard and cayenne pepper. Toss to mix well.

★ Remove from the heat and stir in ¼ cup (¾ oz/20 g) of the cracker crumbs, the pecans and the parsley. Then stir in as much of the cream as is necessary to make the mixture slightly moist. Divide the crab mixture evenly among 2 or 3 buttered scallop shells or ramekins.
★ In a small pan, melt the remaining 2 tablespoons butter. Sprinkle the remaining ¼ cup (¾ oz/20 g) cracker crumbs evenly over the tops of the crab mixture and then drizzle evenly with the melted butter.
★ Bake until heated through and the crumbs are lightly browned, 20–25 minutes. Serve immediately.

SERVES 2 OR 3

Left to right: Hot Crackered Texas Crab with Pecans, Fall Floral Salad

AGUAS FRESCAS

Aguas frescas are thirst-quenching, colorful, low-calorie fresh-fruit beverages enjoyed throughout Mexico and popular in Texas as well. They are made with fruit juice and pulp, water and a hint of sugar and lime juice. Typically, these drinks are served in clear glass crocks for ladling over ice cubes in glasses.

★ Select fruits when they are at their peak of flavor. Cantaloupes, honeydew melons, kiwifruits, mangoes, oranges, strawberries, watermelons, and guavas are all good choices. In a blender or juicer, smoothly purée fruit of choice (fruits may be prepared alone or in any combination) with sugar and fresh lime juice to taste. Add this flavored fruit mixture to water; the usual proportion is 1–2 cups (8–16 fl oz/250–500 ml) fruit mixture to 3–4 cups (24–32 fl oz/750 ml–1 l) water and ¼ cup (2 oz/60 g) sugar. Then add fresh lime juice to taste. Refrigerate until well chilled or as long as overnight.

★ To serve, pour the well-chilled fruit juice over ice cubes in tall clear glasses. For a decorative touch, add slices or chunks of the fruit used for making the drinks and garnish with fresh mint sprigs.

Photograph page 4

*Top to bottom: Apricot Tequila Sunrise, Smoked Duck
and Goat Cheese Nachos with Mango Pico*

Gulf Coast

APRICOT TEQUILA SUNRISE

This refreshing drink takes its name from the beautiful multicolored layers of a Texas sunrise. The grenadine must not be stirred into the drink, but allowed to remain on the bottom. Grenadine was originally based on pomegranate juice, but now it contains other fruit juices and artificial coloring. If at all possible, substitute fresh pomegranate juice for the grenadine and garnish the drink with pomegranate seeds. If you can't make it to West Texas or the Gulf Coast for a sunrise, this is the next best thing.

1½ fl oz (45 ml) gold tequila
½ cup (4 fl oz/125 ml) apricot or peach nectar or freshly
 squeezed orange juice
2 teaspoons fresh lime juice
ice cubes
1 fl oz (30 ml) grenadine
1 kumquat, lime peel strip or strawberry, or peach and
 borage blossoms for garnish

★ In a cocktail shaker, combine the tequila, fruit nectar or orange juice, lime juice and ice cubes. Shake until well chilled. Strain into a tall Champagne flute.
★ Carefully pour the grenadine down the inside of the glass so that it runs to the bottom; do not stir. Garnish the rim of the glass with a kumquat, lime peel strip or strawberry, or peach and borage blossoms. Serve immediately.

SERVES 1

San Antonio

SMOKED DUCK AND GOAT CHEESE NACHOS WITH MANGO PICO

Chef Phillip Rice takes the typical nacho several steps further with this intriguing combination. Smoked chicken may be substituted for the duck, and experimenting with various Mexican cheeses will produce other, equally interesting results. The mango pico adds a particularly refreshing flavor to this substantial appetizer. Guacamole (see glossary) and sour cream can be served in place of the mango pico.

4 boneless, skinless duck breasts, 6–8 oz (185–250 g) each
1 tablespoon minced garlic
2 tablespoons salt
1½ teaspoons freshly ground black pepper
1½ teaspoons sugar
1½ teaspoons cayenne pepper
½ lb (250 g) fresh goat cheese, *queso fresco* or Chihuahua
 cheese, at room temperature (see glossary)
8 *chalupa* shells or large triangular tortilla chips (see glossary)
6 oz (185 g) pepper Jack cheese, shredded (see glossary)
2 tablespoons chopped fresh cilantro (fresh coriander)

FOR THE MANGO *PICO*:

3 mangoes, peeled, pitted and diced
6 plum (Roma) tomatoes, seeded and diced
4 green (spring) onions, including tender green tops, chopped
2 fresh serrano chili peppers, seeded (if desired) and minced
 (see glossary)
juice of 2 limes
¼ cup (⅓ oz/10 g) chopped fresh cilantro (fresh coriander)
salt and freshly ground pepper

★ Lay the duck breasts in a single layer in a shallow dish or on a baking sheet. In a small bowl, combine the garlic, salt, black pepper, sugar and cayenne pepper, mixing well. Coat the duck breasts on all sides with the seasoning mixture. Let stand, uncovered, in the refrigerator overnight.
★ Prepare a smoker according to the manufacturer's instructions, or prepare an indirect-heat fire in a charcoal grill and oil the grill rack. Brush off any excess seasoning from the duck breasts. Place the breasts in the smoker or on the oiled charcoal-fire grill rack, cover and cook until tender and cooked through, about 1 hour.
★ Meanwhile, to make the mango *pico*, in a bowl, stir together all the ingredients, including salt and pepper to taste.
★ Preheat a broiler (griller). To assemble the nachos, cut the smoked duck breasts into long, narrow strips. Spread the goat cheese, *queso fresco* or Chihuahua cheese on the *chalupa* shells or tortilla chips, then sprinkle evenly with the pepper Jack cheese, cilantro and duck breast. Place under the broiler and broil (grill) until the cheeses melt and the ingredients are heated through, 3–4 minutes.
★ Remove from the broiler and serve immediately with the mango *pico* on the side.

SERVES 8

Austin

MEXICAN MAY WINE

This is an adaptation of Austin cookbook author Lucinda Hutson's German May wine recipe with a Texas accent. In place of the traditional sweet woodruff, the nutmeg-scented herb that usually flavors German May wine, Hutson substitutes anise-scented Mexican marigold mint and uses a blush-colored white Zinfandel. Pineapple sage, lemon verbena, lemon mint and/or lemon thyme can be substituted or used in combination with the Mexican marigold mint. To make the herbal ice cubes, freeze fresh herb leaves of choice in ice-cube trays filled with distilled water.

1 cup (1 oz/30 g) loosely packed, stemmed fresh Mexican
 marigold mint leaves (see glossary)
1 tablespoon coriander seeds, lightly crushed
4 bottles (3 cups/24 fl oz/750 ml each) lightly fruity white
 or blush wine, chilled
4 cups (1 lb/500 g) strawberries, stemmed
1–2 tablespoons sugar
1 orange, thinly sliced
1 lime, thinly sliced
18–20 fresh Mexican marigold mint sprigs and flowers
1 bottle (3 cups/750 ml) Champagne or other high-quality
 sparkling wine, chilled
herbal ice cubes (see note) and fresh marigold mint sprigs
 for garnish

★ In a large pitcher, combine the 1 cup (1 oz/30 g) Mexican marigold mint, the coriander seeds and 1 bottle of the wine. Let stand overnight at room temperature.
★ Strain the wine-mint mixture through a fine-mesh sieve lined with cheesecloth (muslin) into another pitcher. Add the remaining 3 bottles wine. In a bowl, slightly mash together 2 cups (8 oz/250 g) of the strawberries (reserving the rest for garnish) and the sugar. Add to the wine and stir to mix. Cover and chill for up to 3 days.
★ To serve, slice the remaining 2 cups (8 oz/250 g) strawberries, if desired. Strain the wine-strawberry mixture through a fine-mesh sieve into a glass pitcher. Add the sliced or whole strawberries, orange and lime slices, and marigold mint and flower sprigs. At the last moment, add the Champagne or sparkling wine and herbal ice cubes.
★ Pour the punch into glasses and serve.

SERVES 18–20   *Photograph page 32–33*

PEARSALL SALAD WITH FLOWER-FILLED PASTA ROUNDS

The tasty mixture of garden-fresh greens and the dressing for this salad were created by Patty Johnson, owner of Patty's Herbs, a well-known commercial herb farm in Pearsall. The flower-filled pasta rounds are particularly attractive additions. For filling the pasta rounds, select edible flowers such as nasturtiums, Johnny-jump-ups, pansies and/or dianthus. Make sure that the flowers have not been treated with any pesticides or other chemicals. Fresh herb leaves such as cilantro (coriander), basil and flat-leaf (Italian) parsley can be used in place of, or along with, the flowers. The pasta rounds can also be cooked and served in a rich chicken stock as a first course, with flower shapes cut from carrot slices as a garnish, or cooked in stock or water, drained well and tossed with a pesto made from pineapple sage. If you are short of time, you can omit the pasta rounds from the salad and it will still be delicious.

FOR THE PASTA ROUNDS WITH FRESH FLOWERS AND/OR HERBS:

1 tablespoon cornstarch (cornflour)
1 tablespoon water
16 square wonton wrappers or round potsticker wrappers
fresh edible flowers and/or herbs (see note)

FOR THE DRESSING:

3 tablespoons mayonnaise
1 tablespoon chopped fresh flat-leaf (Italian) parsley
2 teaspoons chopped fresh herbs, such as basil
Mexican marigold mint (see glossary), tarragon, oregano
    and lemon thyme in any combination
juice of ½ lime
salt and freshly ground white pepper
2 teaspoons Dijon-style mustard

2 cups (2 oz/60 g) French sorrel leaves, stemmed and torn
    into bite-sized pieces
¼ cup (¼ oz/15 g) salad burnet leaves, stemmed and torn
    into bite-sized pieces
2 cups (2 oz/60 g) arugula (rocket) leaves, stemmed and torn
    into bite-sized pieces

★ To make the pasta rounds, in a small bowl, stir together the cornstarch and water until smooth. Place 1 wonton or potsticker wrapper on a work surface and lightly brush the surface with some of the cornstarch mixture. Place 1 or 2 flowers or leaves in the center of the wrapper. Brush another wrapper with the cornstarch mixture and gently place it, brushed side down, on top of the first wrapper. Using a rolling pin, gently roll out any air bubbles. If using square wrappers, with a ravioli wheel or cookie cutter, trim the squares into circles. As soon as the pasta round is finished, place it on a waxed paper–covered plate. Repeat with the remaining wonton wrappers and flowers and leaves, separating the layers with additional waxed paper, if necessary. Cover and chill for 1–2 hours before cooking.
★ To cook the pasta rounds, bring a large saucepan three-fourths full of water to a boil. Add the rounds, a few at a time, and simmer gently, until slightly translucent, about 2 minutes. Drain well, let cool, cover and chill well.
★ To make the dressing, in a small bowl, combine all the ingredients and, using a whisk, stir until well mixed.
★ In a salad bowl, combine the sorrel, salad burnet and arugula and toss to mix. Divide the greens evenly among individual plates. Garnish with the pasta rounds and serve the dressing alongside.

SERVES 4

PEACH ICED TEA WITH PEACH ICE CUBES

Spring and summer make Texans dream of glasses of iced tea with mint sprigs from the garden, served under live-oak trees brushed with warm breezes and surrounded by wildflowers. Plums, nectarines or pears can be used in place of the peaches,

*Top to bottom: Peach Iced Tea with Peach Ice Cubes,
Pearsall Salad with Flower-Filled Pasta Rounds*

*and fresh mint sprigs or slices of carambola (star fruit) and
hibiscus blossoms can be substituted for the garnish of peach
slices and geranium leaves.*

4 orange pekoe tea bags
4 cups (32 fl oz/1 l) water, boiling
4 peaches, peeled and pitted
1 tablespoon fresh lemon juice
1 can (12 fl oz/375 ml) citrus- or peach-flavored soda water,
  chilled
peach slices and peach-scented geranium leaves for garnish

★ Place the tea bags in a saucepan and pour the boiling water
over the top. Refrigerate until cold.
★ Meanwhile, in a food processor fitted with the metal
blade or in a blender, combine the peaches and lemon juice.
Purée until smooth. Pour into 1 or 2 ice cube trays and
freeze solid.
★ When ready to serve, divide the tea among 4 tall glasses. Fill
with peach ice cubes and a splash of the soda water. Garnish
with peach slices and geranium leaves and serve at once.

SERVES 4

Left to right: Fiesta Tequila, Margaritas

T e x a s

MARGARITAS

Many stories exist on the origin of the margarita. Among them is one that it was created in Jalisco, Mexico, in the town of Tequila. Others credit it to a bartender at a racetrack in Tijuana or to a bar in Taxco. This is the version served throughout Texas today.

1 lime, quartered, plus lime slices or lime peel
   for garnish
kosher salt
cracked ice
3 fl oz (90 ml) white tequila
1 fl oz (30 ml) Triple Sec
1 fl oz (30 ml) fresh lime juice

★ Rub the rims of 2 chilled stemmed cocktail glasses with the cut sides of the lime quarters. Sprinkle salt onto a small plate and invert a glass onto the salt. Twist the glass to coat the rim. Repeat with the second glass.
★ In a cocktail shaker, combine the cracked ice, the tequila, the Triple Sec and the lime juice. Shake briskly. Strain carefully into the prepared glasses. Garnish with lime slices or peel and serve.

SERVES 2

A u s t i n

FIESTA TEQUILA

Tequila authority Lucinda Hutson frequently serves a variation of this festive drink to highlight both the indigenous ingredients and the spirit of Texas. To be sure that the block of ice is clear rather than cloudy, use distilled water or bring tap water to a boil and then let it cool. If Mexican marigold mint or pineapple sage is not available, substitute bright yellow daisies and fern fronds. Hutson also sometimes freezes small cactus in the block of ice.

1 bottle (33.8 fl oz/1 l) gold tequila
2 or 3 limes, unpeeled, sliced
6 fresh red and/or green serrano chili peppers
   (see glossary)
6 fresh green jalapeño chili peppers
several Mexican marigold mint sprigs with flowers
   (see glossary)
several pineapple sage flowers
lime and salt wedges for serving

★ Place the bottle of tequila in a milk carton. Add water (see note) to the carton to a depth of 2 in (5 cm) and place some of the lime slices and some of the peppers around the bottom. Press a few sprigs of Mexican marigold mint and pineapple sage flowers close to the sides. Add 1–2 in (2.5–5 cm) water and freeze until slightly frozen. Then again add 1–2 in (2.5–5 cm) water and more chilies and flowers in the same fashion and return to the freezer. Repeat until the carton is full.
★ When completely frozen and just before serving, remove the carton from the block of ice by cutting or tearing it off. Place the ice mold in a Mexican pottery dish or other attractive dish. Surround the dish with lime wedges, a small bowl of salt and small shot glasses.
★ The traditional way to drink tequila is to pour a shot, rub lime juice on the back of one hand and then sprinkle salt on it. In quick succession, bite into a lime wedge, lick the salt from your hand and down the shot of tequila.

MAKES ABOUT THIRTY-THREE 1–FL OZ (30-ML) SHOTS

S a n A n t o n i o

SANGRÍA

No celebration would be complete without sangría! This festive drink is not only refreshing, but pretty; its name, which is Spanish for bleeding, was inspired from its blood-red color. As with most things Texan, there are many variations on this traditional drink. Here is one of the best.

1 bottle (3 cups/24 fl oz/750 ml) dry red wine
¼ cup (2 fl oz/60 ml) brandy
¼ cup (2 oz/60 g) sugar
1 lemon, thinly sliced
1 orange, thinly sliced
1 apple, halved, cored and cut into thin wedges
club soda, chilled
ice cubes
orange slices and mint leaves for garnish

★ In a glass pitcher or punch bowl, combine the wine, brandy, sugar, lemon, orange and apple. Stir until the sugar dissolves and all the ingredients are well mixed. Cover and refrigerate until thoroughly chilled.
★ Just before serving, pour in chilled club soda to taste. Pour the sangría over ice cubes in glasses. Garnish each glass with an orange slice and mint leaf.

SERVES 6

Sangría

FRIED OKRA SALAD

Everyone who loves fried okra will love this salad, which takes a favorite dish—fried okra—one step further in color, texture and flavor.

6 slices bacon, coarsely chopped
yellow cornmeal for coating
salt and cayenne pepper
1 lb (500 g) okra (lady's fingers), cut crosswise into slices ½ in (12 mm) thick
vegetable oil, if needed
1 large ripe tomato, cut into ½-in (12-mm) dice
1 small yellow onion, cut into ½-in (12-mm) dice
1 small green bell pepper (capsicum), seeded and cut into ½-in (12-mm) dice
salt and freshly ground black pepper

★ In a frying pan over medium-high heat, fry the bacon until crisp, 3–5 minutes. Using a slotted spoon, transfer to paper towels to drain. Reserve the bacon drippings in the pan. Place the cornmeal in a shallow bowl and season to taste with salt and cayenne pepper. Toss the sliced okra in the cornmeal to coat evenly. Reheat the bacon drippings over high heat, adding vegetable oil if needed to cover the bottom of the pan lightly. Add the okra and fry, turning as needed to ensure even browning, until tender and crisp, 6–7 minutes.

★ Using a slotted spoon, transfer the okra to a serving bowl and add the tomato, onion and bell pepper. Toss to mix. Add salt and black pepper to taste and toss again. Sprinkle with the bacon and serve.

SERVES 6

SWEET-AND-SOUR COLESLAW

In Texas, from Columbus to El Campo and from Taylor to Temple, this coleslaw, commonly known as nine-day slaw because it keeps so well, is a must at an old-fashioned fish fry or a ranch-style barbecue.

1 small head green cabbage, about 1 lb (500 g), coarsely shredded
1 small head red cabbage, about ¾–1 lb (375 g– 500g), coarsely shredded
4 celery stalks, diced
1 yellow onion, diced
1 green bell pepper (capsicum), seeded and chopped
1 red bell pepper (capsicum), seeded and chopped, or ¾ cup (4 oz/125 g) chopped jarred pimiento
1 or 2 pickled jalapeño chili peppers, diced (optional; see glossary)
1 cup (8 oz/250 g) sugar
1 cup (8 fl oz/250 ml) corn or vegetable oil
1 cup (8 fl oz/250 ml) cider vinegar
1½ teaspoons salt, or to taste
1 teaspoon dry mustard
1 teaspoon celery seeds
1 teaspoon poppy seeds (optional)
¼ cup (1½ oz/45 g) whole roasted peanuts

★ In a large bowl, combine the 2 cabbages, celery, onion, bell peppers, jalapeños (if using) and sugar. Toss to mix and set aside.

★ In a saucepan over medium heat, combine the oil, vinegar, salt, dry mustard, celery seeds and the poppy seeds, if using; stir to mix well. When hot, pour it over the cabbage mixture and toss and stir well. Cover and refrigerate overnight.

★ Just before serving, garnish the coleslaw with the peanuts.

SERVES 12

SMOKED SHRIMP FRITTERS WITH CHARRED GREEN SALSA

The confetti and fiesta colors of this innovative recipe from San Antonio chef Michael Bomberg make these fritters especially appealing and fun to eat. Typically, they are served with guacamole and salsa, but they are equally delicious with San Antonio chef Phillip Rice's charred green salsa.

FOR THE CHARRED GREEN SALSA:

6 fresh poblano chili peppers (see glossary)
1 lb (500 g) tomatillos, brown husks removed (see glossary)
1 large yellow onion
½ bunch fresh cilantro (fresh coriander)
1 head romaine (cos) lettuce
2 or 3 cloves garlic, chopped
4 cups (32 fl oz/1 l) chicken stock
salt

FOR THE FRITTERS:

⅓ cup (2 oz/60 g) grilled or smoked large shrimp (prawns), finely diced
⅓ cup (2 oz/60 g) corn kernels
⅓ cup (2 oz/60 g) cooled and drained, cooked black beans (see glossary) or drained canned black beans
2 tablespoons chopped green (spring) onion, including tender green tops
2 tablespoons diced red bell pepper (capsicum)
1 cup (5 oz/155 g) *masa harina* (see glossary)
½ cup (2½ oz/75 g) all-purpose (plain) flour
½ teaspoon baking powder
2 eggs
¾ cup (6 fl oz/80 ml) dark bock beer
salt, freshly ground pepper and ground cumin
vegetable oil for deep-frying

★ To make the salsa, preheat a broiler (griller), or prepare a hot direct-heat fire in a charcoal grill and oil the grill rack. Place the chili peppers and tomatillos on a baking sheet and slip under the broiler, or place the chilies and tomatillos on the grill rack. Char evenly on all sides, turning as necessary.

★ Transfer the chilies and tomatillos to a cutting board. Remove and discard the seeds and stems from the poblanos. (The charred skin may be peeled, but you can also leave it attached, as it heightens the flavor of the salsa.) Roughly chop the chilies and tomatillos, along with the onion, cilantro and lettuce, and place in a saucepan. Add the garlic and chicken stock and place over medium heat. Bring to a fast simmer and cook until the liquid is reduced by about one-fourth, 10–15 minutes.

★ Remove from the heat and transfer to a food processor fitted with the metal blade or to a blender. Process to form a purée. Season to taste with salt. Set aside to cool to room temperature.

★ To make the fritters, in a small bowl, combine the shrimp, corn, black beans, green onion and bell pepper. Mix well. In another bowl, combine the *masa harina,* flour and baking powder. In a third bowl, combine the eggs and beer and whisk to mix. Pour the egg mixture into the flour mixture and mix until smooth. Then fold in the shrimp mixture until evenly combined. Season to taste with salt, pepper and cumin.

★ In a deep, heavy frying pan or in a heavy saucepan, pour in oil to a depth of 3 in (7.5 cm). Heat the oil to 375°F (190°C), or until a small bit of the batter sizzles upon contact with the oil. Working in batches so as not to crowd the pan, drop spoonfuls of the batter into the oil and deep-fry until crisp and golden brown, 2–3 minutes. Using a slotted utensil, transfer to paper towels to drain briefly.

★ Arrange the fritters on a serving plate and serve immediately, accompanied with the salsa.

SERVES 6–8   *Photograph page 54*

Top to bottom: Fried Okra Salad, Sweet-and-Sour Coleslaw

Left to right: Smoked Shrimp Fritters with Charred Green Salsa (recipe page 52), Seafood Quesadillas

SEAFOOD QUESADILLAS

These tortilla-based turnovers are an excellent way to utilize little bits of leftover grilled shrimp or chicken. The simplest filling (and my favorite) is a freshly roasted and peeled long green chili (see glossary) and a slice of Monterey Jack cheese sprinkled lightly with salt. But the possibilities are endless. A filling of lobster and papaya accompanied with a mango salsa is currently popular. Another delectable combination brings together strips of Brie and roasted chilies, chopped mango and fresh cilantro. If you have time, make chili flowers for garnishing the quesadillas. A light, fruity Chardonnay will complement this dish.

4 flour tortillas, each 8 in (20 cm) in diameter
olive oil
1½ cups (6 oz/185 g) shredded pepper Jack cheese (see glossary)
1 green (spring) onion, including tender green tops, thinly sliced
½ cup (3 oz/90 g) diced cooked shrimp (prawns) or flaked fresh-cooked crab meat

¼ cup (1½ oz/45 g) thinly sliced green, red or yellow bell pepper (capsicum)
1 small fresh jalapeño chili pepper, seeded (if desired) and minced
1 small tomato, diced
guacamole (see glossary), sour cream and fresh cilantro (fresh coriander) sprigs for garnish (optional)

★ Preheat a griddle or cast-iron frying pan until medium-hot.
★ Rub 1 side of each tortilla with olive oil. Place 2 tortillas, oiled sides down, on the hot griddle or pan and evenly top with the cheese, green onion, shrimp or crab meat, bell pepper, jalapeño and tomato. Place the remaining 2 flour tortillas on top, oiled sides up. Cook until browned on the bottom, 2–3 minutes. Carefully turn the filled tortillas over and brown on the second side, 2–3 minutes longer.
★ Garnish with dollops of guacamole and sour cream, and cilantro sprigs, if desired. Serve at once.

SERVES 2

54

Gulf Coast

SHRIMP PUFFS WITH BLACK SESAME SEEDS

A large Asian population lives along the Texas Gulf Coast, and this dish reflects the influence of their culinary heritage. The recipe calls for black sesame seeds, but white sesame seeds can be used in their place. The same batter may be used with snow peas (mangetouts), green (spring) onions, thin slices of peeled sweet potato, eggplant (aubergine) slices or carrots. The sweet-hot mustard sauce is the perfect accompaniment to the shrimp. A semidry Gewürztraminer or Chenin Blanc will stand up to the distinctive flavors of the chilies and mustard in the dish.

8 jumbo shrimp (prawns), peeled, deveined and butterflied with tail section intact (see glossary)
¼ teaspoon salt
2 teaspoons dry sherry

FOR THE MUSTARD SAUCE:

3 tablespoons Dijon-style mustard
¼ cup (2 fl oz/60 ml) heavy (double) cream
2 tablespoons jalapeño jelly
1 tablespoon black sesame seeds, toasted

FOR THE BATTER:

1 cup (5 oz/155 g) all-purpose (plain) flour
1 teaspoon baking powder
1 tablespoon black sesame seeds
1 cup (8 fl oz/250 ml) water

peanut oil for deep-frying
2 tablespoons cornstarch (cornflour)

★ Place the shrimp in a bowl and sprinkle evenly with the salt and sherry. Let stand for 10 minutes.
★ To make the sauce, in a small bowl, combine the mustard, cream, jalapeño jelly and black sesame seeds and, using a whisk, mix well. Set aside.
★ To make the batter, in a bowl, stir together the flour, baking powder, black sesame seeds and water until smooth. Pour the peanut oil into a deep, heavy frying pan or heavy saucepan to a depth of 1½ in (4 cm). Heat to 360°F (182°C), or until a small bit of the batter sizzles upon contact with the oil.
★ Spread the cornstarch on a plate. Working in batches so as not to crowd the pan, hold each shrimp by the tail and dip it first into the cornstarch, coating both sides and shaking off any excess, and then into the batter. Slip the shrimp into the oil and deep-fry until lightly browned and cooked through, 2–3 minutes. Using a slotted utensil, transfer to paper towels to drain briefly.
★ Serve the shrimp piping hot with the mustard sauce on the side.

SERVES 4

Shrimp Puffs with Black Sesame Seeds

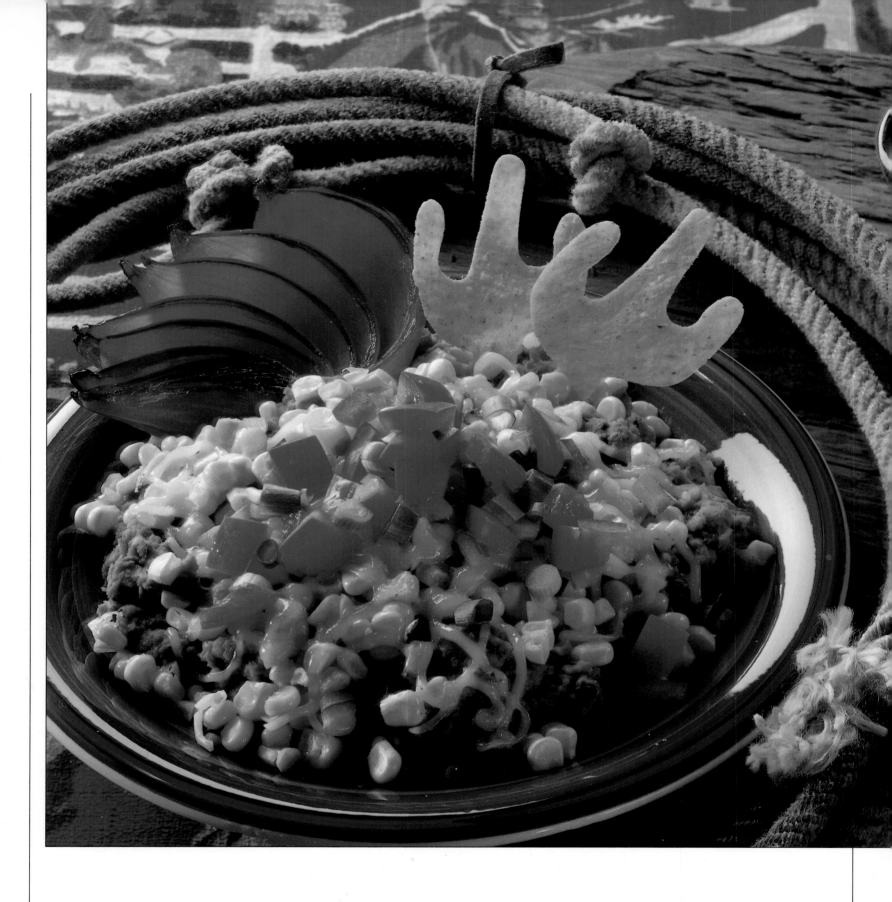

REFRIED BLACK-EYED PEAS WITH CORN AND CHEESE

Athens, Texas, a farming community some sixty miles (one hundred kilometers) east of Dallas, calls itself the Black-eyed Pea Capital of the World and is the source of most of the black-eyed peas sold throughout the state. That boast is important in Texas, where the typical country meal includes black-eyed peas, corn bread and sliced tomatoes topped with green (spring) onions. Texans love to graze and snack. This elaborate variation on old-fashioned South Texas refried pinto beans is a perfect opportunity to do just that. Under a layer of melting cheese and fresh crunchy corn kernels, you will find refried black-eyed peas ready for scooping onto blue corn tortilla chips and topping with a little tomato salsa. This dish defines the heart of Texas food: corn, chilies, cumin, garlic and cilantro.

2 teaspoons bacon drippings or vegetable oil
2 cans (15½ oz/485 g each) black-eyed peas, undrained
2 cloves garlic, minced
1 green (spring) onion, including the tender green tops, minced
¾ teaspoon ground cumin
¾ teaspoon chili powder
salt
juice of ½ lemon
corn kernels cut from 1 or 2 ears of corn
1 cup (4 oz/125 g) shredded pepper Jack cheese (see glossary)

FOR SERVING:

2 green (spring) onions, including the tender green tops, minced
1 cup (8 fl oz/250 ml) fresh tomato salsa (see glossary)
minced fresh cilantro (fresh coriander) (optional)
1 fresh jalapeño chili pepper, seeded (if desired) and minced (optional)
cactus-shaped tortilla chips (optional; see glossary)
blue corn tortilla chips (optional; see glossary)

Clockwise from top right: Cilantro and Pumpkin Seed Butter, Charred Onion and Garlic Spread, Refried Black-eyed Peas with Corn and Cheese

★ Preheat an oven to 425°F (220°C).
★ In a nonstick frying pan over medium heat, warm the bacon drippings or vegetable oil. Add the undrained black-eyed peas, garlic and green onion. Stir well and season with the cumin, chili powder, salt to taste and lemon juice. Using a potato masher, mash the beans. Continue cooking and mashing over medium heat until the black-eyed peas are slightly thickened, 6–8 minutes.
★ Pour the black-eyed peas onto an oval ovenproof platter and sprinkle with the corn kernels. Top the corn evenly with the cheese. Bake until the cheese melts and is quite hot, 8–10 minutes.
★ To serve, remove from the oven and immediately sprinkle with the green onions, the tomato salsa and the cilantro and jalapeño, if using. If desired, stand cactus-shaped tortilla chips upright over the surface and surround the edge of the plate with the blue corn tortilla chips.

SERVES 6–8

High Plains

CILANTRO AND PUMPKIN SEED BUTTER

Serve this cilantro-flecked butter with hot flour tortillas for a wonderful appetizer or snack. It is also delicious brushed onto fish, shellfish or chicken on the grill or slathered on hot ears of corn. Sunflower seeds can be substituted for the pumpkin seeds.

½ cup (2 oz/60 g) salted, roasted pumpkin seeds
½ cup (½ oz/15 g) fresh cilantro (fresh coriander) leaves
4 cloves garlic, minced
1½ cups (12 oz/375 g) butter or margarine, at room temperature
juice of ½ lime
freshly ground pepper

★ In a food processor fitted with the metal blade, combine the pumpkin seeds, cilantro and garlic. Process until minced. Add the butter, lime juice and pepper to taste and process until smooth.
★ Spoon the butter into a crock and serve at room temperature.

MAKES ABOUT 1¾ CUPS (14 OZ/440 G)

South Texas

CHARRED ONION AND GARLIC SPREAD

Onions are plentiful and sweet in Texas. This heady spread is delicious on crackers or French bread slices. It is also good in place of butter on baked potatoes or on angel-hair pasta that is then garnished with toasted pine nuts and minced parsley. Cajun-style seasoning, a blend of cayenne pepper, oregano, onion, garlic, thyme and nutmeg, can be found in well-stocked food stores. For a special presentation, hollow out large purple onions or the softball-sized Texas 1015 onions and use as serving containers for this unique spread.

1 whole head garlic
olive oil, to cover
1 yellow onion, cut into slices ½ in (12 mm) thick
½ lb (250 g) cream cheese or Neufchâtel cheese, at room temperature
salt and freshly ground pepper
2 green (spring) onions, including tender green tops, minced
2 tablespoons minced fresh parsley
1 teaspoon Cajun-style seasoning
salted, roasted pumpkin seeds or toasted pine nuts for garnish

★ Separate the garlic cloves and peel them. Place the garlic cloves in a small saucepan and add olive oil to cover. Place over low heat and bring to a simmer. Cook until the cloves are softened but not browned, about 10 minutes. Remove from the heat and set aside.
★ Place a heavy frying pan or cast-iron griddle over medium-high heat. Add the yellow onion slices in a single layer. Press down on them, turning when they begin to caramelize and char, after about 15 minutes. Turn, repeating the process on the second side. Remove from the heat and set aside.
★ Drain the garlic cloves. Engage the motor in a food processor fitted with the metal blade and drop the garlic cloves down the feed tube. When the garlic is puréed, add the onion slices and use on-off pulses to combine. Add the cream cheese or Neufchâtel cheese, salt and pepper to taste, green onions, parsley and Cajun-style seasoning. Process until smooth.
★ Serve at room temperature garnished with pumpkin seeds or pine nuts.

MAKES ABOUT 1½ CUPS (12 FL OZ/375 ML)

SOUTH TEXAS

SOUTH TEXAS

A medley of Spanish, German and Old South lifestyles has contributed to the character of South Texas, which includes the coastline along the Gulf of Mexico. This area known locally as the Coastal Plains is the bridge between plantation and hacienda lifestyles. San Antonio, the oldest large city in the area, is considered every Texan's symbolic second home, as well as a favorite location for the actual second homes of many Mexican nationals. The spirit of *mi casa es su casa* prevails in this most festive of Texas cities.

Historically important structures lure visitors again and again: the Alamo (San Antonio de Valero Mission) and the four other missions that formed the nucleus for settlement in the 1700s, the Spanish governor's house, the homes and buildings of Fort Sam Houston built in the 1800s, and the grande dame hotels of the same period (the Menger, the St. Anthony and the Gunter) all create the city's unforgettably romantic ambience. The beautiful San Antonio River and the San Fernando Cathedral, the oldest continually operating parish church in the nation, are wonderful visual focal points and tributes to the dreams of early generations.

This area long has been important in the food world also, for here, in the eighteenth century, missionaries first introduced Old World crops, fed by more than fifteen miles (twenty-five kilometers) of irrigation ditches and

Previous pages: The venerable Mission San José, built in the mid-1700s, is considered one of the finest examples of Spanish mission architecture in the United States. Left: An array of restaurants, cafes and shops lines the cobblestone paths of the Paseo del Rio, or River Walk, along the San Antonio River.

61

aqueducts, and built huge granaries. Cattle barons established their presence on vast stretches of mesquite- and cactus-inhabited land, built their mansions in town and ruled their domains in a manner that may have set the scene for all times—bigger is better.

German settlers founded milling empires, and Mexican vaqueros introduced foods that forever changed North America's menus. Food experts credit San Antonio with making chili, fajitas and gorditas famous, and salsa has reached new heights of perfection as a result of the efforts of San Antonio–based companies. The French, Poles and South Africans made their way to this beautiful spot known for its hospitality and food. Those early days set the stage for the international hub the city is today. Then and now, El Camino Real (the King's Highway) leads from San Antonio, south through Laredo to Mexico, and then to Central and South America.

The Gulf Coast merges with the arid reaches of South Texas so seamlessly that at first you are not aware that you have transitted from one area to the other. Corpus Christi, the gateway from Europe to inland destinations of Mexico, Texas and beyond, joins the Port of Houston in welcoming products from around the globe. Houston's collection of megabusinesses continues the legacy of New York's Allen brothers, who purchased two thousand acres (eight hundred hectares) for five thousand dollars in the 1800s. They established a city on the land and named it after the hero of the 1836 Battle of San Jacinto, General Sam Houston, who was once the governor of Tennessee, chief advisor to the Cherokee nation and the leader of the colonists in their fight for freedom from Mexico.

The "rose window" of the Mission San José exemplifies the desire of the Spanish to imbue a functional architectural element with beauty.

When the famous Spindletop gusher roared into being in 1901, it heralded the beginning of an age founded on energy-based businesses, paved the streets with "black gold" and provided a natural habitat for the aggressive "can-do" attitude of the wildcatters that continues to this day. Houston is known as the only city that "dared to dig a ditch to the sea." Today, a modern waterway allows ships to travel the short distance between Houston and Galveston. Houston took over Galveston's position as the state's wealthiest city when a hurricane virtually destroyed Galveston in 1900. Prior to this time Galveston was known as the Wall Street of the South.

The Spanish ranches were confined largely to South Texas as a result of the Comanches' and Apaches' dedicated resistance to the white settlers' advancement northward. The descendants of these early conquistadors exerted great influence on other ranchers, and it is they who are credited with establishing the techniques and sharing the skills that became the basis for western ranching. The huge King Ranch is a typical example of this legacy, with vast herds that occupy more than eight hundred thousand acres (three hundred thousand hectares). Known throughout the world for beef, King Ranch led the way in conquering the arid land in other ways as well.

Highly productive farming in the Rio Grande Valley is possible because of sophisticated irrigation techniques, aided by the year-long growing season that makes the battle with nature worthwhile. Land that once was thorn forest, home to jaguars, javelinas, ocelots and similar exotic creatures, now boasts orange and grapefruit groves as well as Asian and other vegetable crops grown on experimental cooperatives overseen by Israel, China, the Texas Department of Agriculture and private business.

A stretch of South Texas produces much of the nation's supply of winter spinach, watermelons and cantaloupe. The Franciscan priests who battled superstition, Comanche and Apache war bands and hostile Mexican inhabitants to establish farming outposts in this part of the world would be gratified to know of the importance of farming in these modern times.

With the founding of La Villita (the village that was to become San Antonio) on the banks of the San Antonio River came street vendors who sold chili, families who prepared typical south-of-the-border foods and served them in tiny cafes or in the open-air *mercado,* and the evolution of Tex-Mex cooking. Although some people decry the term *Tex-Mex,* it is impossible to deny its existence. Various adaptations of tacos and nachos are examples of what many people perceive as Mexican food, when in actuality they are Tex-Mex variations of foods made with ingredients found in many Mexican recipes. No self-respecting restaurant in Mexico will lay claim to having originated chili, a dish that probably came about as a method of cooking meat that was no longer fresh, but it includes several items that are staples of the Mexican pantry.

But it was not until the 1950s that Tex-Mex food showed up in towns and cities across the state, and now there are fast-food chains with drive-in service, charming rustic cafes and upscale restaurants with white tablecloths serving Mexican fare. Frito Lay developed the

The Santa Ana Wildlife Refuge preserved the dense, subtropical forests of the Rio Grande delta before they could be cleared for cultivation.

A storefront near Engels dates to the 1890s, when much of south-central Texas consisted of general stores and other small businesses interspersed along the major roadways.

famed Fritos corn chips, and machinery produces tons of tortillas in companies large and small. Schools, hospitals and cafeterias regularly include enchiladas, tacos, fajitas, beans and rice on their menus, and nachos are a passion for people of all ages. The "Mexican" food that is gaining such popularity nationally and internationally is frequently more Tex-Mex than true Mexican cuisine.

It has taken many years for restaurants that prepare authentic Mexican cuisine to become major influences on the food scene. A number include cactus fruits and leaves among the interesting, somewhat unfamiliar ingredients used, as do establishments that specialize in southwestern menus. Of any single plant, the humble prickly pear cactus may have the most dramatic and far-reaching influence on food trends for years to come. It is plentiful and inexpensively and easily grown, is the most water-efficient plant in Texas, produces almost year-round and is nourishing. These attributes are important, for many experts forecast that in the twenty-first century much of Texas will become hotter and drier. Prickly pear, a plant that thrives in hot, dry conditions, may someday become a mainstay in the diets of a large segment of the population.

Cooking with cactus is an ancient tradition that uses the sweet fruit known as *tunas,* which have a flavor somewhat similar to that of the kiwifruit. They can be used in much the same way as cooks around the world use peaches, apricots, pears and apples. The paddles, or leaves, taste like tart green beans and are good served hot as a vegetable or cold in salads, and the blossoms are delicious additions to green salads. The prickly pear is an untapped low-cost source of vitamin C, calcium, crude protein, phosphorus and natural sugars, is low in calories and sodium, and contains no cholesterol. New spineless varieties with a fruity flavor akin to honeydew melon are being developed for nationwide distribution.

The Doguet family of China, Texas, southeast of Beaumont, provides an excellent example of the type of diversified farming now being developed. They combine crayfish, beef, grass, rice and milling into a single interactive approach to farming. Immediately after harvesting the rice, they flood the fields and grow five hundred to eight hundred pounds (250 to 400 kilograms) of crayfish per acre (about two-fifths of a hectare). The crayfish eat all the stubble and algae, every weed, every root, every seed and even insects, so there is no need for artificial chemicals. The Doguets produce and market 25 to 30 million pounds (13 to 15 million kilograms) of rice and many tons of beef annually.

It has taken Texans years to decide to grow crayfish commercially. It is sometimes difficult to think of delib-

erately cultivating the creature that is responsible for mud chimneys and burrows in East Texas front lawns, but crayfish farms have become a key element in the regional economy.

Nowhere is the "gone to Texas" refrain of old felt more than in this part of the state. Asians, Hispanics from the Caribbean and Central and South America, and Americans from other states continue to flock to South Texas and the Coastal Plains. This international mix of inhabitants has given rise to markets, restaurants and cooking schools that incorporate the culinary traditions of these newcomers.

Foremost among the high-profile South Texas chefs making their mark on the new Texas cuisine is Bruce Auden. Not to be outdone, Debra Auden is making headlines in the baking world, and Jay McCarthy creates innovative recipes including Thai and Caribbean seasonings and cactus as key ingredients. Michael Bomberg, Alec Baratin, Thierry Burkle, Mark Bliss and Kim Swendson-Cameron are among the many chefs generating excitement on a daily basis. Their work promises a particularly bright future for Texas cuisine.

Left: Houston, with a population of over 4 million, is noted for its modernity and relative lack of tradition—most of the buildings were constructed after 1960. Below: The Gulf Coast, which once harbored pirates, is now the playground for anglers and water-sports enthusiasts.

CULINARY COMFORTS

A pan of biscuits, cooked over an open fire, adds the final touch to a simple Texas meal.

CULINARY COMFORTS

The Llano Estacado is an area so flat and lacking in landmarks that the Spanish explorer Francisco Coronado left piles of bones as markers for his return journey. It was here that the army finally defeated the Comanches in Palo Duro Canyon, which opened the way for ranchers whose spreads eventually encompassed vast tracts. There remains little evidence of the terror, hardships and bloodshed that preceded the development of ranching here. Today, the land is a rich kaleidoscope of irrigated wheat and cotton fields; less than 120 years ago, only the Comanches knew where to find the few water holes.

Food was simple, often scarce. Meat was cooked in an open pot over a campfire, and seasonings masked the rancid tastes. Of these trail-born foods—the results of cooking with whatever was on hand and of adding a large dose of hot chili peppers to stave off disease, to cover undesirable flavors and to appease the requests of the Mexican cowhands known as vaqueros—only chili has evolved into a national passion. There are as many recipes for a "bowl o' red" as there are cooks preparing it. Entire books have been written about chili, and any number of festivals tout its glories. From the white chili sold by Neiman Marcus to chili guru Wick Fowler's recipe served at Austin's La Zona Rosa, ingredients have been chopped, ground, pounded and stirred into preparations that range from mild to fiery.

Passion exists, too, in the debate over how to serve chili. There are the proponents of a large bowl of just the plain soup-stew served with Indian fry bread or a wedge of butter-slathered, down-home-style corn bread. Some folks are equally certain that chili is best when smothered in chopped onions and shredded Cheddar cheese, crowned with dollops of sour cream and salsa and served with fresh tortillas on the side. Others say that there must be a scoop of white rice or crumbled saltines or corn chips in the bottom of the bowl, the chili ladled over the top and then the bowl garnished to your heart's content. Still other "experts" claim that griddle-cooked, English muffin–style corn bread made by Barnaby's Beanery in Amarillo is the only extra needed.

The best beverage to accompany hearty chili or stew is beer, preferably a dark Shiner Bock or other locally produced brew. One of the most important food developments of the 1990s has been the emergence of brew pubs throughout the state. The first such pub in Texas was Austin's Waterloo Brewing Company, named for the outpost on the Colorado River that later was renamed Austin. Waterloo's flagship beers commemorate the names of famous Austinites. Edwin Waller (Ed's Best Bitter) signed the Texas Declaration of Independence and was the first mayor of Austin; Clara Driscoll (Clara's Clara) was a wealthy matron who saved the Alamo in San Antonio by purchasing it in 1903; and writer William Sydney Porter, popularly known as O. Henry (O. Henry's Porter), needs no introduction.

Ed's Best Bitter is an American version of a traditional British bitter, while O. Henry's Porter is a rich, coal-

Previous pages, clockwise from top left: Country Biscuits with Apple-Tequila Jelly (recipe page 85), Frank Tolbert's Original Texas Chili (recipe page 88), Bock Black Bean Soup (recipe page 90)

68

Above: Growing cotton, wheat and other grains and raising cattle constitute the agrarian economy of the Texas Panhandle. Left: The incendiary "bowl o' red" derives its name from the lavish use of ground dried chili pepper.

colored ale known stylistically as a black beer. Black beer is darker and more bitter than most porters and sweeter and less roasted than most dry stouts. Clara's Clara is a mild golden ale, with a slightly sweet malt flavor, a good example of the trend to freshly brewed, flavorful beers.

Chef Bruce Auden has opened a brew pub in San Antonio that serves fabulous food as well as great brews. He and wife Debra have been pacesetters in the evolution of the state's cuisine since the early 1980s. The emergence of brew pubs is in turn encouraging the opening of European-style coffeehouses and small playhouses, phenomena not previously seen in the Lone Star State, where the favorite watering holes have traditionally been huge dance halls.

Whether because they are reminders of how things once were or a means of comfort in a fast-paced lifestyle, soups, stews, chilis and breads are loosely placed in a category called comfort foods. They are somewhat old-fashioned, are simple to prepare, are rib-stickin' good and stand on their own merits. But there is always room for a little experimentation, even with old favorites, and the recipes that follow are a blending of the old and the new.

CARNE GUISADA

This popular south-of-the-border stew is most often served with refried beans, tomato slices topped with cool, creamy guacamole and hot flour tortillas. For heat lovers, add jalapeños, or Texas okra as they are sometimes called. In South Texas, this stew is also often served in wrapped flour tortillas for a delicious, portable breakfast.

3 tablespoons vegetable oil
2 lb (1 kg) beef round steak, cut into 1-in (2.5-cm) cubes
2 tablespoons all-purpose (plain) flour
½ green bell pepper (capsicum), seeded and finely chopped
½ yellow onion, finely chopped
1 large tomato, finely chopped
1 fresh jalapeño chili pepper, thinly sliced crosswise
3 cloves garlic, finely chopped
½ teaspoon ground cumin
1 teaspoon chili powder
½ teaspoon salt and ¼ teaspoon freshly ground pepper
½ cup (4 fl oz/125 ml) beef stock or water, or as needed

★ In a large saucepan or heavy pot over medium-high heat, warm the vegetable oil. Add the beef cubes and sauté until lightly browned, 8–10 minutes. Sprinkle with the flour and then add the bell pepper, onion and tomato. Stir well and then mix in the jalapeño, garlic, cumin, chili powder, salt and pepper and the ½ cup (4 fl oz/125 ml) beef stock or water. Reduce the heat to low, cover and simmer gently until the meat is very tender, 2–2½ hours. Add additional stock or water if the stew begins to stick to the pan bottom.
★ Serve the stew piping hot in warmed bowls.

SERVES 4–6

CACTUS JACK BISCUITS WITH ANCHO-CINNAMON BUTTER

San Antonio chef Michael Bomberg created this distinctive biscuit recipe using the highly versatile cactus, which imparts an enticing flavor and texture. The ancho-cinnamon butter is the perfect partner to the biscuits. It is also delicious on grilled chicken. The biscuits can also be served with honey.

FOR THE BISCUITS:

1 cup (8 oz/250 g) chopped fresh or canned cactus paddles (see glossary)
1 cup (4 oz/125 g) grated pepper Jack cheese (see glossary)
3 tablespoons chopped fresh cilantro (fresh coriander)
1 cup (5 oz/155 g) all-purpose (plain) flour
2 teaspoons baking powder
½ cup (4 oz/125 g) unsalted butter, at room temperature

FOR THE ANCHO-CINNAMON BUTTER:

1 large or 2 small dried ancho chili peppers (see glossary)
2 tablespoons fresh orange juice
1½ cups (¾ lb/750 g) unsalted butter, at room temperature
½ teaspoon ground cinnamon
¾ teaspoon ground cumin
2½ teaspoons honey
⅛–¼ teaspoon Asian sesame oil
salt

★ Place a baking sheet in an oven and preheat the oven to 400°F (200°C).
★ In a large bowl, combine the cactus, cheese and cilantro. Sprinkle in the flour and baking powder, and then stir to mix well. Using a fork; work in the butter until a ball of sticky dough forms.
★ Grease the hot baking sheet with vegetable shortening. Using a spoon, drop mounds of dough about the size of

Left to right: Cactus Jack Biscuits with Ancho-Cinnamon Butter, Carne Guisada

unshelled walnuts onto the baking sheet, spacing them about 1½ in (4 cm) apart. Flatten slightly with the back of a fork. Bake until slightly browned and crisp, 30–40 minutes.

★ Meanwhile, make the ancho-cinnamon butter. In a bowl, combine the chilies with hot water to cover and let stand for 15–20 minutes to soften. Drain, squeeze out the excess water and remove the stems and seeds. In a blender or food processor fitted with a metal blade, combine the soaked chilies,

orange juice and about one-third of the butter and purée until smooth. Add the remaining butter and the cinnamon, cumin and honey, and stir in the sesame oil and salt to taste. Taste and adjust the seasoning. Transfer to a small bowl and set aside at room temperature.

★ Serve the biscuits hot from the oven with the ancho-cinnamon butter.

MAKES 20–24 BISCUITS; MAKES 1¾ CUPS (14 OZ/440 G) BUTTER

DESERT FLAT BREAD

With flavors reminiscent of Italian focaccia, this delicious bread can be topped with fresh herbs, cheese, sun-dried tomatoes and grilled onions for a first course or light supper. It also makes a good base for sandwiches filled with Mexican queso fresco and prosciutto.

2 eggs
1 cup (8 fl oz/250 ml) milk
¼ teaspoon dried oregano leaves, crumbled
½ teaspoon fresh rosemary leaves, crushed
1 teaspoon salt
1¼ cups (6½ oz/200 g) all-purpose (plain) flour
3 oz (90 g) spicy green olives, coarsely chopped
3 oz (90 g) spicy black olives, coarsely chopped
½ teaspoon crushed red pepper flakes (optional)
½ cup (4 fl oz/125 ml) olive oil

★ Preheat an oven to 350°F (180°C). Generously oil a cast-iron frying pan or baking dish 12 in (30 cm) in diameter.
★ In a bowl, whisk together the eggs and milk. Add the oregano, rosemary, salt and flour and stir to form a smooth batter. Stir in the green and black olives, the pepper flakes, if using, and the olive oil. Pour into the prepared pan or dish.
★ Bake until lightly browned, 25–35 minutes. Remove from the oven and serve hot or at room temperature.

MAKES ONE 12-IN (30-CM) ROUND

MASHED POTATO SOUP

Comforting and wonderfully flavored, this Texas-style vichyssoise is an adaptation of a soup at the Peach Tree Tea Room in Fredericksburg. It is equally delicious when prepared with red potatoes. For a more substantial soup, add 1 cup (6 oz/185 g) shredded chicken and ½ cup (3 oz/90 g) roasted corn kernels.

¼ cup (2 oz/60 g) butter or margarine
1 yellow onion, minced
4 large russet potatoes (about 2 lb/ 1 kg), peeled and cut into ¾-in (2-cm) cubes

Fresh Corn Soup with Roasted Poblano Chilies and Crab Meat

2 cups (16 fl oz/500 ml) chicken stock
3 cups (24 fl oz/750 ml) water
1 teaspoon ground cumin
¼ cup (1½ oz/45 g) pickled jalapeño chili peppers and juice, minced (see glossary)
pinch of baking soda (bicarbonate of soda)
½ cup (4 fl oz/125 ml) evaporated milk
salt and freshly ground pepper
sliced green (spring) onions, cilantro pesto (optional; see glossary) and crisp-cooked bacon pieces for garnish

★ In a large pot over medium-high heat, melt the butter or margarine. Add the onion and sauté until just tender, about 5 minutes. Add the potatoes, chicken stock, water and cumin. Stir well, bring to a boil, cover and cook over medium-high heat until the potatoes are tender, 20–30 minutes.
★ Stir in the jalapeños, baking soda and evaporated milk. Remove from the heat and, using a potato masher, mash the potatoes coarsely. Stir well, taste and adjust the seasoning. Return the pot to medium heat, bring to a simmer and simmer for 15 minutes to blend the flavors. Ladle into small warmed soup bowls and garnish with green onions, cilantro pesto, if using, and bacon. Serve immediately.

SERVES 6–8

FRESH CORN SOUP WITH ROASTED POBLANO CHILIES AND CRAB MEAT

In Dallas, you will find everything from Texas chili to French haute cuisine. Here is a soup that can be either simple home cooking or, with the addition of the crab meat, a sophisticated first course.

4–6 large ears of corn, husks and silks removed
4 tablespoons butter
½ yellow onion, chopped
2 cloves garlic, minced
2 cups (16 fl oz/500 ml) milk
2 cups (16 fl oz/500 ml) heavy (double) cream
salt
1 cup (6 oz/185 g) flaked lump crab meat, picked over for cartilage and shell fragments and shredded, for garnish
thin strips of roasted poblano chili (see glossary) and tiny triangles of red bell pepper (capsicum) for garnish

★ Using a sharp knife, slice enough corn kernels from the ears of corn to measure 3 cups (18 oz/560 g). Transfer to a food processor fitted with the metal blade or to a blender.
★ In a small frying pan over medium heat, melt 2 tablespoons of the butter. Add the onion and garlic and sauté until translucent, 3–4 minutes. Add the onion-garlic mixture to the corn with ¼ cup (2 fl oz/60 ml) of the milk. Purée until smooth.
★ In a saucepan over medium heat, melt the remaining 2 tablespoons butter. Add the puréed corn mixture and cook, stirring occasionally, until quite thick, 8–10 minutes. Gradually whisk in the remaining 1¾ cups (14 fl oz/440 ml) milk. When it is fully incorporated, cover and simmer over medium heat until the mixture is smooth and slightly thickened, about 15 minutes.
★ Pour the mixture through a sieve into a clean bowl. Then return it to the saucepan over medium heat. Stir in the cream and add salt to taste. Heat to serving temperature and ladle into soup bowls. Garnish with the crab, chili strips and bell pepper triangles. Serve at once.

SERVES 4–6

Top to bottom: Mashed Potato Soup, Desert Flat Bread

East Texas

SOURDOUGH BISCUITS WITH SPICY PEACH CHUTNEY

These flaky sourdough biscuits can be served with mesquite honey or jalapeño jelly, but you'll find the spicy peach chutney worth the extra effort. Peaches were planted at the Spanish missions in Texas in the sixteenth century, and at one time East Texas commercial growers boasted 15 million Elberta peach trees. The chutney recipe yields enough for serving with several batches of biscuits, but since it can be processed in a hot-water bath for long-term storage, you can tuck it away until you bake again. The sweet yet tart chutney also complements Cheddar cheese–flavored biscuits, Black Forest ham or even egg rolls. The recipe is adapted from one developed by Sylvia and Bill Varney, who use their own pepper-garlic herb vinegar from the Fredericksburg Herb Farm. The starter left over, once the biscuits have been made, can be kept indefinitely in the refrigerator to use in other recipes calling for sourdough starter, such as waffles, rolls and breads.

FOR THE SOURDOUGH STARTER:

1 tablespoon active dry yeast
3½ cups (17½ oz/545 g) all-purpose (plain) flour
2¾ cups (22 fl oz/680 ml) warm water (105°–115°F/41°–46°C)

FOR THE SPICY PEACH CHUTNEY:

3 tablespoons crushed red pepper flakes
2 lb (1 kg) peaches, pitted, peeled and sliced
2 cups (16 fl oz/500 ml) pepper-garlic herb vinegar or cider vinegar
1¼ cups (9 oz/280 g) firmly packed light brown sugar
¼ cup (2 fl oz/60 ml) fresh lemon juice
1 white onion, minced
½ cup (3 oz/90 g) raisins
2 teaspoons yellow mustard seeds
1 teaspoon ground ginger or 3 oz (90 g) crystallized ginger, chopped
1 teaspoon ground cinnamon
¼ teaspoon ground allspice

FOR THE BISCUITS:

½ cup (4 fl oz/125 ml) sourdough starter
1 cup (8 fl oz/250 ml) milk
2½ cups (12½ oz/390 g) all-purpose (plain) flour
2 tablespoons sugar
1 teaspoon salt
1 teaspoon baking powder
1 teaspoon baking soda (bicarbonate of soda)
¼ cup (4 oz/125 g) unsalted butter, melted and cooled

★ To make the starter, in a bowl, combine the yeast, 1 cup (5 oz/155 g) of the flour and ¾ cup (6 fl oz/180 ml) of the water. Stir to mix well, cover and let stand in a warm place for about 3 days, stirring occasionally. When it begins to smell sour, it is ready. Refrigerate, well covered, until needed.
★ In a large bowl, combine the above mixture, the remaining 2½ cups (12½ oz/390 g) flour and the remaining 2 cups (16 fl oz/500 ml) warm water. Stir to mix well, cover and let stand overnight in a warm place. You should have about 1 qt (1 l) starter. Store in the refrigerator following fermentation.
★ While the starter is fermenting, make the chutney. In a nonreactive saucepan over high heat, combine all of the ingredients and bring to a boil. Reduce the heat to low and simmer, uncovered, stirring occasionally and skimming off any foam that forms, until the mixture is the consistency of thick fruit preserve, 45–60 minutes.
★ Ladle the hot chutney into hot, sterilized jars, leaving ¼ in (6 mm) headspace. Cover with canning lids and screw on ring bands. Process the jars in a hot-water bath (see glossary) for 15 minutes. Remove from the bath, let cool completely and check to see that the seals are good. Store in a cool, dry place

for up to 6 months. If a seal is not good, store the chutney in the refrigerator for up to 3 weeks, or store uncanned chutney in the refrigerator for the same amount of time.
★ To make the biscuits, in a large bowl, combine the ½ cup (4 fl oz/125 ml) starter, the milk and 1 cup (5 oz/155 g) of the flour. Using a wooden spoon, stir until well mixed, then cover the bowl with a clean, dry towel and let rise in a warm place until the mixture rises and puffs, 45–60 minutes.
★ In a sifter, combine the sugar, salt, baking powder and soda, and the remaining 1½ cup (7½ oz/235 g) flour. Sift the mixture over the top of the dough.
★ Using your hands, mix the flour mixture into the soft dough, kneading lightly until a soft, smooth consistency forms, 1–2 minutes.
★ Turn out the dough onto a floured work surface. Roll it out into a round ½ in (12 mm) thick. Using a floured biscuit cutter 2 in (5 cm) in diameter, cut out the biscuits. You should have about 24.
★ Dip each biscuit in the melted butter to coat both sides well, then arrange the biscuits in a 9-in (23-cm) square pan. They will fit snugly. Let rise, uncovered, in a warm place until puffed, 20–30 minutes.
★ Preheat an oven to 375°F (190°C).
★ Bake until golden brown, about 30 minutes. Remove from the oven and serve hot with the spicy peach chutney.

MAKES 24 BISCUITS; MAKES 4 CUPS (2½ LB/750 G) CHUTNEY

West Texas

VENISON CHILI WITH CHILI-FLAVORED CRÈME FRAÎCHE

This is but one version of the dish that made Texas famous. Venison is leaner than beef and may require a bit more oil for cooking. It also needs to be slowly simmered for up to 2 hours or longer to become tender. If possible, use a cactus-shaped cookie cutter for cutting the flour or corn tortillas for chips. The chili can be served in a chafing dish, with the chips alongside for guests to dip. You can also use plain crème fraîche or minced green (spring) onions and shredded Cheddar cheese in place of the chili crème fraîche. A traditional Texas beer, such as Shiner Bock or Lone Star, would be the perfect accompaniment.

2 lb (1 kg) venison or beef, coarsely ground (coarsely minced)
2–3 cups (16–24 fl oz/500–750 ml) milk
2 tablespoons vegetable oil
1 large yellow onion, diced
4 cloves garlic, minced
1 tablespoon dried oregano
1 tablespoon cumin seed
2 tablespoons chili powder
3 cans (10 oz/315 g each) diced or whole tomatoes with hot green chilies, undrained
1 cup (8 fl oz/250 ml) beef stock
salt
2–3 tablespoons sugar

FOR THE CHILI-FLAVORED CRÈME FRAÎCHE:

1 cup (8 fl oz/250 ml) crème fraîche (see glossary)
dash of ground cumin
¼ teaspoon chili powder
2 teaspoons fresh lime juice
2 tablespoons minced fresh cilantro (fresh coriander)
2 tablespoons minced fresh flat-leaf (Italian) parsley

tortilla chips (see glossary)

★ In a bowl, combine the venison and as much milk as needed to cover. Cover and refrigerate overnight. The next day, drain

Top to bottom: Sourdough Biscuits with Spicy Peach Chutney, Venison Chili with Chili-Flavored Crème Fraîche, Hunter's Stew with Refrigerator Yeast Rolls (recipe page 76)

the venison and pat it dry with paper towels. (This step helps to eliminate the gamy flavor of the meat.)

★ In a large, heavy pot over medium heat, warm the oil. Add the onion, garlic and venison and sauté until lightly browned, 15–20 minutes. Add the oregano, cumin, chili powder, tomatoes with chilies, beef stock and salt and sugar to taste. Stir well, bring to a gentle boil, reduce the heat to low and cook gently until the venison is tender, 1–2 hours.

★ While the chili is simmering, make the chili-flavored crème fraîche. In a bowl, stir together all ingredients until well mixed. Cover and refrigerate until serving.

★ Ladle the chili into warmed soup mugs or bowls and top with the chili-flavored crème fraîche and tortilla chips. Serve at once.

SERVES 6–8

75

HUNTER'S STEW WITH REFRIGERATOR YEAST ROLLS

The ranchlands of South Texas and the Hill Country provide Texans with wild game and beef for informal entertaining. This hearty and fragrant hunter's stew is prepared with venison and the wonderful German sausage found deep in the heart of Texas Hill Country, but beef can be substituted. The Pedregons of Fredericksburg, who operate the Peach Tree Tea Room, serve the stew in hollowed-out rolls. The award-winning Sister Creek Winery, in nearby Sisterdale, bottles a blend of Cabernet Franc and Sauvignon that is sufficiently full-flavored for this game stew.

FOR THE ROLLS:

2 tablespoons active dry yeast
⅓ cup (3 fl oz/80 ml) warm water (105°–115°F/41°–46°C)
½ cup (4 oz/125 g) butter
1 cup (8 fl oz/250 ml) milk

4¼–4¾ cups (21½–24 oz/675–755 g) unbleached all-purpose (plain) flour
⅓ cup (3 oz/90 g) sugar
2 teaspoons salt
3 eggs, at room temperature
melted butter

FOR THE STEW:

3 tablespoons vegetable oil
2½ lb (1.25 kg) boneless venison, cut into ½-in (12-mm) cubes
¾ lb (325 g) smoked sausage, cut into slices ½ in (12 mm) thick
1 large yellow onion, chopped
½ cup (2½ oz/75 g) chopped celery
2 cans (28 oz/875 g each) tomatoes, chopped and juices reserved
1 can (12 fl oz/375 ml) beer
1 teaspoon salt
1 teaspoon crushed red pepper flakes
1 teaspoon sugar

workable dough, mixing it in by hand. The dough will be soft and sticky. Form into a ball, place in an oiled bowl, turn to coat the surface and cover the bowl with plastic wrap. Refrigerate for at least 4 hours (or as long as overnight). The dough will rise until doubled in volume.

★ Turn out the dough onto a generously floured work surface. Pinch off pieces the size of a small apple and form into balls. You should have 10 balls in all. Place the balls on an ungreased baking sheet 2–3 in (5–7.5 cm) apart. Brush generously with melted butter. Allow to rise at room temperature until doubled in volume, 45–60 minutes.

★ About 30 minutes before you begin to form the rolls, make the stew. In a large, heavy pot over medium-high heat, warm the vegetable oil. Add the venison and sausage and brown well on all sides, 8–10 minutes. Add the onion and celery and sauté until tender, about 10 minutes.

★ Add the tomatoes and their juices, beer, salt, red pepper flakes, sugar, rosemary, basil and ground pepper. Stir well, cover, reduce the heat to low and simmer for 30 minutes. Add the carrots and cook, uncovered, for 30 minutes. Then stir in the potatoes and cook until the meats and vegetables are tender when pierced with a fork, about 30 minutes longer.

★ While the stew simmers, preheat an oven to 400°F (200°C).

★ Just before the stew is ready, bake the rolls until lightly browned, about 10 minutes. Remove from the oven and, using a fork, hollow out the center of each roll. (Reserve the removed bread to use in a stuffing or other dish.)

★ Place the hot rolls on individual plates and ladle the hot stew into them. Garnish with fresh basil sprigs. Serve immediately.

SERVES 8–10   *Photograph page 75*

S o u t h   T e x a s

TORTILLA SOUP

Here is a basic yet flavorful tortilla soup that has all the nuances of the culinary traditions of Texas and Mexico. The Mexican white cheese and crispy corn tortillas add flavor and texture to the rich stock.

8 cups (64 fl oz/2 l) rich chicken stock
4 green (spring) onions, including tender green tops, minced
2 large, ripe tomatoes, chopped
¼ cup (2 fl oz/60 ml) vegetable oil
6 corn tortillas, halved and cut crosswise into ¼ in (6 mm) wide thin strips
2–3 dried pasilla chili peppers (see glossary)
1 cup (4 oz/125 g) cubed *queso fresco* (see glossary) or Monterey Jack cheese
1 ripe avocado, halved, pitted, peeled and diced
6 tablespoons (3 fl oz/90 ml) tablespoons *crema,* sour cream, or crème fraîche (see glossary)
fresh cilantro (fresh coriander) sprigs

★ Pour the chicken stock into a large soup pot and bring to a simmer over medium heat. Stir in the green onions and tomatoes.

★ Meanwhile, in a small frying pan over high heat, warm the vegetable oil. Add the tortilla strips and sauté until browned and crisp, about 2 minutes. Using a slotted spoon, transfer to paper towels to drain. Add the pasilla chilies to the same oil and fry over medium heat, turning once, until puffed and crisp, 20–30 seconds; do not allow to burn. Using the slotted spoon, transfer to paper towels to drain and cool. When cool enough to handle, crumble coarsely.

★ Divide the tortilla strips among 6 individual bowls, reserving some for garnish. Add an equal amount of the cheese and avocado to each bowl. Ladle the stock into each bowl. Garnish with *crema,* sour cream or crème fraîche, cilantro sprigs and the reserved crumbled pasillas and tortilla strips. Serve immediately.

SERVES 6

Tortilla Soup

½ teaspoon dried rosemary
½ teaspoon dried basil
½ teaspoon freshly ground pepper
3 carrots, peeled and cut into 1–2-in (2.5–5-cm) lengths
3 russet potatoes, peeled and cut into 1–2-in (2.5–5-cm) pieces

fresh basil sprigs for garnish

★ To make the rolls, in a small bowl, dissolve the yeast in the warm water. Set aside until bubbly, 5–10 minutes. Meanwhile, in a small saucepan over low heat, combine the butter and the milk and heat just until the butter melts. Remove from the heat and let cool until just warm to the touch, 105°–110°F (41°–43°C).

★ In a large bowl, combine 2¾ cups (14 oz/430 g) of the flour and the sugar, salt, eggs, dissolved yeast and warm milk-butter mixture. Using a wooden spoon, beat until smooth and the batter pulls away from the sides of the bowl, about 3 minutes. (This step can also be done in a food processor fitted with the plastic blade.)

★ Add as much of the remaining flour as needed to form a

Top to bottom: Coriander Bolillos, Potato Soup with Green Chilies and Cheese

ACADIANA SEAFOOD GUMBO

"Jambalaya, crawfish pie and filé gumbo" is a delightful refrain from a bayou ballad. It is often hummed by Cajun cooks in East Texas and along the Gulf Coast as they prepare their own favorite versions of gumbo. They even say that Cajuns of the Golden Triangle, Beaumont, Port Arthur and Orange, look to Louisiana as the "old country." Oil-boom jobs brought thousands of Cajuns to Texas during the Great Depression. With them came hot boudin, steaming crawfish and, of course, seafood gumbo. The secret of a great gumbo is the rich taste of the roux and the freshness of the seafood. This gumbo can also be brought to the table in a large pot, with seafood on one side and the rice on the other.

½ cup (4 fl oz/125 ml) vegetable oil
½ cup (2½ oz/75 g) all-purpose (plain) flour
¼ cup (2 oz/60 g) butter
½ lb (250 g) okra (lady's fingers), sliced ½ in (12 mm) thick
1 yellow onion, chopped
1 green bell pepper (capsicum), seeded and chopped

2 celery stalks, chopped
3 cloves garlic, finely chopped
¼ cup (⅓ oz/10 g) minced fresh parsley
4 cups (32 fl oz/1 l) chicken stock
3 cups (18 oz/560 g) chopped, peeled tomatoes
2 bay leaves
½ teaspoon dried thyme leaves, crumbled
¼ teaspoon dried oregano leaves, crumbled
1 teaspoon salt, or to taste
1 lb (500 g) peeled shrimp (prawns) or crayfish tails
12 oysters, shucked (optional)
1 teaspoon fresh lemon juice
1 teaspoon Worcestershire sauce
crushed red pepper flakes or cayenne pepper
4–5 cups (1¾–2¼ lb/8.75 g–1.1 kg) freshly cooked long-grain white rice

★ In a heavy saucepan over low heat, combine the oil and flour. Cook, stirring frequently with a wire whisk, until the mixture (the roux) is a deep copper brown, 35–40 minutes. Do not allow to burn. Set aside.

★ In a large frying pan over medium heat, melt the butter. Add the okra and cook, stirring, until softened, 3–4 minutes. Add the onion, bell pepper, celery, garlic and parsley. Cook, stirring often, until the vegetables are tender, about 5 minutes.

★ Stir in the stock, tomatoes, bay leaves, thyme, oregano, salt and reserved roux. Cook, uncovered, over low heat until well blended and thickened, 30–45 minutes.

★ Stir in the shrimp or crayfish and cook until they begin to turn pink, 3–4 minutes. Add the oysters, if using, and simmer until the edges just begin to curl, about 3 minutes. (If you have not used oysters, continue to simmer the gumbo until the shrimp or crayfish are cooked through.) Season with the lemon juice, Worcestershire sauce and red pepper flakes or cayenne to taste.

★ To serve, ladle into shallow soup bowls and top each serving with a spoonful of rice. Pass additional red pepper flakes or cayenne.

SERVES 6

High Plains

POTATO SOUP WITH GREEN CHILIES AND CHEESE

Like Mexican menudo, *this soup is known as a hangover cure. Serve it with crispy blue corn tortilla chips.*

2 tablespoons vegetable oil
1 yellow onion, chopped
2 garlic cloves, finely chopped
2 cups (10 oz/315 g) cubed, peeled potatoes (¾-in/2-cm cubes)
3 cups (24 fl oz/750 ml) chicken stock
½ cup (4 fl oz/125 ml) milk
4 fresh poblano or anaheim chili peppers, roasted, peeled, seeded and chopped (see glossary)
salt and freshly ground pepper
6 oz (185 g) Monterey Jack cheese, shredded
blue or yellow corn tortilla chips (see glossary)

★ In a large saucepan over medium heat, warm the vegetable oil. Add the onion and garlic and sauté until tender, 3–4 minutes. Stir in the potatoes, stock, milk, chilies and salt and pepper to taste. Bring to a simmer and cook, uncovered, until the potatoes are tender, 20–25 minutes.

★ To serve, place an equal amount of the soup in each of 6 small soup bowls. Sprinkle with the cheese and garnish with the corn tortilla chips. Serve immediately.

SERVES 6

Dallas

CORIANDER BOLILLOS

This is Dallas chef Stephen Pyles's recipe for those wonderful crusty oval rolls found in most Mexican and Texan bakeries. The unique addition of ground coriander is highly successful. These rolls can be served as tortas, *halved, spread with hot refried beans and then stuffed with cooked chicken, turkey or ham slices, shredded Cheddar cheese, tomato and avocado slices, lettuce, mayonnaise and pickled jalapeños (see glossary).*

1 tablespoon active dry yeast
4½ cups (22½ oz/700 g) all-purpose (plain) flour
2 tablespoons sugar
1 teaspoon salt
½ cup (4 oz/125 g) plus 1 tablespoon vegetable shortening
1½ cups (12 fl oz/375 ml) water

1½ teaspoons ground coriander
1 egg
2 tablespoons milk

★ In a large bowl, combine the yeast, 2 cups (10 oz/315 g) of the flour, the sugar and the salt. In a saucepan over low heat, combine the shortening and the water and heat until the shortening melts. Remove from the heat and let cool to 105°–110°F (41°–43°C). Add the shortening-water mixture to the flour mixture and stir with a wooden spoon to combine.

★ Add the coriander and then the remaining flour, ½ cup (2½ oz/75 g) at a time, beating with the dough hook of a heavy-duty electric mixer until a soft dough forms that pulls away from the sides of the bowl, 5–6 minutes. The dough should be soft and elastic, but not sticky. (If making by hand, beat in the flour with the spoon and then turn out the dough onto a lightly floured work surface and knead until soft and elastic, about 10 minutes.) Gather the dough into a ball, place in an oiled bowl, turn to coat the surface and cover with a damp kitchen towel. Let the dough rise in a warm place until doubled in volume, 1½–2 hours.

★ Punch down the dough and turn out onto a lightly floured work surface. Divide the dough into 12 equal portions of about 3 oz (90 g) each. Using your palms, roll each portion into an elongated shape and pull and pinch each end into a point. Place 2–3 in (5–7.5 cm) apart on a baking sheet lined with parchment (baking) paper. Press on the top of each roll to flatten slightly and, using a sharp knife, make 2 diagonal parallel slashes. Cover loosely with a damp kitchen towel and let rise until doubled in volume, 45–60 minutes.

★ Preheat an oven to 375°F (190°C).

★ In a small bowl, whisk together the egg and milk and gently brush onto the rolls. Bake until golden brown, 15–18 minutes. Transfer to a rack to cool completely before serving.

MAKES 12 ROLLS

Acadiana Seafood Gumbo

Amarillo

POSOLE

In Amarillo, the flavor of the West can be sampled on Cowboy Mornings, organized tours held from May to September. Following a ride across the plains to Palo Duro Canyon, a geologic formation more than 200 million years old, breakfast is served from a chuck wagon. It is here that you'll find cowboy stews and the always popular posole. Posole is a Christmas Eve favorite in Mexico, but in Texas it is enjoyed anytime.

3 tablespoons vegetable oil
2 lb (1 kg) lean boneless pork, cut into ½-in (12-mm) cubes
1½ cups (7½ oz/235 g) chopped yellow onion
6 cloves garlic, minced
½ teaspoon ground cumin
1 tablespoon chili powder
2 teaspoons dried oregano
2 cans (15 oz/470 g each) white or yellow hominy, drained
salt and freshly ground pepper
¼ cup (⅓ oz/10 g) minced fresh cilantro (fresh coriander)
6–8 cups (48–64 fl oz/1.5–2 l) chicken stock
shredded lettuce; sliced radishes, green (spring) onions and avocado; lime wedges; minced fresh cilantro; and pumpkin seeds for garnish

★ In a large, heavy pot over medium-high heat, warm the vegetable oil. Add the pork, onion and garlic and sauté until lightly browned, 6–8 minutes. Stir in the cumin, chili powder, oregano, hominy, salt and pepper to taste, cilantro and chicken stock. Bring to a boil, reduce the heat to low and simmer, uncovered, until the pork is tender, about 1 hour.
★ Ladle into warmed bowls and serve the garnishes in separate bowls alongside for guests to add as desired.

SERVES 8

Palo Duro Canyon

BLUE CORNSTICKS WITH BLACK OLIVE BUTTER

Yellow cornmeal can be substituted for the blue cornmeal in these delicious cornsticks. The butter, which yields about ½ cup (4 oz/ 125 g), can be used on other savory breads.

FOR THE CORNSTICKS:

½ cup (2½ oz/75 g) blue cornmeal
½ cup (2½ oz/75 g) all-purpose (plain) flour
1 tablespoon sugar
1¼ teaspoons baking powder
1 teaspoon salt
½ cup (3 oz/90 g) corn kernels, blanched in boiling water for 2–3 minutes, drained and cooled
¼ green bell pepper (capsicum), seeded and minced
4 slices bacon, fried until crisp, drained well and crumbled
3 tablespoons fresh cilantro (fresh coriander)
1 egg, separated
1 cup (8 fl oz/250 ml) less 2 tablespoons heavy (double) cream
⅓ cup (3 oz/90 g) butter, melted

FOR THE BLACK OLIVE BUTTER:

½ cup (4 oz/125 g) unsalted butter, at room temperature
8 Kalamata olives, pitted

fresh green corn husks (optional; see glossary)

★ Place 2 cornstick pans (enough to bake 14 cornsticks) in an oven and preheat to 475°F (245°C). In a large bowl, stir together the cornmeal, flour, sugar, baking powder and salt. Stir in the corn, bell pepper, bacon and cilantro.

★ In a small bowl, whisk together the egg yolk and cream. Whisk in all but 1 tablespoon of the melted butter. Stir the cream mixture into the cornmeal mixture just until fully combined.
★ In another bowl, using an electric mixer, beat the egg white until stiff. Fold it into the batter, being careful not to deflate it.
★ Brush the hot cornstick molds with the remaining 1 tablespoon melted butter. Spoon about ¼ cup (2 fl oz/60 ml) of the batter into each mold, filling almost half full. Bake until golden brown, about 15 minutes. Remove from the oven and let stand for 5 minutes before removing from the pans.
★ While the cornsticks are baking, make the olive butter. In a food processor fitted with the metal blade, combine the butter and olives and process until smooth and the olives are evenly distributed. Transfer to a small bowl. Serve the cornsticks wrapped in green corn husks or on a plate lined with green corn husks, if desired. Pass the black olive butter.

MAKES 14 CORNSTICKS   *Photograph page 82*

Left to right: Posole, Spoonbread

SPOONBREAD

This is a Texas variation on a southern favorite. Garnish the dish with thin avocado slices dipped in lemon juice and arranged in a circle on the bread; place a cluster of tiny yellow and red cherry tomatoes in the center. Serve the spoonbread for breakfast with Canadian bacon, or with smoked pork chops and collard greens cooked with ham hocks, East Texas style. For an interesting presentation, line the baking dish with soaked, dried corn husks, allowing the ends to extend over the rim of the dish, before pouring in the spoonbread batter.

¾ cup (4 oz/125 g) fine-grind yellow cornmeal
¼ cup (1½ oz/45 g) *masa harina* (see glossary)
½ teaspoon salt
½ teaspoon baking soda (bicarbonate of soda)
1 teaspoon baking powder
½ teaspoon garlic powder
1 teaspoon dried oregano, crumbled

1½ cups (6 oz/185 g) shredded Cheddar cheese
¾ cup (6 fl oz/180 ml) milk or buttermilk
⅓ cup (3 fl oz/80 ml) vegetable oil
2 eggs, well beaten
1 can (15 oz/470 g) cream-style corn
1 can (4 oz/125 g) chopped poblano chili peppers, drained (see glossary)

★ Preheat an oven to 350°F (180°C).
★ In a large bowl, stir together the cornmeal, *masa harina*, salt, baking soda, baking powder, garlic powder and oregano. Add the cheese and stir to distribute evenly. Add the milk or buttermilk, vegetable oil, eggs, cream-style corn and chilies, mixing well.
★ Pour the batter into a 13-by-9-by-2-in (33-by-23-by-5-cm) baking pan or an oval gratin dish of similar dimensions. Bake until golden brown and the top springs back when touched in the center, about 45 minutes.
★ Remove from the oven and serve hot directly from the pan.

SERVES 6–8

Top to bottom: Blue Cornsticks with Black Olive Butter (recipe page 80),
Chicken and White Bean Chili

CHICKEN AND WHITE BEAN CHILI

In the early days of Texas, there was always a pot of beans simmering on the back burner, ready to serve to any stranger who happened by. Today, casual entertaining and warm hospitality still reign throughout the state, with dishes just like this one ladled up for unexpected guests. This dish goes together quickly, as it calls for canned beans and cooked chicken.

2 cans (15½ oz/485 g each) Great Northern or other large
    white beans
6 cups (48 fl oz/1.5 l) chicken stock, or as needed
4 cloves garlic, minced
1 yellow or white onion, diced
2 or 3 fresh serrano chili peppers, minced (see glossary)
1 tablespoon ground cumin
1 tablespoon dried oregano
¼ teaspoon cayenne pepper

4 fresh poblano chili peppers, roasted, peeled, seeded and
    finely diced (see glossary)
4 cups (1½ lb/750 g) cubed, cooked chicken (¾-in/
    2-cm cubes)
salt
1 cup (4 oz/125 g) shredded Monterey Jack cheese
tortilla chips (optional; see glossary)

★ In a large, heavy pot, combine the beans, 6 cups (48 fl oz/ 1.5 l) stock, garlic and onion. Bring to a boil, reduce the heat to low and simmer, uncovered, mashing the beans occasionally to thicken the stew slightly, for 1 hour.

★ Add the serrano chilies, cumin, oregano, cayenne pepper, poblano chilies and chicken and continue to simmer, uncovered, until the flavors are established, about 1 hour longer. Add additional stock, if necessary, to prevent the chili from sticking.

★ Season to taste with salt and ladle into soup bowls. Top each serving with some of the shredded cheese and garnish with tortilla chips, if using. Serve immediately.

SERVES 8

SAUSAGE-FILLED KOLACHES

Between 1850 and 1920, thousands of Czechs left their homes in Moravia and Bohemia to come to Texas in search of a better life. They brought with them their folk customs, music and food, then adapted the foods they found in their new home. In Fayetteville, Praha, Hallettsville and Rosenberg-Richmond, many residents continue to speak Czech. The latter hosts a popular festival where the Klobasniky, a foot-long sausage encased in an airy kolache dough and served with butter and a dollop of mustard, is one of the highlights. Czech sausage and kolaches are traditionally found on menus that include baked pork loin, sauerkraut and boiled potatoes. Kolaches are the best-known Czech contribution to Texas cuisine. Caldwell is the Kolache Capital of Texas, but you will also find these pastries in wildflower-rich Schulenburg, the Gateway to the Rolling Hills. The latter town is as well-known for the "painted churches" located in the surrounding rural communities as it is for its kolaches.

FOR THE KOLACHE DOUGH:

2 cups (16 fl oz/500 ml) milk
½ cup (4 oz/125 g) plus 2 tablespoons vegetable shortening
2 tablespoons active dry yeast
½ cup (4 oz/125 g) sugar, plus 1 tablespoon sugar
½ cup (4 fl oz/125 ml) warm water (105°–115°F/ 41°–46°C)
2 teaspoons salt
2 egg yolks
6¼ cups (2 lb/1 kg) all-purpose (plain) flour, sifted

FOR THE FILLING:

6 smoked link sausages, each 6 in (15 cm) long, cut into slices 1 in (2.5 cm) thick

★ In a saucepan over low heat, combine the milk and short-ening and heat until the shortening melts. Remove from the heat and let cool to 100°F (38°C).

★ In a small bowl, sprinkle the yeast and the 1 tablespoon sugar over the warm water and stir to dissolve. Set aside until foamy, 5–10 minutes.

★ In a large bowl, combine the cooled milk mixture, the yeast mixture, the ½ cup (4 oz/125 g) sugar, the salt and the egg yolks. Using a wooden spoon, stir to mix. Add the flour and stir until well combined and glossy, soft and elastic. Turn out onto a lightly floured work surface and knead gently for 3–4 minutes. Cover with a damp kitchen cloth and let rise in a warm place until doubled in volume, 1–2 hours.

★ Line a baking sheet with aluminum foil or parchment (baking) paper.

★ Punch down the dough, pinch off pieces and form into 2-in (5-cm) balls. Place on the prepared baking sheets 2 in (5 cm) apart. Cover with a slightly dampened kitchen towel and let rise in a warm place until doubled in bulk, about 40 minutes.

★ Preheat an oven to 425°F (200°C).

★ Make a depression in the center of each ball and fill the depression with a sausage slice. Bake until the kolaches are a light golden brown, about 15 minutes. Remove from the oven and serve hot or transfer to a rack, let cool and serve. Any kolaches that are not eaten the day they are baked should be frozen. They will keep for up to 1 month.

MAKES 3 DOZEN

Sausage-Filled Kolaches

Top to bottom: Ancho Bread, Rosemary and Oregano Bread

Pearsall

ROSEMARY AND OREGANO BREAD

*This bread has a chewy, yeasty quality and a crunchy crust. Try
your own versions, using different grains and herbs. If you like,
make a crosshatch pattern in the top of the loaves before baking.
A chive-laced butter goes well with this fragrant bread. The recipe
is adapted from an herb bread made by Patty Johnson of Patty's
Herbs in Pearsall.*

1½ tablespoons sugar
2 tablespoons active dry yeast
1¼ cups (2 fl oz/60 ml) warm water (105°–115°F/41°–46°C)
3¼–4 cups (16–20 oz/500–625 g) unbleached all-purpose
  (plain) flour
2 teaspoons salt
¼ cup (1½ oz/45 g) chopped shallots
4 tablespoons chopped fresh oregano or garlic chives
2 tablespoons minced fresh rosemary
¼ cup (1½ oz/45 g) chopped white onion (optional)
¼ cup (2 fl oz/60 ml) olive oil

★ In a large bowl, dissolve the sugar and yeast in the warm
water. Set aside until bubbly, 5–10 minutes. Using a wooden
spoon, stir in 3 cups (15 oz/470 g) of the flour and the salt.
When the dough comes away from the sides of the bowl, turn
it out onto a lightly floured work surface. Knead, adding in the
remaining flour as necessary to form a workable dough, until
elastic, 6–8 minutes. Add the shallots, the herbs and the onion,
if using. Knead until evenly distributed. Shape into a ball and
place in a lightly oiled bowl. Turn to coat the surface with oil,
cover the bowl with a clean, dry towel and let the dough rise
in a warm place until doubled in volume, 45–60 minutes.
Punch down the dough and turn out onto a lightly floured
work surface. Divide in half and shape into two freeform
loaves or place in two 8½-by-4½-by-2½-in (21.5-by-11.5-by-
6-cm) loaf pans. Let rise, uncovered, in a warm place until
doubled in volume, 45–60 minutes.
★ Preheat an oven to 325°F (165°C).
★ Brush the loaves with the olive oil. Bake the loaves until
they are brown and sound hollow when tapped on the
bottom, about 30 minutes. Transfer to a rack and remove from
the pans. Let cool completely before serving.

MAKES 2 SMALL LOAVES

Texas

TEXAS CORN BREAD

Cornmeal is a staple of the Texas table. Serve this spicy corn bread as a side dish to grilled meats or chili. It also freezes beautifully for up to 3 months. If you like, add 2 or 3 canned chipotle chilies in adobo (see glossary), well drained and puréed or minced, to the batter. Baking the corn bread in a preheated cast-iron frying pan gives it a deliciously crispy crust. If you do not have a cast-iron pan, use a regular baking pan.

2 eggs
¼ cup (2 fl oz/60 ml) vegetable oil
1 can (4 oz/125 g) chopped poblano chilies, drained (see glossary)
1 fresh jalapeño chili pepper, minced
1½ teaspoons minced jarred pimiento
1 can (15 oz/470 g) cream-style corn
½ cup (4 fl oz/125 ml) sour cream
1 cup (5 oz/155 g) fine-grind yellow cornmeal
2 teaspoons baking powder
½ teaspoon salt
2 cups (8 oz/250 g) shredded sharp Cheddar cheese

★ Grease a 9-in (23-cm) cast-iron frying pan and place in an oven. Preheat to 350°F (180°C).
★ In a large bowl, using a fork, beat together the eggs and oil until well blended. Add the poblano chilies, jalapeño, pimiento, corn, sour cream, cornmeal, baking powder, salt and 1½ cups (6 oz/185 g) of the cheese. Using a wooden spoon, stir until well combined.
★ Remove the frying pan from the oven and pour the batter into it. Sprinkle the top with the remaining ½ cup (2 oz/60 g) cheese. Return to the oven and bake until golden brown and a toothpick inserted into the center comes out clean, 45–60 minutes.
★ Remove from the oven, cut into wedges and serve hot directly from the pan.

SERVES 6–8   *Photograph page 12*

East Texas

COUNTRY BISCUITS WITH APPLE-TEQUILA JELLY

A book on Texas cuisine would not be complete without this East Texas biscuit recipe. The jelly recipe, which is popular in South Texas, yeilds 5 cups (3 pounds/1.5 kilograms) and leaves plenty left over for other uses.

FOR THE APPLE-TEQUILA JELLY:

¼ cup (2 fl oz/60 ml) gold tequila
1¾ cups (14 fl oz/440 ml) apple cider
2 tablespoons crème de cassis
3½ cups (1¾ lb/875 g) sugar
¾ cup (6 fl oz/180 ml) liquid fruit pectin

FOR THE BISCUITS:

¼ cup (2 oz/160 g) unsalted butter
2 cups (10 oz/315 g) all-purpose (plain) flour
½ teaspoon salt
¼ teaspoon baking soda (bicarbonate of soda)
1 tablespoon baking powder
5 tablespoons (2½ oz/75 g) vegetable shortening, chilled
1 cup (8 fl oz/250 ml) buttermilk

★ To make the jelly, in a large, nonreactive saucepan over high heat, stir together the tequila, apple cider, crème de cassis and sugar. Bring to a boil and stir in the pectin. Return to a rolling boil and boil for 1 minute.
★ Remove from the heat and ladle into hot, sterilized jelly jars or glasses, leaving ¼ in (6 mm) headspace. Let cool and seal with melted paraffin (see glossary). The jelly can be stored in a cool, dark place for up to 6 months, or, once opened, in the refrigerator for up to 3 weeks.
★ To make the biscuits, preheat an oven to 400°F (200°C). Place the butter in a cast-iron frying pan or baking dish 9 in (23 cm) in diameter. Place the pan or dish in the oven to melt the butter, then remove from the oven.
★ In a bowl, stir together the flour, salt, baking soda and baking powder. Add the shortening and, using a pastry blender or 2 knives, work together all the ingredients until the mixture is the consistency of small peas. Make a well in the center and pour in the buttermilk. Mix gently with a fork until the buttermilk is fully absorbed; do not overbeat. The dough will be sticky and hold together.
★ Turn out the dough onto a floured work surface and lightly flour the top of the dough. Knead gently 2 or 3 times, then pat or roll out the dough into a round about ½ in (12 mm) thick. Using a floured biscuit cutter 2½ in (6 cm) in diameter, cut out the biscuits. Dip each biscuit in the melted butter to coat both sides well and arrange in the heated pan or dish. They will fit snugly.
★ Bake until the biscuits have risen and are browned, 8–10 minutes. Remove from the oven and serve warm with the apple tequila jelly.

MAKES 12 BISCUITS   *Photograph pages 66–67*

South Texas

ANCHO BREAD

Chef Jay McCarthy recommends using his delicious bread for making sandwiches with habanero-marinated turkey breast (recipe page 121) or as a stand-in for hamburger buns. Any leftover bread can later be processed in a food processor with garlic, dried chilies and a dash of sugar to make bread crumbs for using with chicken or pork.

2 dried ancho chili peppers (see glossary)
3 tablespoons active dry yeast
1 cup (8 fl oz/250 ml) warm water (100°–115°F/41°–46°C)
¾ cup (5 oz/155 g) lightly packed light brown sugar
2 teaspoons salt
1½ cups (12 fl oz/375 ml) cold water
4 cups (1¼ lb/625 g) all-purpose (plain) flour

★ Remove the stems and seeds from the chilies and discard.
★ In a food processor fitted with the metal blade, process the chilies until they form small flakes. Set aside.
★ In a large bowl, dissolve the yeast in the warm water. Set aside until bubbly, 5–10 minutes.
★ When the yeast is ready, add the sugar, salt and cold water and, using a wooden spoon, stir to combine. Then stir in the flour and chili flakes. Using an electric mixer fitted with a dough hook, knead until a soft dough forms, about 5 minutes. Form the dough into a ball, place in an oiled bowl, turn to coat the surface with oil and cover the bowl with a lightly dampened cloth. Let rise in a warm place until doubled in bulk, 45 minutes–1¼ hours.
★ Punch down the dough and turn out onto a lightly floured board. Divide the dough in half and form each half into a loaf shape. Place each loaf in a 9-by-5-in (23-by-13-cm) loaf pan and let rise, uncovered, in a warm place until doubled in bulk, 20–30 minutes.
★ Preheat an oven to 350°F (180°C).
★ Bake the loaves until they are browned and sound hollow when tapped on the bottom, 35–45 minutes.
★ Transfer to a rack and remove from the pans. Let cool completely before slicing.

MAKES 2 LOAVES

Heart of Texas

CREAM OF TOMATILLO SOUP

The tomatillo is also known as tomate de bolsa, *or "tomato in a bag," because of its papery husk. Despite the fact that there is no cream in the soup, the name is traditional. Fresh tomatillos will make a superior soup, but you may use canned tomatillos if fresh are unavailable. You can also serve this low-calorie, beautifully colored soup icy cold. A few pesticide-free edible blossoms would make a lovely garnish in addition to those suggested here. A semidry Riesling will stand up nicely to the acidity of the tomatillos.*

2 teaspoons vegetable oil
⅓ cup (2 oz/60 g) minced yellow onion
1 clove garlic, minced
1 lb (500 g) tomatillos, brown husks removed and coarsely chopped
1 or 2 fresh jalapeño chili peppers, seeded and minced
2–3 cups (16–24 fl oz/500–750 ml) rich chicken stock
2 tablespoons minced fresh cilantro (fresh coriander)

FOR GARNISH:

minced fresh cilantro (fresh coriander)
sour cream or plain yogurt, optional
South Texas crab grass (see glossary)

★ In a soup pot over medium heat, warm the vegetable oil. Add the onion and garlic and sauté until slightly softened, about 2 minutes. Stir in the tomatillos and jalapeños and cook, stirring occasionally, until softened, 5–6 minutes.
★ Remove from the heat and let cool slightly. Place in a food processor fitted with the metal blade or in a blender, and process until smooth. Add 2 cups (16 fl oz/500 ml) of the chicken stock to the processor or blender and process to mix. Return the purée to the saucepan and add as much of the remaining 1 cup (8 fl oz/250 ml) stock as needed to achieve a smooth consistency. Return to medium heat and heat to serving temperature. Stir in the 2 tablespoons cilantro.
★ Ladle the soup into warmed bowls and garnish each serving with cilantro, sour cream or yogurt (if using), and South Texas crab grass. Serve at once.

SERVES 4

Clockwise from top left: Cream of Tomatillo Soup, Chilled Avocado Soup with Papaya-Pepper Relish, Seafood Gazpacho

1 fresh poblano chili pepper, roasted, peeled, seeded and finely diced (see glossary)
1 tablespoon fresh lime juice
2 tablespoons finely chopped fresh cilantro (fresh coriander)
2 fresh jalapeño chili peppers, seeded (if desired) and minced
salt

salt
finely chopped fresh jalapeño chili pepper for garnish

★ In a blender or a food processor fitted with the metal blade, combine the avocados, stock, chili powder, coriander and cayenne. Purée until very smooth. Pour into a saucepan and place over low heat just until the mixture is hot to the touch. Immediately remove from the heat and let cool to lukewarm. Transfer to a bowl and stir in the cream, crème fraîche or yogurt. Cover and refrigerate until well chilled, 3–4 hours.
★ To make the relish, in a bowl, combine all the ingredients, including salt to taste, and stir to combine. Cover and refrigerate until serving.
★ To serve, taste the soup and add salt as needed. Ladle the soup into chilled bowls. Top with dollops of the relish and a sprinkling of jalapeño. Serve at once.
SERVES 6

Corpus Christi

SEAFOOD GAZPACHO

Corpus Christi stands in a lush, semitropical setting with immaculate white sandy beaches kissing the palm-studded waterfront—the perfect spot to enjoy a cool and refreshing gazpacho. The addition of the state's wonderful Gulf Coast shrimp sets this gazpacho apart from all the rest. Cooked scallops, crab or lobster are equally delicious substitutions. For an attractive garnish, freeze 1 part fresh lemon thyme leaves to 20 parts water in ice-cube trays and float the cubes in the soup in place of the herb sprigs. A light-bodied, herbal Sauvignon Blanc makes a refreshing accompaniment.

1 clove garlic, halved
1 cup (6 oz/185 g) cooked shrimp, peeled and deveined
5 ripe tomatoes, peeled, seeded and cut up
1 large cucumber, peeled, seeded and cut up
1 green bell pepper (capsicum), seeded and cut up
1 large yellow onion, cut up
1 fresh jalapeño chili pepper, seeded (if desired) and minced (optional)
1 clove garlic, minced
5 cups (40 fl oz/1.25 l) tomato juice
⅓ cup (3 fl oz/80 ml) olive oil
⅓ cup (3 fl oz/80 ml) red wine vinegar
Tabasco sauce
1 teaspoon salt, or to taste
½ cup (4 fl oz/125 ml) vodka, or to taste (optional)
croutons and fresh oregano, watercress or fresh cilantro (fresh coriander) leaves for garnish

★ Rub a large wooden salad bowl with the halved garlic clove and place the shrimp in the bowl. Working in batches if necessary, coarsely chop the tomatoes, cucumber, bell pepper and onion in a food processor fitted with the metal blade. Transfer to a large bowl and add the jalapeño, if using, minced garlic, tomato juice, olive oil, vinegar, Tabasco sauce to taste, salt and the vodka, if using. Mix well. Pour the mixture over the shrimp, cover and chill thoroughly several hours.
★ Ladle the gazpacho into iced bowls and garnish with croutons and oregano, watercress or cilantro. Serve immediately.
SERVES 8–10

Houston

CHILLED AVOCADO SOUP WITH PAPAYA-PEPPER RELISH

This light and refreshing soup is especially good on hot summer days. Use a rich chicken stock for the best results. For a formal occasion, omit the papaya-pepper relish and instead float a thin slice of avocado topped with a dab of red caviar on the soup.

2 small ripe Haas avocados, halved, pitted, peeled and chopped
2 cups (16 fl oz/500 ml) chicken stock
½ teaspoon chili powder
¼ teaspoon ground coriander
⅛ teaspoon cayenne pepper, or to taste
1 cup (8 fl oz/250 ml) heavy (double) cream, crème fraîche (see glossary) or plain yogurt

FOR THE PAPAYA-PEPPER RELISH:

1 small ripe papaya, peeled, seeded and finely diced
1 red bell pepper (capsicum), roasted, peeled, seeded and finely diced (see glossary)

West Texas

FRIJOLES A LA CHARRA

Always popular at any Tex-Mex occasion, these pinto beans can be turned into frijoles borrachos, *or "drunken beans," by adding ¾ cup (6 fl oz/180 ml) beer with the seasonings. Serve either version topped with* pico de gallo *(see glossary) and offer crispy tortilla chips (see glossary) on the side, if you like. For a delicious soup, thin the beans slightly with additional water or chicken stock and top with grated cheese and crumbled bacon. Serve with Texas corn bread (recipe on page 85).*

8 slices lean bacon, coarsely chopped
6 cups (2½ lb/1.25 kg) cooked pinto beans (see glossary)
4–5 cups (32–40 fl oz/1.1 l) water
3 cloves garlic, minced
1 teaspoon ground cumin
2 teaspoons chili powder
1 teaspoon salt
pico de gallo (see glossary)

★ In a heavy-bottomed saucepan over medium-high heat, fry the bacon until slightly crisp, 3–5 minutes. Add the cooked beans and water, just to cover. Bring to a boil, reduce the heat to a simmer and add the garlic, cumin, chili powder and salt. Simmer gently for 20–30 minutes to blend flavors.
★ Ladle into bowls and serve topped with a generous spoonful of *pico de gallo.*

SERVES 10–12

Terlingua

FRANK TOLBERT'S ORIGINAL TEXAS CHILI

Chili, the official state dish, has become show business in Texas, where a typical "bowl o' red" ranges from hot to hotter. It is a refinement of a Mexican Indian dish invented before refrigeration, when chilies and spices were used to mask the flavor of tainted meat. Today, there is great controversy as to the correct way to prepare chili, with beans versus no beans the subject of the most heated arguments.

There are a number of chili cookoffs, such as the Chilympiad in San Marcos, but the grandfather of all contests is the annual ritual held in Terlingua. Frank Tolbert was one of the founders of this championship chili cookoff, and his writing did much to popularize chili far beyond the state's borders. Terlingua is a ghost town that boasts a population of thousands one weekend in early November every year, all of them there to attend the World Championship Chili Cookoff. This is one of the chili recipes that put Terlingua on the map.

2–4 ancho chili peppers (see glossary), 4–8 small dried red chili peppers or 2–4 tablespoons chili powder
4 tablespoons (2 fl oz/60 ml) vegetable oil
3 lb (1.5 kg) lean beef chuck, cut into bite-sized pieces
1–2 cups (8–16 fl oz/250–500 ml) beef stock or water
⅓ cup (2 oz/60 g) finely chopped garlic
1 yellow onion, finely chopped
2 tablespoons ground cumin
1 tablespoon ground oregano
salt
½ cup (1½ oz/45 g) paprika
1 or 2 fresh cilantro (fresh coriander) sprigs, chopped

★ If using the chili peppers, trim the stems. Remove the seeds as well, if using ancho chilies. Place in a small saucepan and add water to cover barely. Bring to a boil, remove from the

heat, cover and let stand for 15 minutes. Transfer the chilies and their soaking water to a blender or a food processor fitted with the metal blade. Purée until smooth. Set aside.
★ In a large frying pan over high heat, warm 2 tablespoons of the vegetable oil. Brown half of the meat on all sides until it loses its pinkness, 6–8 minutes.
★ Transfer the meat and accumulated juices in the frying pan to a heavy pot and add the puréed chilies, or the chili powder, if using. Place over low heat and bring to a simmer. Mean-

Frijoles a la Charra

while, brown the remaining beef in the same manner, then transfer it and the juices to the pot.

★ Add enough stock or water just to cover the meat. Bring to a boil, reduce the heat to low and simmer, uncovered, for 30 minutes.

★ Add the garlic, onion, cumin, oregano, salt to taste, paprika and cilantro and continue to simmer uncovered, stirring occasionally, until the meat is very tender, another 30 minutes. Add a bit more liquid if the chili starts to stick or too much of the liquid cooks away. When the chili is ready, using a large kitchen spoon, skim off any fat from the surface. (Or make the chili a day in advance of serving, remove from the heat, let cool, cover and refrigerate overnight. The next day, skim off and discard any fat that has settled on the surface and reheat to serving temperature.)

★ Ladle the chili into shallow bowls and serve.

SERVES 4–6   *Photograph pages 66–67*

Shiner

BOCK BLACK BEAN SOUP

Black bean soup is more commonly found in Mexico than in Texas, but it has gained in popularity in the state. The addition of bock beer comes from the Spoetzl Brewery in Shiner. The brewery, a registered Texas Historical Landmark, lies eighty-five miles from San Antonio. It was founded in 1909 by German and Czech farmers who longed for a beer with Old World taste, and has been in continuous operation ever since. The people at Spoetzl, producer of the famous Shiner Premium and Shiner Bock beers, proudly boast of brewing just one beer at a time with one of the smallest brew kettles in the country. This soup is also delicious made without the beer.

2 cups (14 oz/440 g) dried black beans
2–3 qt (2–3 l) water
1 large yellow onion, minced
4 cloves garlic, minced
1 teaspoon dried oregano, crumbled
1 tablespoon chopped fresh epazote (optional; see glossary)
3–4 tablespoons chili powder
1–2 teaspoons ground cumin
1 ham hock (optional)
1 can (12 fl oz/375 ml) bock beer
sliced radishes, shredded lettuce, shredded red cabbage, minced fresh serrano chili peppers (see glossary), cheese, sour cream, lime wedges, chive blossoms and/or *pico de gallo* (see glossary) for garnish

★ Rinse the black beans and discard any misshapen ones and any stones. Place in a large bowl, add water to cover by 2 in (5 cm) and let soak a few hours or as long as overnight. Drain the beans.
★ Place the beans in a large, heavy pot and add water to cover. Add the onion, garlic, oregano, epazote (if using), chili powder, cumin, ham hock (if using) and beer. Bring to a boil, reduce the heat to low, cover and simmer until the beans are tender, about 2 hours. If necessary, add additional water to maintain original level of liquid.
★ Bring to the table in a soup tureen or ladle into warmed soup bowls. Serve one or more of the garnishes in separate bowls alongside for guests to add as desired or garnish as desired before serving.

SERVES 6   *Photograph pages 66–67*

South Texas

CREAM OF CHICKEN SOUP IN TORTILLA BOWLS

Delicately spiced, with just a hint of hot chili, this delectable soup is imaginatively served in tortilla bowls. The bowls will hold less than 1 cup (8 fl oz/250 ml) of soup, so you may need to serve any remaining after the bowl has "wilted." White beans, carrots, zucchini (courgettes) or green beans and red bell pepper (capsicum) can be added along with all the other ingredients. Extra chicken stock will make a lighter soup. Or you can omit the tortilla bowls and serve in regular bowls with Texas corn bread (recipe page 85) on the side.

FOR THE TORTILLA BOWLS:

vegetable oil for deep-frying
6 flour tortillas

FOR THE SOUP:

2 cups (16 fl oz/500 ml) rich chicken stock
2 cups (16 fl oz/500 ml) milk or heavy (double) cream

2 cups (12 oz/375 g) shredded, cooked chicken
1 cup (6 oz/185 g) freshly cut corn kernels
1 can (15 oz/470 g) chickpeas (garbanzo beans), rinsed and drained
½ cup (3½ oz/105 g) cooked white rice
2 tomatoes, peeled, seeded and chopped
½ yellow or white onion, diced
2 green (spring) onions, including tender green tops, minced
1 or 2 fresh jalapeño chili peppers, seeded (if desired) and minced
¼ cup (⅓ oz/10 g) minced fresh cilantro (fresh coriander)

diced avocado, lime wedges, minced green (spring) onions and shredded Cheddar or Monterey Jack cheese and crispy flour tortilla (see glossary) strips for garnish

★ To make the tortilla bowls, in a deep-fat fryer or heavy, narrow saucepan, pour in oil to a depth of 3–4 in (7.5–10 cm). Heat to 360°F (185°C) on a deep-fat thermometer or until a small bit of bread turns golden within moments of contact with the oil.
★ Gently lower a tortilla into the oil and, using a soup ladle, press on the center of the tortilla so the sides come up and form a bowl shape about 2 in (5 cm) high. Fry until crispy and lightly browned, 3–4 minutes. Using tongs, transfer to paper towels to drain. Repeat with the remaining tortillas. (The bowls can be fried ahead of time and stored in an airtight container at room temperature for up to 2 days.)
★ To make the soup, in a large saucepan over medium heat, combine all ingredients. Bring to a simmer and simmer very gently until the flavors are blended and the soup is heated to serving temperature, about 15 minutes.
★ Place a tortilla bowl inside a soup bowl and ladle the soup into the bowl. Serve at once with the garnishes alongside for guests to add as desired.

SERVES 6

High Plains

INDIAN FRY BREAD

Texas has been the home of more different Native American tribes than any other state. The best known are the Plains Indians— Comanches, Apaches and Kiowas—famed mounted buffalo hunters who lived in tepees. Today, Texans enjoy their traditional golden fry bread, which can be used in a variety of ways. Split the bread rounds and serve with honey or jam, use as hamburger buns or stuff with meat, beans and/or cheese. You can also top the bread rounds with a thin layer of cooked pinto or black beans followed by mixed salad greens, cherry tomatoes, corn kernels, roasted chili pepper strips, green (spring) onions, radishes, avocados and a garnish of crumbled fresh goat cheese and whole fresh oregano leaves. Omit the cumin seeds if serving with jams, honey or syrups.

2 cups (10 oz/315 g) all-purpose (plain) flour
⅓ cup (2 oz/60 g) instant nonfat dry milk powder
2½ teaspoons baking powder
½ teaspoon salt
2 teaspoons cumin seeds (optional)
3 tablespoons vegetable shortening
⅔–¾ cup (5–6 fl oz/160–180 ml) lukewarm water
vegetable oil for deep-frying

★ In a bowl, stir together the flour, milk powder, baking powder and salt and the cumin seeds, if using. Add the shortening and, using a pastry blender or fork, mix the ingredients together until the mixture is the consistency of pea-sized crumbs. Stir in the water, a little at a time, using just enough for the mixture to form a ball.

Top to bottom: Indian Fry Bread, Cream of Chicken Soup in Tortilla Bowls

★ Turn out the dough onto a lightly floured work surface and knead until it is soft and no longer sticky, 3–4 minutes. Divide the dough into 6 equal portions. Cover with a damp kitchen towel and let stand for 1 hour.

★ Shape each dough portion into a round ¼ in (6 mm) thick. On the floured surface, pat or roll out each round into a larger round 6–7 in (15–18 cm) in diameter. Poke a hole through the center with a finger or a thimble. This will prevent the round from bursting during frying and allows it to fry evenly.

★ In a frying pan, pour in oil to a depth of 1 in (2.5 cm). Heat to 365°–370°F (185°–187°C) on a deep-fat thermometer, or until a small bit of bread turns golden within moments of contact with the oil. One at a time, gently slip the bread rounds into the oil. Fry, turning once, until golden brown and puffy, 1–2 minutes on each side.

★ Using tongs, transfer the bread rounds to paper towels to drain. Serve immediately, or let cool and refrigerate if they are to be used later. To reheat, preheat an oven to 325°F (165°C) and warm the breads in the oven for 8–10 minutes.

MAKES 6 ROUNDS

ANCHO CHILI WITH BEANS

Chili booths were common on the plazas in San Antonio during the latter part of the nineteenth century, particularly on the plaza called El Mercado. Here, chili con carne was cooked and ladled up into bowls by señoritas who flirted with the many customers. By 1893, these "chili queens" had made the dish so popular that there was a San Antonio chili stand at the Chicago World's Fair that year. In 1898, William Gebhardt of New Braunfels produced the first canned chili con carne, with the Gebhardt label, a brand still in existence today. The food of the chili queens was banned from San Antonio in 1937 for health reasons, but in 1977, chili con carne was

proclaimed the state dish by the legislature. Even today there are disputes over the size and grind of the meat and whether the dish should contain beans and tomatoes.

Enjoy this traditional Texas chili with hot Texas corn bread (recipe page 85), spoonbread (recipe page 81), or chili-and-cheese corn husk muffins with pumpkin-seed topping (facing page) and grilled red bell peppers (capsicums).

5 dried ancho chili peppers (see glossary)
2 cups (16 fl oz/500 ml) water, or to cover
2 tablespoons vegetable oil
1 yellow or white onion, diced
3 cloves garlic, minced

★ Rinse the ancho chilies and remove the stems, seeds and ribs. Place in a saucepan, add the water to cover barely and bring to a boil. Turn off the heat and let stand until quite soft, about 30 minutes. Transfer the chilies and liquid to a blender or a food processor fitted with the metal blade. Process until smooth. Set aside.

★ In a sauté pan over medium heat, warm the vegetable oil. Add the onion and garlic and sauté until translucent, 3–4 minutes. Stir in the beef and pork cubes and sauté briefly. Add the jalapeños, salt, oregano, cumin, beer and ancho chili purée. Stir well, cover and simmer over low heat until the meat is very tender, about 2 hours.

★ Stir in the beans, if using, and simmer until the mixture is slightly thickened, about 20 minutes. In a small bowl, stir together the *masa harina*, if using, and 2 tablespoons liquid from the chili. Then stir the mixture into the chili and simmer until thickened, just a few minutes.

★ Ladle into heated bowls and garnish with cilantro leaves, Cheddar cheese and green onions, if desired. Accompany with warm tortillas.

SERVES 10 WITH BEANS, 8 WITHOUT BEANS

W e s t   T e x a s

CHILI-AND-CHEESE CORN HUSK MUFFINS WITH PUMPKIN-SEED TOPPING

These moist and flavorful muffins are baked and served in corn husks. If corn husks are unavailable, paper muffin-tin liners can be used.

12–15 dried corn husks (see glossary)
boiling water, as needed
1 cup (5 oz/155 g) yellow or blue cornmeal
1 cup (5 oz/155 g) all-purpose (plain) flour
2 tablespoons sugar
4 teaspoons baking powder
½ teaspoon salt
½ teaspoon cumin seeds
1 egg
¼ cup (2 fl oz/60 ml) vegetable oil
1 cup (8 fl oz/250 ml) milk
1 cup (4 oz/125 g) shredded pepper Jack cheese (see glossary)
1 cup (6 oz/220 g) freshly cut corn kernels
1 can (7 oz/220 g) chopped poblano chilies, drained (see glossary)
6 tablespoons (2 oz/60 g) finely minced pumpkin seeds

★ Preheat an oven to 400°F (200°C).

★ Separate the corn husks and place them in a large bowl. Add boiling water to cover and weight down with any heavy item that will keep them submerged. Let soak until soft and pliable, about 15 minutes. Drain and pat dry. Tear lengthwise into strips 2 in (5 cm) wide. Set aside.

★ In a large bowl, stir together the cornmeal, flour, sugar, baking powder, salt and cumin seeds. In another bowl, stir together the egg, vegetable oil, milk, cheese, corn kernels and chilies. Add the egg mixture to the cornmeal mixture, stirring just until moistened.

★ Grease 18 standard muffin-tin cups, each about 2 in (5 cm) in diameter. Place 2 or 3 strips of corn husk in the bottom of each cup, crossing them and extending them upward 2–4 in (5–10 cm). As you line each cup, carefully spoon in the batter, filling two-thirds full, and sprinkle the top with about 1 teaspoon of the minced pumpkin seeds.

★ Bake until lightly browned and a toothpick inserted into the center comes out clean, 10–12 minutes. Turn the muffins out of the pan(s) and serve immediately.

MAKES 18 MUFFINS

Left to right: Ancho Chili with Beans, Chili-and-Cheese Corn Husk Muffins with Pumpkin-Seed Topping

1 lb (500 g) lean boneless beef, cut into small cubes
1 lb (500 g) lean boneless pork, cut into small cubes
2 fresh jalapeño chili peppers, seeded (if desired) and minced
1 teaspoon salt, or to taste
1 teaspoon oregano leaves, crushed
1 teaspoon ground cumin
½ cup (4 fl oz/125 ml) beer
3 cups (21 oz/655 g) cooked pinto beans (optional; see glossary)
2 tablespoons *masa harina* (optional; see glossary)
fresh cilantro (fresh coriander) leaves, shredded Cheddar cheese and sliced green (spring) onions for garnish (optional)
flour tortillas, warmed

HIGH PLAINS

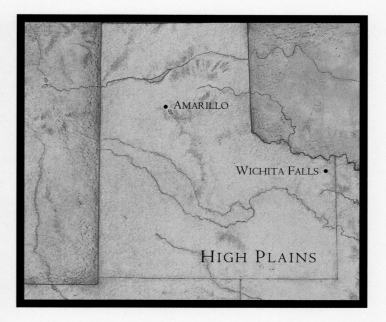

- AMARILLO
- WICHITA FALLS

HIGH PLAINS

HIGH PLAINS

The Mission Trail, believed to have been established by Montezuma and the Spanish and French explorers in the 1500s, is still a fascinating attraction in this windswept part of the Lone Star State. Other interesting trails that provided a route for hundreds of thousands of "snail-footed" longhorn cattle are the Old Spanish Trail, Butterfield Trail, Goodnight Cattle Trail, Chisholm Trail and Blue Star Memorial Trail—names that conjure up visions of Native Americans on horseback, weather-hardened cowboys and endless chains of wagon trains. Tourists who travel the modern highways that follow some of these same paths find it difficult to visualize the hardships endured by the brave souls who walked or rode horseback over the rugged terrain more than two hundred years ago.

Buffaloes roamed the area, game birds were in abundance, and the chest-high grasslands provided grain for the cattle. Food was plentiful, if somewhat limited in variety, and stagecoach stops sprang up near water supplies. Farmers later cleared so much land that today the landscape is drastically changed. Seven hundred miles (eleven hundred kilometers) separate today's short-grass and crop fields of the Panhandle from the marshes of the Coastal Plains; even more miles separate the northern boundaries from the southernmost tip of the state, which noses into Mexico.

Previous pages: Millions of years of erosion formed the majestic buttes and dramatic ravines of Palo Duro Canyon. Left: Alibates National Monument preserves the land once occupied by prehistoric game hunters. Native Americans later mined the area's highly valued flint.

The expanses of prairie land in the Texas Panhandle end abruptly at the multicolored chasm known as Palo Duro Canyon.

The northernmost tip, with Dalhart as its seat, is part of the some 3 million acres (1.25 million hectares) of land that was once the gigantic XIT spread. It was created in 1882, when the state of Texas granted a Chicago corporation the acreage in exchange for the construction of Austin, the state capital. The unbelievably large operation was known as the XIT—*X* signifying the ten members of the corporation and *IT* for "in Texas." Today a winery of the same name is making a mark in culinary circles, and the area is known as The Golden Spread because of rich agricultural, mineral and industrial developments.

The shallow soil here supports fields of vegetables and of buffalo grass, which is being developed as an ecologically sound yard cover. Prairie dogs, which eat the hordes of grasshoppers that plague the land each year, barn owls, rattlesnakes and red-tailed hawks still stake out their territories. Perhaps the most impressive sight is the annual migration of millions of monarch butterflies as they pass this way on their journey to the one and only mountain in Mexico where they lay their eggs. The Lubbock Lake Archaeological Site, the National Ranching Heritage Center and Lubbock's three wineries—Pheasant Ridge Winery, Teysha Cellars and Llano Estacado Winery—all play starring roles in the area's modern-day fame. The first settlement in the Texas High Plains was in Blanco Canyon, Crosby County, by Henry Clay Smith in 1876, who recognized the potential of the land.

Abilene, one of the busiest cities in Texas, thrives today just as it did in the mid-1800s, when it was first a stopping place on the trail drives north and, later, a fort town. Tough, reliant frontiersmen came face to face here with the Native Americans, who resisted their claim on the land.

Grapevines now flourish where the Spanish and Native Americans once roamed. Founded in 1976, the award-winning Llano Estacado Winery is comfortably at home in the High Plains. As the products of the first modern Texas winery, the wines of Llano have garnered more awards than any of its state competitors, and France is one of the largest customers of these vintages. La Escarbada XIT Winery is the northernmost winery in the state. Located just outside Amarillo, in the heart of the historic XIT Ranch, it is known as the Winery of the Panhandle.

Pheasant Ridge Winery and Teysha Cellars are both just outside Lubbock. Pheasant Ridge is named for the wild birds often seen in the vineyard. The Cox family makes its estate wines in the typical French method, with all of them except the blush aged in French oak barrels. Although the family is best known for their reds—Merlot, Pinot Noir, Cabernet Sauvignon, Cabernet Franc—the whites also are award winners. Teysha Cellars is the newest winery in the High Plains. The first crush in 1988 produced more awards than any new Texas winery has ever received.

Three million beef cattle are raised annually in the region. Flocks of migratory waterfowl so large they blot out the sun descend on the fields and wetlands on their way north and south. Massive grain elevators tower to the skies, and oil derricks dot the land. This section of the state produces 450 million pounds (200 million kilograms) of grain sorghum and more than 3 million bushels of wheat each year. Potatoes, carrots, lettuce and onions are shipped coast to coast. Here you also will find Holly Sugar Corporation's huge plant and fields of corn, castor beans and sugar beets. And everywhere countless miles of irrigation systems, whether ditches, long rows of pipe or wheeled sprinkler systems, supplement the meager seventeen to eighteen inches (forty-five centimeters) of annual rainfall.

Small herds of buffalo are again appearing on the horizon. Texas, like Montana and South Dakota, has begun raising these legendary animals for the tender and surprisingly flavorful meat they yield, which is said to be 25 percent lower in cholesterol than beef.

Buffalo grass is a modern-day commercial product that has a long history in the state. Over the years, during which it suffered from the effects of heavy grazing by bison and periodic prairie fires, buffalo grass developed three characteristics that enabled it to survive: seeds that are produced on stems and in seed burrs close to the ground, surface runners with joints that put out new roots, and roots that search deeply for moisture. The same reasons the grass survived on the prairie make it attractive to contemporary homeowners, who are seeking yard covers that require little upkeep and water, resist insects and tolerate drought and freezing temperatures.

It is this part of the state that has remained the most conservative in its embrace of new culinary trends. The residents favor the foods that offer robust tastes and a link with the land: hamburgers; corned beef; gargantuan steaks and sumptuous roasts; chili; stews loaded with potatoes, onions and carrots; thick, fudgy chocolate cakes; strawberry chantilly; banana cream–filled cakes garnished with chocolate chips and chocolate icing.

Dotting the Texas countryside are modest towns often consisting of little more than a general store, a church and a service station.

FROM THE GRILL

Dishes cooked over an open fire acquire a distinctive flavor and aroma.

FROM THE GRILL

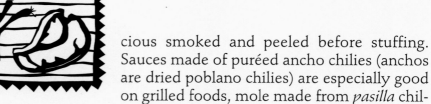

Grilling is so popular in Texas in part because many homes have yards, but also because it celebrates the basic flavors that have nourished Texans for centuries. The natural accompaniments to foods cooked over an outdoor fire are the myriad of piquant salsas. Fresh salsas have taken on a new and exciting identity in the past few years. Previously limited to one basic recipe in most restaurants and cafes, or possibly two or three combinations in upscale dining establishments, salsas in as many as ten different blends now appear on Texas menus. Fresh fruits, exotic as well as ordinary—still laced with the lime and chili peppers that are traditional in the basic fresh vegetable salsas—have found their way into these popular concoctions, adding a refreshing, low-fat, nourishing zest to grilled foods.

Serrano (which translates literally as "medium hot") peppers are the chilies of choice for fresh salsas. Jalapeño peppers, sometimes called the "state pepper of Texas," are equally good. Both are used fresh and green in salsas; canned or pickled jalapeño or serrano peppers are not used in fresh salsas, nor is bottled lime juice. Mangoes, peaches and avocados should be just short of fully ripe so that they will hold their shape when diced into tiny pieces, and the dicing must be done by hand for a successful result.

Fully three-quarters of the world's population use chilies in their cooking, and they can be prepared in many ways. A chipotle chili pepper is a jalapeño that has been smoked over mesquite wood; poblano peppers are deli-cious smoked and peeled before stuffing. Sauces made of puréed ancho chilies (anchos are dried poblano chilies) are especially good on grilled foods, mole made from *pasilla* chilies is found on many upscale menus, and ground chili powder seasoning composed of Anaheim-type chilies, garlic, oregano, cumin, cayenne and paprika, first produced in New Braunfels, Texas, in the early 1890s by William Gebhardt, remains popular throughout the world.

Of the over two hundred varieties of chili, only about two dozen are used in Texas kitchens.

Previous pages, left to right: Grilled Fruit Quesadillas with Cinnamon-Ricotta Filling (recipe page 117), Grilled Jalapeño-Minted Lamb Chops (recipe page 111), Habanero-Marinated Turkey Breast with Pineapple Salsa (recipe page 121), Grilled Grits with Pork Cubes and Gazpacho Salsa (recipe page 114)

Texas is famous for its dude ranches, which offer trail-style cooking from modern-day chuck wagons.

Grilling, popular almost year-round in most parts of Texas because of the balmy climate, cooks meats evenly and imparts an unequaled taste. Everyone looks forward to the first grilled corn of the season, as well as juicy hamburgers and fajitas. Vegetables, seafood, bread and even slices of polenta are also delicious cooked over coals. Woods range from apple to pecan to the ever-popular mesquite, and skewers of fresh rosemary or other flavorful woods lend a subtle flavor that permeates the food. Brushes made from fresh herb sprigs can be dipped into garlic butter or other basting sauces and used for mopping foods.

Herb vinegars are important in the preparation of interesting vinaigrettes, and many homes and apartments have at least one pot of fresh herbs ready for plucking. Indeed, kitchen gardens are enjoying renewed popularity and some contain as many as fifteen different herbs. All the best chefs have their secret, or not so secret, sources for fresh herbs and grow many of their favorites themselves, either at home or on the grounds of the restaurant. Texas soil is good for growing Mexican marigold mint, which is often substituted for hard-to-grow tarragon. Basil, mint, oregano and sage are widely cultivated throughout the state, and rosemary thrives in the areas that resemble the Mediterranean in climate. Epazote, appearing in sidewalks and other places where weeds usually sprout, and cilantro (fresh coriander) are essential for preparing Tex-Mex, Thai and Mexican recipes.

Commercial herb growers are constantly investigating new herbs to brighten the culinary horizon. For example, South Texas herb grower Patty Johnson has introduced a beautiful green-and-white variegated Cuban oregano with fleshy, slightly fuzzy leaves, which promises to add excitement to the kitchen as well as beauty to the garden.

Texans eat heartily on weekends and on special occasions, but more and more cooks are relying on fresh herbs and healthful methods of preparing lean meats and fresh vegetables for daily fare. An enormous breakfast of steak, eggs and flapjacks is, for the most part, a fable left over from trail days. And because most people are concerned with health and fitness, grilling and flavoring foods with herbs and salsas have become de rigueur in food preparation.

Hamburgers, popular since the 1880s when they first appeared in Athens, Texas, are made from venison and buffalo as well as beef. Little did Fletcher Davis know when he "invented" the sandwich made of a ground meat patty served between two slices of bread with hot mustard, a thick onion slice and a large fresh cucumber pickle on the side that he would start a trend that would result in billions of such sandwiches being consumed by people of all ages, from all walks of life. In an early example of joint-venture investment, local business leaders raised the capital to send Davis to the 1904 World's Fair, where, Texas food buffs say, hamburgers were introduced and thus culinary history was made.

As concern with health and wise eating habits continues to grow, grilling—whether indoors over a stove-top burner or outdoors over a portable grill or built-in barbecue pit—is likely to assume a more major role in Texas cuisine than ever before.

Del Rio

BEST-OF-THE-BORDER BARBECUE BRISKET

Cowboys and traders came to the Southwest in great numbers during the nineteenth century. They introduced their distinctive chuck-wagon chow, which featured meat cooked over mesquite fires. This tradition of trail life continues in today's Texas cookouts, both simple and elaborate.

Bob Matzig and Bill Langford, members of the Del Rio Chuckwagon Gang, a group of dedicated cooks, created this recipe, and they insist that using a dry rub is the way real Texans barbecue brisket. Of course, other Lone Star cooks will argue that a wet marinade produces the only authentic brisket. The type of grill you use can range from an elaborate brick pit or kettle grill to a large metal drum with a hinged lid. The heat is regulated by dampers on the firebox and/or chimney. You will need to place a metal pan half full of water beneath the rack holding the brisket and arrange the hot coals, plus presoaked wood chips, alongside it. You will also need to watch the heat level carefully, so that the meat cooks slowly.

9–10 lb (4.5–5 kg) beef brisket

FOR THE DRY RUB:

¾ cup (6 oz/185 g) salt
½ cup (4 oz/125 g) black pepper
⅓ cup (1 oz/30 g) chili powder
4½ teaspoons cayenne pepper

¼–⅓ cup (2–3 fl oz/60–80 ml) full-flavored beer

FOR THE BARBECUE SAUCE:

¼ cup (2 oz/60 g) bacon drippings, butter or margarine
1 yellow onion, coarsely chopped
1 cup (8 fl oz/250 ml) ketchup
2 tablespoons Worcestershire sauce
¼ cup (2 fl oz/60 ml) wine vinegar
1 cup (8 fl oz/250 ml) water or full-flavored beer
2 tablespoons chili powder
1 tablespoon dry mustard
1 teaspoon salt
1 teaspoon freshly ground black pepper
½ teaspoon cayenne pepper or 2 pickled jalapeño chili
    peppers, minced (see glossary)
2 cloves garlic, minced

★ Prepare an indirect-heat fire in a charcoal grill and oil the grill rack (see note).
★ Remove the fat wedge from the side of the large end of the brisket. To make the dry rub, in a small bowl, stir together all the ingredients. Generously rub the brisket on all sides with the dry rub and place it in the grill rack, fat side up. Pack any remaining dry rub on top.
★ Cook at 250°–275°F (120°–135°C) for 4 hours.
★ Remove the brisket from the pit. Make a bag large enough to accommodate the brisket from heavy-duty aluminum foil, leaving one side open. Put the brisket in the middle of the bag and add the beer. Seal all edges of the bag securely.
★ Return the foil-wrapped brisket to the grill rack. Raise the temperature to 300°F (150°C). Cook the brisket, letting the heat cool down to 225°–250°F (107°–120°C), for another 3 hours.
★ To make the barbecue sauce, in a saucepan, combine all the ingredients and bring to a boil, stirring to mix well. Reduce the heat to medium and simmer, uncovered, until thickened, 20–25 minutes.
★ Remove the brisket from the pit. Slice against the grain and arrange on a platter. Serve the warm barbecue sauce alongside for spooning over the top.

SERVES 10–12

Texas

BABY BACK RIBS WITH CHIPOTLE BARBECUE SAUCE

This delicious homemade "ketchup" also complements barbecued chicken or country-style pork ribs. The seductive smoky flavor produced by the addition of presoaked hickory, mesquite, oak, pecan, peach or piñon chips to the fire is essential for really great Texas ribs.

6 lb (3 kg) baby beef back ribs, in one piece
2 cups (16 fl oz/500 ml) distilled white vinegar

FOR THE BARBECUE SAUCE:

3 cups (18 oz/560 g) peeled, seeded and chopped tomatoes,
    with their juices
1 tablespoon salt

Left to right: Baby Back Ribs with Chipotle Barbecue Sauce,
Best-of-the-Border Barbecue Brisket

1½ teaspoons freshly ground pepper
2 tablespoons ground cinnamon
⅛ teaspoon ground cloves
pinch of ground allspice
2 tablespoons firmly packed brown sugar
⅔ cup (5 fl oz/160 ml) cider vinegar
½ chipotle chili in adobo plus ½ teaspoon of the adobo
   sauce (see glossary)
4 teaspoons honey, or to taste

★ In a large pot, combine the ribs, vinegar and water to cover. Bring to a boil, reduce the heat to medium-low and simmer until the meat pulls away from the bones, 35–45 minutes. (This helps remove the fat and tenderize the ribs.) Remove from the heat and drain. Let the ribs cool.
★ Meanwhile, to make the sauce, in a nonreactive saucepan over medium-high heat, cook the tomatoes, stirring occasionally, until they are soft and the liquid has evaporated, about 20 minutes. Remove from the heat.

★ In another saucepan over medium-high heat, combine the salt, pepper, cinnamon, cloves, allspice, brown sugar and vinegar. Stir until the sugar dissolves. Add to the tomatoes, along with the chipotle chili and adobo sauce. Bring to a boil over high heat, reduce the heat to medium and simmer, stirring occasionally, until thickened, about 10 minutes. Transfer to a blender or a food processor fitted with the metal blade and purée until smooth. Strain through a fine-mesh sieve into a bowl, if desired. Add the honey and stir well.
★ While the sauce is cooking, prepare an indirect-heat fire in a charcoal grill and oil the grill rack.
★ Place the ribs on the grill rack and baste with the barbecue sauce. Grill, turning once and basting often, until tender and no longer pink in the center, about 15 minutes on each side.
★ Cut the ribs apart and place on a warmed serving platter.
SERVES 6

CHICKEN SLIVERS WITH CHIPOTLE-PEANUT SAUCE

Canned chipotle chilies come packed in a vinegary tomato-based sauce called adobo. They are dark red and have an addictive smoky, hot flavor. Store unused chilies in a jar in the refrigerator. Orzo (rice-shaped pasta) flavored with Parmesan cheese and fresh basil makes a nice accompaniment. A crisp, dry Riesling or Sauvignon Blanc would be a tangy partner to these bright flavors.

FOR THE CHIPOTLE-PEANUT SAUCE:

1 tablespoon olive oil
3 cloves garlic, chopped
1 yellow onion, coarsely chopped
2 tomatoes, cut up
4 chipotle chilies in adobo (see glossary)
½ cup (3 oz/90 g) unsalted peanuts or pumpkin seeds
½ cup (4 fl oz/125 ml) chicken stock
salt

4 boneless, skinless chicken breast halves
lime wedges for garnish (optional)

★ Prepare an indirect-heat fire in a charcoal grill and oil the grill rack. Soak bamboo skewers in water for 20–30 minutes.
★ To make the chipotle-peanut sauce, in a small frying pan over medium heat, warm the olive oil. Add the garlic and onion and sauté until just softened, 2–3 minutes. Transfer the onion mixture to a blender and add the tomatoes, chilies, peanuts or pumpkin seeds and stock. Purée until smooth. Return to the frying pan and simmer for 5 minutes to blend the flavors. Season to taste with salt. Remove from the heat and set aside.
★ Slice the chicken into long, thin strips. Drain the skewers and thread the chicken strips onto them. Place the skewers on the grill rack and grill, turning once, until opaque throughout when cut into with a knife, about 2 minutes on each side.
★ Place the skewers on a warmed platter or individual plates and garnish with the lime wedges, if using. Serve the sauce in a bowl alongside.

SERVES 4

⅓ cup (3 fl oz/80 ml) peanut oil
1 teaspoon red pepper flakes
salt and freshly cracked black pepper
chilled Bibb lettuce (butterhead) cups, chiffonade of
   radicchio and deep-fried julienne-cut wonton wrappers
   for serving

★ Prepare an indirect-heat fire in a charcoal grill and oil the grill rack.
★ When the coals are ready, place the beef on the grill rack and grill, turning once, until cooked to taste, 10–12 minutes on each side for medium-rare. Transfer to a cutting board and let cool.
★ Slice the cooled beef into julienne strips and place in a bowl. Add the carrots, green onions and bell pepper and toss well. Sprinkle with the black and white sesame seeds.
★ In a small bowl, whisk together the chili oil, cilantro, sesame oil, peanut oil, red pepper flakes and salt and black pepper to taste. Pour the mixture over the beef and vegetables. Cover and chill thoroughly.
★ Place the lettuce cups on individual plates. Place a heaping spoonful of the beef mixture in each lettuce cup. Garnish with radicchio chiffonade and wonton strips. Serve immediately.

SERVES 4–6

Clockwise from left: Chicken Slivers with Chipotle-Peanut Sauce, Texas Beef Tapas, Grilled Chicken with Garlic and Cilantro

Texas

TEXAS BEEF TAPAS

In 1870, the first Chinese were brought to Calvert to build a railroad from the Brazos Valley to Dallas. Once the railroad was finished, many of the Chinese stayed on to farm. The influences of their cuisine are very much in existence today, as evidenced in this recipe by Texas chef Kim Swendson-Cameron. A Beaujolais is always a good choice with grilled meats.

1 lb (500 g) beef tenderloin
2 small carrots, peeled and cut into julienne
5 green (spring) onions, including tender green tops, thinly
   sliced on the diagonal
1 red bell pepper (capsicum), seeded and cut into julienne
2 teaspoons black sesame seeds, toasted
2 teaspoons white sesame seeds, toasted
1 teaspoon chili oil
½ bunch fresh cilantro (fresh coriander), chopped
2 teaspoons Asian sesame oil

Houston

GRILLED CHICKEN WITH GARLIC AND CILANTRO

Chinese influences are strong in Texas, particularly in Houston. Don't be surprised to find flour tortillas often used in place of traditional Chinese pancakes, however. A spicy Gewürztraminer, such as Cap Rock's, will work with the Asian flavors of this dish.

3 tablespoons rice wine vinegar
1 tablespoon Asian sesame oil
2 tablespoons peanut oil
2 tablespoons low-sodium soy sauce
juice of ½ lime
2 cloves garlic, minced
¼ cup (2 fl oz/60 ml) plum wine
freshly ground pepper
4 boneless, skinless chicken breast halves
radicchio leaves, stir-fried snow peas (mangetouts) and
   red bell pepper (capsicum) strips, fresh cilantro (fresh
   coriander) sprigs (optional) and warmed flour tortillas
   for serving

★ In a small bowl, whisk together the vinegar, sesame oil, peanut oil, soy sauce, lime juice, garlic, plum wine and pepper to taste. Arrange the chicken breasts in a single layer in a dish and pour the vinegar mixture evenly over the top. Turn to coat evenly, cover and marinate in the refrigerator for 1–2 hours.
★ Prepare an indirect-heat fire in a charcoal grill and oil the grill rack.
★ When the coals are ready, remove the chicken from the marinade and place on the grill rack. Grill, turning once, until opaque throughout when cut into with a knife, 4–5 minutes on each side.
★ Line 4 individual plates with radicchio leaves and place the chicken breasts on top. Top with the snow peas, the peppers and the cilantro sprigs, if using. Pass the flour tortillas.

SERVES 4

South Texas

LAMB WITH LIME-JALAPEÑO BUTTER

Beef, pork, chicken, shrimp, fish and vegetables are also good basted with this butter mixture. Serve the lamb with green chili and red onion salsa (recipe page 112) and an apple-spinach salad. Rounds of prepared cactus paddles (see glossary) can be used for garnish.

FOR THE LIME-JALAPEÑO BUTTER:

¾ cup (1 oz/30 g) tightly packed fresh cilantro (fresh coriander) leaves, minced
2 fresh jalapeño chili peppers, minced
1 tablespoon fresh lime juice
1 teaspoon grated lime zest
½ cup (4 oz/125 g) unsalted butter

salt
cayenne pepper

1½ lb (750 g) boneless leg of lamb, cut into rounds about 1 in (2.5 cm) thick
sliced green or red bell pepper (capsicum) for garnish

★ Prepare a direct-heat fire in a charcoal grill and oil the grill rack generously.
★ To make the lime-jalapeño butter, in a saucepan over low heat, combine all the ingredients, including salt and cayenne to taste. Heat, gently stirring, until the butter is melted and the flavors are blended.
★ Baste the lamb liberally with the butter and place on the grill rack. Grill, turning once and basting often, until cooked to taste, about 3 minutes on each side for medium-rare.
★ Transfer to warmed individual plates, garnish with bell pepper and serve at once.

SERVES 4–6

Lamb with Lime-Jalapeño Butter

108

King Ranch Jalapeño-Stuffed Quail

K i n g s v i l l e

KING RANCH JALAPEÑO-STUFFED QUAIL

This is a variation on a South Texas classic from the Santa Gertrudis Ranch, where doves are used for this simple dish. The quail may be boned and only the breasts used, in which case the breasts are wrapped around the jalapeño and onion and then the breast is wrapped in the bacon. You can also omit the jalapeño and stuff the cavity with finely chopped apple. The chilitipiques sprigs—small green leaves punctuated by tiny, round, red chilies—make a stunning garnish. Serve the quail with jalapeño potato salad (recipe page 39).

12 quail
6 pickled jalapeño chili peppers, halved and seeded (see glossary)
12 white onion slices
6 slices bacon, halved crosswise

FOR THE MARINADE:

2 tablespoons balsamic vinegar
1 teaspoon minced garlic
1 tablespoon Dijon-style mustard
½ cup (4 fl oz/125 ml) olive oil
salt and freshly ground pepper
South Texas crab grass (see glossary) or shredded spinach
    leaves and chilitipiques sprigs for serving

★ Place in the cavity of each quail half of a jalapeño and an onion slice and then wrap each quail with a piece of the bacon; secure in place with a toothpick. Place in a shallow glass dish in a single layer.
★ To make the marinade, in a small bowl, whisk together the vinegar, garlic and mustard until well mixed. Whisk in the olive oil until an emulsion forms and then season to taste with salt and pepper. Pour the marinade over the quail and turn the birds to coat well. Cover and refrigerate for 1–2 hours.
★ Prepare an indirect-heat fire in a charcoal grill and oil the grill rack.
★ When the coals are ready, remove the quail from the marinade and place on the grill rack. Grill, turning frequently, until the bacon is browned and crispy and the quail are tender when pierced, about 20 minutes total.
★ Transfer to a platter lined with South Texas crab grass or spinach and garnish with chilitipiques sprigs. Serve at once.

SERVES 6

South Texas

BACON-AND-BASIL-WRAPPED GRILLED SHRIMP

Chef Randy Babcock developed this for the famous Grey Moss Inn in Helotes, just outside of San Antonio. It combines fresh basil and rosemary from the Hill Country, shrimp from the Gulf Coast and the fiery zest of South Texas jalapeños. If the rosemary sprigs are not available, use bamboo skewers, presoaking them for 20–30 minutes. A crisp, lively herbal Sauvignon Blanc such as the Gold Medal Slaughter-Leftwich will complement this tangy shrimp appetizer.

8 long, woody fresh rosemary sprigs

FOR THE BARBECUE SAUCE:

1½ teaspoons unsulfured light molasses
2 cups (16 fl oz/500 ml) bottled chili sauce
1 chipotle chili pepper, soaked in hot water to soften, drained and diced (see glossary)
¼ cup (2 oz/60 g) butter
1 tablespoon Worcestershire sauce

3 fresh serrano chili peppers, thinly sliced lengthwise and seeded (see glossary)
2 lb (1 kg) large shrimp (prawns), peeled, deveined and butterflied (see glossary)
large fresh basil leaves, one for each shrimp
½ lb (250 g) venison prosciutto or bacon

★ Place the rosemary sprigs in water to cover for 2–3 hours.
★ Prepare an indirect-heat fire in a charcoal grill and oil the grill rack.
★ To make the barbecue sauce, combine all the ingredients in a saucepan and place over medium heat. Bring to a simmer, stirring to mix well. Remove the sauce from the heat and keep warm until serving.
★ Place a small sliver of serrano chili inside each shrimp, press closed and then wrap first with a basil leaf and then with a piece of the venison prosciutto or bacon. Drain the rosemary sprigs and thread the shrimp onto them.
★ Place the skewers on the grill rack and grill, turning twice and basting frequently with the warm sauce, until just cooked, 3–4 minutes.
★ Serve the shrimp immediately. Serve any remaining sauce in a bowl on the side.

SERVES 8

Heart of Texas

GRILLED SALMON IN BOURBON-HERB MARINADE WITH CUCUMBER-DILL SAUCE

Here is a delightful recipe with which to welcome spring. Serve this fragrant salmon with butter-tossed orzo flecked with lemon zest and fresh parsley. Tender asparagus spears sprinkled with hard-cooked eggs and toasted bread crumbs would be a perfect companion. The cucumber-dill sauce calls for an herbal wine such as Sauvignon Blanc.

4 salmon steaks, each about 6 oz (185 g) and 1 in (2.5 cm) thick
¾ cup (6 fl oz/180 ml) olive oil
⅓ cup (3 fl oz/80 ml) red wine vinegar

4 cloves garlic, minced
1 small white onion, sliced
1 tablespoon Dijon-style mustard
1 teaspoon fresh oregano leaves
½ teaspoon minced fresh basil
1 bay leaf, crumbled
¼ cup (2 fl oz/60 ml) bourbon whiskey

FOR THE CUCUMBER-DILL SAUCE:

1 small cucumber, unpeeled, seeded, shredded and squeezed dry in a kitchen towel
1 cup (8 fl oz/250 ml) sour cream or plain yogurt
1 tablespoon minced fresh dill or 1 teaspoon dried dill
1 green (spring) onion, including tender green tops, finely minced
2 tablespoons finely minced fresh parsley
salt

★ Place the salmon steaks in a single layer in a shallow glass dish. In a bowl, stir together the oil, vinegar, garlic, onion, mustard, oregano, basil, bay leaf and bourbon and pour evenly over the salmon. Turn to coat, cover and refrigerate, turning occasionally, for at least 1 hour or for up to 2 hours.
★ Meanwhile, to make the cucumber-dill sauce, in a bowl, stir together all the ingredients, including salt to taste. Cover and refrigerate until serving.
★ Prepare a direct-heat fire in a charcoal grill and oil the grill rack.
★ Remove the salmon steaks from the marinade, reserving the marinade, and place on the grill rack. Grill, turning once and basting occasionally, until the fish just flakes easily with a fork, about 5 minutes on each side.
★ Transfer the salmon to warmed individual plates and serve immediately with the sauce on the side.

SERVES 4

Rio Grande Valley

GRILLED MAHIMAHI WITH CITRUS AND MIXED BERRY SALSA

Grapefruit had its beginning in Texas in 1919, when Texas citrus growers made a discovery, the Ruby Red grapefruit. Today, we have the Ruby Sweet and the Rio Star varieties, both naturally sweet and delicious. The popularity of the Texas red grapefruit has become so great that it has been proclaimed the state fruit. The state's current billion-dollar citrus industry began from a single orange in the saddlebag of an itinerant Catholic priest. Seven trees grew from the seeds he planted a century ago. This delightful lime-and-grapefruit-marinated fish, topped with a superb fresh berry salsa, beautifully showcases the fresh fruits of Texas. A full-bodied oak-aged Chardonnay will complement the fruit flavors and smokiness of the fish.

FOR THE MIXED BERRY SALSA:

¼ cup (1 oz/30 g) minced red (Spanish) onion
1 fresh jalapeño chili pepper, seeded, if desired, and finely minced
1 small fresh poblano chili pepper, seeded, if desired, and minced (see glossary)
3 tablespoons minced yellow bell pepper (capsicum)
3 tablespoons minced red bell pepper (capsicum)
3 tablespoons minced green bell pepper (capsicum)
3 tablespoons minced fresh cilantro (fresh coriander)
½ cup (2 oz/60 g) blueberries
½ cup (2 oz/60 g) strawberries, stems removed and sliced

Clockwise from left: Bacon-and-Basil-Wrapped Grilled Shrimp, Grilled Salmon in Bourbon-Herb Marinade with Cucumber-Dill Sauce, Grilled Mahimahi with Citrus and Mixed Berry Salsa

3 tablespoons fresh orange juice
1 tablespoon olive oil
salt

1 teaspoon grated lime zest
3 tablespoons fresh lime juice
2 teaspoons grated grapefruit zest
3 tablespoons fresh grapefruit juice
1 teaspoon grated orange zest
3 tablespoons fresh orange juice
½ cup (4 fl oz/125 ml) olive oil
1 fresh jalapeño chili pepper, sliced
½ cup (2 oz/60 g) thinly sliced red (Spanish) onion
2 cloves garlic, minced
salt
6 mahimahi fillets, 6–8 oz (185–250 g) each

★ About 2 hours before serving, make the salsa. In a bowl, stir together all the ingredients, including salt to taste, mixing well. Cover and refrigerate.
★ In a small bowl, whisk together the citrus zests and juices, olive oil, jalapeño, red onion, garlic and salt to taste. Place the fillets in a shallow glass dish in a single layer and spoon the marinade evenly over the top. Cover and refrigerate for 1–2 hours.
★ Prepare an indirect-heat fire in a charcoal grill and oil the grill rack generously.
★ Remove the fillets from the marinade and place on the grill rack. Grill, turning once, until the fish just flakes, 4–6 minutes on each side.
★ Transfer to individual plates and serve immediately with the salsa.

SERVES 6

GRILLED JALAPEÑO-MINTED LAMB CHOPS

The jalapeño jelly adds a Texas twist to grilled lamb chops with mint jelly. Serve with garlic mashed potatoes and an aged Cabernet.

8 loin lamb chops, each about 6 oz (185 g) and 1 in (2.5 cm) thick
4 cloves garlic, minced
¼ cup (2 fl oz/60 ml) olive oil
½ cup (5 oz/155 g) jalapeño jelly
½ cup (5 oz/155 g) mint jelly
1 tablespoon fresh rosemary leaves
1 tablespoon minced fresh mint
thin jalapeño slices and fresh mint sprigs for garnish

★ Prepare an indirect-heat fire in a charcoal grill and oil the grill rack.
★ Pat the lamb chops dry with paper towels. In a small bowl, stir together the garlic and olive oil and then brush the mixture over both sides of the chops.
★ In a small saucepan over low heat, melt together the jalapeño and mint jellies. Stir in the rosemary and mint.
★ Place the chops on the grill rack and grill, basting with the jelly mixture and turning once, until cooked to taste, 5 minutes on each side for medium-rare.
★ Transfer the chops to a warmed platter and glaze each chop with an additional teaspoon of the jelly mixture. Garnish with jalapeño slices and mint sprigs and serve at once.

SERVES 4 *Photograph pages 100–101*

GRILLED POLENTA WITH GREEN CHILI AND RED ONION SALSA

In East Texas, fried cornmeal mush served with maple syrup is a common breakfast menu item, and this hot and hearty dish is reminiscent of that tradition. Use a strong, sweet mesquite fire for grilling the polenta and, if you like, add 1 teaspoon chopped fresh rosemary to the cornmeal mixture. A garnish of chopped ripe tomatoes, minced garlic and fresh basil leaves can be used along with the salsa.

2 cups (16 fl oz/500 ml) chicken stock
2 cups (16 fl oz/500 ml) milk
1 cup (8 fl oz/250 ml) water
1½ teaspoons freshly ground black pepper
1 tablespoon salt
3¼ cups (16½ oz/515 g) medium-grind yellow cornmeal
2 tablespoons butter or margarine

FOR THE GREEN CHILI AND RED ONION SALSA:

5 tomatoes
1 large red (Spanish) onion, unpeeled
3 large fresh jalapeño chili peppers
3 fresh poblano chili peppers (see glossary)
2 garlic cloves, unpeeled

and is no longer grainy, 8–10 minutes. Remove from the heat and stir in the butter or margarine.

★ Pour the cornmeal into the prepared pan. Let cool, cover and chill thoroughly until firmly set.

★ Meanwhile, to make the salsa, preheat a broiler (griller). Place the tomatoes, onion, jalapeños, poblanos and garlic on a broiler pan. Slip under the broiler 4–5 in (10–13 cm) from the heat source and broil (grill), turning as needed, until the skins are evenly blackened. Remove from the broiler, let cool slightly and peel the skins from all the vegetables. Core the tomatoes and stem the jalapeños and poblanos. Cut up the onion. Place the tomatoes, chilies, onion and garlic in a food processor fitted with the metal blade and process to chop coarsely. Pour into a serving bowl. Stir in the avocados, cilantro and lime juice and season to taste with salt. Set aside at room temperature.

★ Prepare an indirect-heat fire in a charcoal grill and oil the grill rack generously.

★ Unmold the cornmeal and cut crosswise into slices ¾ in (2 cm) thick. Brush the slices on both sides with olive oil. Place the slices on the grill rack and grill, turning once, until lightly browned and branded with grill marks, about 5 minutes on each side.

★ Serve the grilled polenta immediately and offer the salsa on the side.

SERVES 8–10

T e x a s

PORK TENDERLOIN WITH ADOBO SAUCE

This multiflavored sauce is equally delicious on boneless chicken breasts grilled over hickory or pecan. Serve with grilled polenta, fried potatoes with cumin ketchup (recipe page 192) or rice. Fall Creek's Emerald Riesling, with its hint of sweetness, will tone the spiciness and blend with the flavor of the pork.

3 or 4 dried ancho or pasilla chili peppers (see glossary)
salt
½ teaspoon ground cumin
1 teaspoon dried oregano
½ teaspoon dried thyme
4 cloves garlic
1 large tomato, coarsely chopped
2 tablespoons fresh lime juice
1 pork tenderloin, 1½ lb (750 g), trimmed of excess fat and butterflied (see glossary)
shredded spinach leaves, cherry tomato halves and green (spring) onion shreds for garnish

★ Place the chilies in a bowl and add hot water to cover. Let stand 30 minutes. Drain the chilies, reserving the soaking water.

★ In a blender, combine the soaked chilies, salt to taste, cumin, oregano, thyme, garlic, tomato and lime juice. Blend until smooth, adding as much of the soaking liquid as needed to make a smooth purée. Set aside.

★ Place the pork between 2 sheets of waxed paper and, using a meat mallet, pound ½–¾ in (12 mm–2 cm) thick. Place in a shallow glass dish and spread the chili purée on both sides. Cover and refrigerate for 2–3 hours.

★ Prepare an indirect-heat fire in a charcoal grill and oil the grill rack.

★ When the coals are ready, place the pork on the grill rack and grill, turning once, until it is no longer pink in the center, 4–5 minutes on each side.

★ To serve, slice the meat on the diagonal into thin strips ½ in (12 mm) wide. Arrange on a warmed platter and garnish with spinach, cherry tomatoes and green onions.

SERVES 4–6

Left to right: Pork Tenderloin with Adobo Sauce, Grilled Polenta with Green Chili and Red Onion Salsa

2 avocados, halved, pitted, peeled and chopped
¼–½ cup (¼–½ oz/7–15 g) fresh cilantro (fresh coriander) leaves, minced
1 tablespoon fresh lime juice
salt

olive oil for brushing

★ Oil a 9-by-5-by-3-in (23-by-13-by-7.5-cm) loaf pan.

★ In a large, heavy pot, combine the chicken stock, milk, water, black pepper and salt. Bring to a boil over high heat and gradually whisk in the cornmeal. Stirring constantly with a wire whisk to prevent sticking and to prevent lumps from forming, cook over medium to medium-low heat until the cornmeal begins to pull away from the sides of the pan

GRILLED GRITS WITH PORK CUBES AND GAZPACHO SALSA

Just as cornmeal has played an important part in the history of Texas food, so too have grits and masa harina. *They come from dried hominy (pozole), which is made by treating corn with lye to remove the hulls from the kernels. In East Texas, the dried kernels are coarsely ground into grits; in West Texas they are finely ground into* masa harina *for making corn tortillas, tamales and the like.*

These grilled grits flecked with pork, onion, garlic and herbs deserve a standing ovation. To serve with roasted pork, omit the pork cubes and add 1 cup (4 oz/125 g) shredded sharp Cheddar cheese to the grits mixture. Minced fresh chives, fresh cilantro (fresh coriander), mint or oregano may also be added.

¼ cup (2 fl oz/60 ml) vegetable oil
½ lb (250 g) boneless pork loin, cut into ⅛-in (3-mm) cubes
4 green (spring) onions, including tender green tops, minced
3 cloves garlic, minced
6 large tomatoes, peeled, seeded and minced
2 bay leaves
1 teaspoon minced fresh Mexican oregano (see glossary)
½ teaspoon fresh thyme leaves
½ teaspoon chopped rosemary leaves
6 cups (1.5 l) chicken stock
2 cups (¾ lb/375 g) quick-cooking grits
salt

FOR THE GAZPACHO SALSA:

2 fresh jalapeño chili peppers, seeded, if desired, and minced
1 bunch radishes, trimmed and diced
1 cucumber, peeled, seeded and diced
5 green (spring) onions, including tender green tops, minced
5 ripe tomatoes, diced
1 cup (6 oz/185 g) small yellow tomatoes, halved
¼ cup (⅓ oz/10 g) minced fresh cilantro (fresh coriander) leaves
¼ cup (2 fl oz/60 ml) olive oil
3 tablespoons fresh lime juice or balsamic vinegar
salt

olive oil for brushing
chives with blossoms attached and diced avocado (optional) for garnish

★ In a large saucepan over medium heat, warm the vegetable oil. Add the pork and sauté until cooked through, 4–5 minutes. Add the green onions, garlic, tomatoes, bay leaves, oregano, thyme and rosemary and stir well. Stir in the chicken stock, grits and salt to taste. Simmer over medium to medium-low heat, stirring occasionally to prevent lumps, until thickened, 10–15 minutes. Remove from the heat.
★ Oil 2 standard loaf pans. Pour the hot cooked grits into the pans, let cool, cover and refrigerate overnight.
★ The next day, make the gazpacho salsa. In a bowl, combine all the ingredients, including salt to taste, and stir well. Set the salsa aside.
★ Prepare a direct-heat fire in a charcoal grill and oil the grill rack generously.
★ Invert the loaf pans onto a cutting board and lift off the pans. Cut the grits vertically into slices ½–¾ in (12 mm–2 cm) thick. Brush both sides of each slice with olive oil. Place on the grill rack and grill, carefully turning once, until golden on both sides, 5–6 minutes on each side.
★ Transfer the grilled grits to a large warmed platter. Garnish each slice with a spoonful of the salsa, the chives and the diced avocado, if using. Serve the remaining salsa in a bowl at the table.

SERVES 10–12   *Photograph pages 100–101*

CHICKEN GRILLED WITH MUSTARD AND FRESH HERBS

Serve these tasty grilled chicken breasts with rosemary and oregano bread (recipe page 84) and spinach-flavored angel hair pasta. If you like, garnish each plate or place setting with individual fresh herbal bouquets. The herb baste used for the chicken is equally delicious on grilled halved game hens (spatchcocks). A homemade herbed mustard can be easily assembled by combining 1 cup (10 oz/315 g) Dijon-style or country-style mustard with ¼ cup (⅓ oz/10 g) minced fresh basil, mint, thyme or rosemary and 1 tablespoon white wine. If using the mustard, lessen the amount of fresh herbs called for in this recipe. A crisp white wine is a great match with all the herb flavors.

¾ teaspoon fresh summer savory leaves
1 tablespoon fresh thyme leaves
1 teaspoon minced fresh pineapple sage leaves
1½ teaspoons fresh whole rosemary leaves
½ teaspoon fresh whole marjoram leaves
3 tablespoons chopped flat-leaf (Italian) parsley
1 teaspoon grated lemon zest
pinch of cayenne pepper
⅓ cup (3 fl oz/80 ml) olive oil
3 tablespoons whole-grain mustard
4 boneless, skinless chicken breast halves

FOR SERVING:

2 cups (4 oz) torn chicory (curly endive)
¼ cup (1 oz/30 g) pine nuts, toasted
¼ cup (2 oz/60 g) well-drained, cooked black beans (see glossary)

salt and freshly ground pepper
fresh herb sprigs (optional) and lemon zest strips for garnish

★ In a glass bowl, combine all the herbs and the lemon zest, cayenne pepper, olive oil and mustard. Mix well. Working with one at a time, place the chicken breast halves between 2 sheets of waxed paper and, using a meat mallet, pound gently until ½ in (12 mm) thick. Generously rub the chicken breasts with the herb mixture and stack in a glass dish. Cover and refrigerate several hours or overnight.
★ Prepare a direct-heat fire in a charcoal grill and oil the grill rack.
★ To prepare individual plates for serving, in a bowl, toss together the chicory, pine nuts and black beans. Divide equally among the plates.
★ Sprinkle the chicken breasts on both sides with salt and pepper and place on the grill rack. Grill, turning once, until opaque throughout when cut into with a knife, 4–5 minutes on each side.
★ Transfer the chicken breasts to the prepared plates and garnish with herb sprigs, if using, and lemon zest strips. Serve at once.

SERVES 4

Chicken Grilled with Mustard and Fresh Herbs

Clockwise from top right: Texas Mixed Grilled Sausages with Cilantro-Chili Salsa, Grilled Chicken with Chipotle Mayonnaise, Texas-Style Burgers, Grilled Shrimp Po' Boy with Olive Mayonnaise

Gulf Coast

GRILLED SHRIMP PO' BOY WITH OLIVE MAYONNAISE

Here is a Texas version of the traditional po' boy sandwich. One of the new microbrewery Texas beers would complement this casual dish.

FOR THE OLIVE MAYONNAISE:

¼ cup (2 fl oz/60 ml) tapenade (see glossary)
½ cup (6 fl oz/180 ml) mayonnaise

6 jumbo shrimp (prawns), peeled and deveined
1 po' boy roll, split horizontally
shredded lettuce, tomato slices and thin red (Spanish) onion
    slices for serving

★ Prepare a direct-heat fire in a charcoal grill and oil the grill rack. Soak bamboo skewers in water to cover for 20–30 minutes.
★ To make the olive mayonnaise, in a small bowl, stir together the tapenade and mayonnaise until well mixed. Cover and refrigerate.
★ Drain the skewers and thread the shrimp onto them. Place the skewers on the grill rack and grill, turning once or twice, until cooked through, 10–12 minutes. Place the roll, cut sides down, on the grill rack as well to toast lightly.
★ To serve, spread the roll generously with the olive mayonnaise. Top with lettuce, tomatoes and onion slices. Remove the shrimp from the skewers and place them on top. Close the roll and cut in half. Serve at once.

SERVES 2

Texas

TEXAS MIXED GRILLED SAUSAGES WITH CILANTRO-CHILI SALSA

There is a tremendous variety of distinctly regional Texas sausages, and they are generally wonderful cooked over a charcoal fire to a succulent and crispy finish. Be sure to prick the skins with a fork to prevent the sausages from splitting during cooking. Serve them with grilled polenta (recipe page 112) or sourdough bread and assorted mustards. Or mix a little minced pickled jalapeño into your favorite mustard and spread it on coriander bolillos (page 79) or hot flour tortillas for encasing the sausages. You can also serve the sausages on a bed of finely shredded cabbage, garnish them with fresh herb sprigs such as rosemary or sage and offer the cilantro-chili salsa on the side.

2–2½ lb (1–1.25 kg) assorted sausages, such as East Texas hot links, New Braunfels bratwurst, Fredericksburg kielbasa, Schulenburg Polish, Castroville Alsatian, Gulf Coast seafood boudin and/or venison, in any combination

FOR THE CILANTRO-CHILI SALSA:

½ cup (4 fl oz/125 ml) fresh lime juice
½ cup (4 fl oz/125 ml) olive oil
2 cups (2 oz/60 g) minced fresh cilantro (fresh coriander) leaves
2 fresh jalapeño chili peppers, seeded, if desired, and minced

116

Left to right: Beef Fajitas with Cactus Salsa, Anticuchos

guacamole (see glossary), lime wedges, *pico de gallo* (see glossary) and sour cream for garnish
flour tortillas, warmed

★ In a shallow glass dish, place the skirt steaks. In a small bowl, stir together the soy sauce, beer, sugar, ground pepper, Worcestershire sauce, lime juice, garlic, green onions and ginger, if using. Pour the mixture evenly over the steaks, turn to coat well, cover and refrigerate for 4–6 hours.
★ To make the salsa, in a bowl, combine all the ingredients, including salt and pepper to taste, and stir well.

★ Prepare a direct-heat fire in a charcoal grill and oil the grill rack. When the coals are ready, remove the steaks from the marinade and place on the grill rack. Grill, turning once, until done to your taste, about 3 minutes on each side for medium-rare. Do not overcook.
★ Transfer to a cutting board and slice thinly on the diagonal. Place on a serving plate. Serve the beef strips with bowls of the salsa, guacamole, lime wedges, *pico de gallo* and sour cream on the side. Pass the tortillas.

SERVES 8–10

119

Top to bottom: Grilled Focaccia with Herbed Oil, Oak-Fired Herb-Wrapped Pork Tenderloin

Hill Country

OAK-FIRED HERB-WRAPPED PORK TENDERLOIN

Serve this sliced tenderloin with grilled tomatoes, whole roasted onions (recipe page 190) and crookneck squash basted with cilantro pesto (see glossary). A fruit-dominated red wine, such as a Pinot Noir, is wonderful with these smoky flavors.

2 pork tenderloins, ½ lb (250 g) each, trimmed of excess fat
6–8 fresh dill, rosemary and thyme sprigs, in any combination
6 slices lean bacon
additional assorted fresh dill, rosemary or thyme sprigs or
    flash-fried parsley (recipe page 123) for garnish

★ Prepare a direct-heat fire in a charcoal grill and oil the grill rack.
★ For uniform cooking, tie the 2 tenderloins together, placing the larger end of one tenderloin against the tapered end of the other. (This will also keep the meat from drying out.) Surround the tenderloins with the herb sprigs and then wrap with the bacon slices. Tie with kitchen twine or secure with toothpicks.
★ Place the tenderloins on the grill rack and cook, turning occasionally, until the meat is no longer pink in the center, 35–40 minutes. Transfer to a cutting board and let rest for 10 minutes before carving.
★ Cut the tenderloins into slices ½ in (12 mm) thick and transfer to a warmed platter or individual plates. Garnish with herb sprigs or flash-fried parsley and serve.

SERVES 4–6

Leon Springs

GRILLED FOCACCIA WITH HERBED OIL

This versatile flat bread is a variation on the popular focaccia made at the Macaroni Grill in Leon Springs. It is a good accompaniment to mixed grilled vegetables with chimichurri sauce (recipe page 126) or assorted cheeses, or it can be the base for an herb pizza. The herbed oil is also excellent in salad dressings or drizzled over steamed vegetables. If grilling isn't possible, the focaccia can be baked in a preheated 400°F (200°C) oven until lightly browned, about 20 minutes.

FOR THE HERBED OIL:

1 teaspoon fresh rosemary leaves, crushed
½ teaspoon red pepper flakes
2 bay leaves, crumbled
1 teaspoon fresh thyme leaves
½ cup (4 fl oz/125 ml) olive oil

FOR THE FOCACCIA:

4 tablespoons (4 fl oz/125 ml) olive oil
3 cups (15 oz/470 g) all-purpose (plain) flour
¾ cup (4½ oz/140 g) semolina flour
½ teaspoon salt
4½ teaspoons active dry yeast
1¼ cups (10 fl oz/310 ml) milk, warmed (105°–115°F/
    41°–46°C)
1 tablespoon fresh rosemary leaves

★ To make the herbed oil, in a bowl, combine all the ingredients, stirring well, and let stand at room temperature for 12 hours.
★ To make the focaccia, pour 2 tablespoons of the olive oil in a 9-in (23-cm) round cake pan. Tip to coat the bottom and then rub the oil on the sides. Set aside.
★ In a large bowl, combine the all-purpose and semolina flours, the remaining 2 tablespoons olive oil, ¼ teaspoon of the salt and the yeast. Using the dough hook on a heavy-duty mixer set at medium speed, beat until mixed. Reduce the speed to low and slowly add the warmed milk, beating until well mixed. Increase the speed to medium and beat until soft and elastic, about 5 minutes.
★ If making by hand, stir together the ingredients with a wooden spoon until well mixed. Turn out onto a lightly floured work surface and knead until soft and elastic, 8–10 minutes.
★ On a lightly floured surface, roll out the dough into a 9-in (23-cm) round and transfer to the prepared pan. Cover loosely with a kitchen towel and let rest for 30 minutes; it will rise slightly.
★ Prepare an indirect-heat fire in a charcoal grill with a cover and oil the grill rack.
★ Remove the towel from the pan and brush the dough with 2 tablespoons of the herbed oil. Sprinkle with the remaining ¼ teaspoon salt and the rosemary, pressing gently on the leaves with your fingertips so that they will adhere. Place the pan on the grill rack, cover the grill and grill until browned and completely cooked, about 15 minutes.
★ Remove from the grill, transfer to a serving plate and drizzle with the remaining herbed oil. Cut into wedges to serve.

MAKES ONE 9-IN (23-CM) ROUND

Buda

HABANERO-MARINATED TURKEY BREAST WITH PINEAPPLE SALSA

The pineapple salsa is a superb contrast to the heat of the habanero-marinated turkey, a preparation that recalls the smoked turkey served at The Salt Lick restaurant in Buda. For an interesting variation, grill the pineapple before adding it to the other salsa ingredients. The grilled peach or mango halves are colorful garnishes and can be put on the grill alongside the turkey breast fillets. The fillets also make great sandwiches. Serve them on cilantro bolillos (recipe page 79), seven-grain bread or ancho bread (page 85) with chipotle mayonnaise (page 117), chipotle butter (page 126) or ancho-cinnamon butter (page 70).

4 skinned turkey breast fillets, each 4–5 oz (125–155 g) and
    ¾ in (2 cm) thick
½ cup (4 fl oz/125 ml) bottled habanero sauce (see glossary)

FOR THE PINEAPPLE SALSA:

1 small pineapple, peeled, cored and chopped
½ cup (2½ oz/75 g) minced red (Spanish) onion
¾ cup (1 oz/30 g) minced fresh cilantro (fresh coriander)
2 tablespoons minced fresh mint
1 tablespoon rice wine vinegar
1 fresh jalapeño chili pepper, minced
salt and freshly ground pepper

grilled peach or mango halves, fresh mint sprigs and whole
    habanero chilies for garnish (see glossary)

★ Place the turkey breasts in a glass dish and coat each with 2 tablespoons of the habanero sauce. Cover and refrigerate for 2 hours.
★ To make the salsa, in a bowl, stir together the pineapple, red onion, cilantro, mint, vinegar, jalapeño and salt and pepper to taste. Cover and refrigerate for 2 hours (or for up to 4 hours).
★ Prepare an indirect-heat fire in a charcoal grill and oil the grill rack.
★ Place the turkey fillets on the grill rack and grill, turning once, until opaque throughout when cut into with a knife, 7–8 minutes on each side.
★ Transfer the turkey fillets to individual plates and garnish with the grilled fruits, mint sprigs and chilies. Serve at once with the salsa.

SERVES 4   *Photograph pages 100–101*

Shrimp with Pumpkin Seed Sauce

SHRIMP WITH PUMPKIN SEED SAUCE

Brown shrimp, which inhabit the deep waters off the Gulf of Mexico, make up about 70 percent of the Texas shrimp catch. Shrimp is clearly big business in Texas. Nearly every Gulf port harbors a shrimp fleet, and the picturesque shrimp basins from Sabine Pass to Port Isabel have become popular attractions for visitors to the Texas coast.

This pumpkin sauce is equally good with chicken or pork skewered with red or yellow bell peppers (capsicums). It can also be thinned with additional stock and used in chicken enchiladas. A Sauvignon Blanc provides the necessary contrast in flavor.

FOR THE PUMPKIN SEED SAUCE:

½ cup (3 oz/90 g) pumpkin seeds
¼ cup (1½ oz/45 g) blanched almonds
¼ teaspoon cumin seeds
1 clove garlic, minced
3 fresh poblano chili peppers, roasted, peeled, seeded and chopped (see glossary)
¼ cup (⅓ oz/10 g) minced fresh parsley
¼ cup (⅓ oz/10 g) minced fresh cilantro (fresh coriander)
1 cup (8 fl oz/250 ml) chicken stock
½ teaspoon fresh lemon or lime juice

3 lb (1.5 kg) large shrimp (prawns), peeled and deveined

★ Prepare a direct-heat fire in a charcoal grill and oil the grill rack. Soak bamboo skewers in water to cover for 20–30 minutes.
★ To make the sauce, in a hot, dry frying pan over low heat, combine the pumpkin seeds, almonds and cumin seeds. Toast, shaking the pan often, until the almonds are golden. Transfer to a blender and grind finely, or place in a mortar and grind with a pestle. Add the garlic, chilies, parsley and cilantro and continue to grind until the mixture is thick and smooth. Pour the stock into a saucepan and gradually stir in the purée. Bring to a boil, stirring occasionally. Remove from the heat and stir in the lemon or lime juice; cover and keep warm.
★ Drain the skewers and thread the shrimp onto them. Place the skewers on the grill rack and grill, turning once, just until cooked through, 1½–2 minutes on each side.
★ Transfer to warmed individual plates and top with some of the sauce. Pass any remaining sauce in a bowl.

SERVES 8–10

Gulf Coast

MUSTANG ISLAND GROUPER WITH FLASH-FRIED PARSLEY

Serve this richly flavored fish garnished with citrus slices and a mound of flash-fried parsley or fresh flat-leaf parsley sprigs. A salad of red, green and yellow bell peppers (capsicums) with a creamy vinaigrette and a pasta dressed with tomato cubes, fresh basil leaves and Kalamata olives will complement the colors as well as the flavors. Serve a crisp Chardonnay or Sauvignon Blanc.

¼ cup (2 fl oz/60 ml) olive oil
2 green (spring) onions, including tender green tops, chopped
1 tablespoon freshly grated Parmesan cheese
½ teaspoon dried basil
¾ teaspoon dry mustard
1 teaspoon fresh oregano leaves
dash of sugar
1 teaspoon salt
freshly ground pepper
2 tablespoons red wine vinegar
1 tablespoon fresh lemon juice
1 grouper or sheepshead fillet, 1½–2 lb (750 g–1 kg) and
    1½–2 in (4–5 cm) thick

FOR THE FLASH-FRIED PARSLEY:

1 bunch fresh flat-leaf (Italian) parsley sprigs

vegetable oil for deep-frying
freshly grated Parmesan cheese (optional)
lemon, orange or lime slices for garnish

★ Prepare an indirect-heat fire in a charcoal grill and oil the grill rack.

★ In a food processor fitted with the metal blade or in a blender, combine the olive oil, green onions, Parmesan cheese, basil, mustard, oregano, sugar and salt and pepper to taste. Process until the onions are finely minced. Add the vinegar and fresh lemon juice and process until fully combined. Pour into a bowl.

★ Place the fish fillet in a wire-hinged basket and place on the grill rack. Grill, turning once and basting repeatedly with the olive oil mixture, just until the fish flakes easily with a fork, about 10 minutes on each side.

★ Meanwhile, make the flash-fried parsley. In a frying pan over medium-high heat, pour in oil to a depth of 1½ in (4 cm). Heat to 360°F (185°C), or until a sprig of parsley begins to color immediately upon being dropped into the oil. Fry the parsley, a few sprigs at a time, until they turn a bright green, about 1 minute. Turn the sprigs, if necessary, to cook evenly. Using a slotted spoon, transfer to paper towels to drain.

★ Transfer the fish fillet to a warmed platter and surround with the parsley. Sprinkle Parmesan cheese over the parsley, if using. Garnish with the citrus slices and serve.

SERVES 4

Mustang Island Grouper with Flash-Fried Parsley

CHILI-AND-CHEESE-STUFFED STEAKS WITH TWO SAUCES

Here is a great way to showcase Texas beef. Serve with grilled polenta triangles, or cut the polenta in cactus shapes before grilling and use as a garnish. The green chili pesto is also delicious with grilled shrimp (prawns) or fish. The rich berry flavors of a Pinot Noir, such as Fredericksburg's Bell Mountain, are a good match for this dish.

2 filets mignons, 6 oz (185 g) each, with pockets cut
   horizontally
¼ cup (2 fl oz/60 ml) olive oil
1 tablespoon balsamic vinegar
1 clove garlic, minced
¼ teaspoon ground cumin

FOR THE GREEN CHILI PESTO:

1 clove garlic
½ cup (2 oz/60 g) drained canned poblano chili peppers,
   coarsely chopped (see glossary)
2 tablespoons freshly grated Parmesan cheese
¼ cup (1½ oz/45 g) pumpkin or sunflower seeds
2–3 tablespoons fresh cilantro (fresh coriander) leaves
2–3 tablespoons fresh parsley leaves
1 small fresh jalapeño chili pepper, seeded and coarsely
   chopped
1 tablespoon olive oil

FOR THE SUN-DRIED TOMATO SAUCE:

1 tablespoon balsamic vinegar
4 dry-packed sun-dried tomatoes, reconstituted in water to
   cover for 10–15 minutes, drained and coarsely chopped
juice of ½ lime
¼ cup (2 fl oz/60 ml) red or blush wine
dash of Worcestershire sauce
½ teaspoon dried oregano

Left to right: Chili-and-Cheese-Stuffed Steaks with Two Sauces, Texas T-Bone with Wild Mushroom Salsa

★ To make the green chili pesto, in a blender or in a food processor fitted with the metal blade, combine all the ingredients and purée until smooth and thick. Pour into a bowl, cover and refrigerate until serving.

★ To make the sun-dried tomato sauce, in a blender or in a food processor fitted with the metal blade, combine all the ingredients except the cream and blend until smooth. Add water if necessary to create a smooth purée. Transfer the purée to a small saucepan and place over low heat. Add the cream, stir to combine and heat slowly. Remove from the heat, cover and set aside.

★ Prepare an indirect-heat fire in a charcoal grill and oil the grill rack.

★ To make the stuffing, in a small bowl, combine the corn kernels, roasted garlic, 1 tablespoon pine nuts, minced sun-dried tomato, roasted chili, Romano cheese and oregano. Mix well. Remove the steaks from the marinade. Stuff an equal amount of the corn mixture into each pocket. Sprinkle the filets mignons with pepper and secure the pockets with toothpicks.

★ Place the steaks on the grill rack and grill, turning once, until cooked to taste, 8–10 minutes total for medium-rare.

★ Meanwhile, reheat the sun-dried tomato sauce gently. Spoon pools of the sun-dried tomato sauce and the green chili pesto on warmed individual plates. Place the steaks on the sauces and sprinkle the pine nuts over the top. Serve immediately, with the remaining sauces in bowls on the side.

SERVES 2

Dallas

TEXAS T-BONE WITH WILD MUSHROOM SALSA

Juicy grilled beef and sautéed mushrooms are a hard combination to beat, especially in Texas. Serve the steaks topped with a pat of herb butter and accompany with horseradish potatoes (recipe page 189). For a simpler dish, brush the whole mushrooms with olive oil and grill them alongside the steak. Or you can sauté the mushrooms as described and add 2 teaspoons chopped fresh cilantro (fresh coriander) and 1 fresh jalapeño chili pepper, seeded and minced, for a spicy variation. Grill the tomatoes and onions alongside the steaks for a pair of easy garnishes, topping the tomatoes with cilantro pesto (see glossary) just before serving, if you like. Match a full-bodied Cap Rock Cabernet Sauvignon from Lubbock with this dish.

4 T-bone steaks, each 1 lb (500 g) and 1½ in (4 cm) thick
salt and freshly ground pepper
2 tablespoons butter
1 teaspoon fresh thyme leaves
2 cloves garlic, minced
1 lb (500 g) fresh mushrooms, such as chanterelle, morel, oyster, or shiitake or a combination, sliced
¼ cup (2 fl oz/60 ml) Cabernet Sauvignon
grilled tomato halves, grilled red (Spanish) onion slices and fresh thyme or marjoram sprigs for garnish

★ Prepare a direct-heat fire in a charcoal grill and oil the grill rack.

★ When the coals are ready, rub the steaks on both sides with salt and pepper to taste. Place on the grill rack and grill, turning once, 6–8 minutes on each side for medium-rare.

★ Meanwhile, in a sauté pan over medium-high heat, melt the butter. Add the thyme and garlic and sauté for 30 seconds. Stir in the mushrooms and sauté until softened, 2–4 minutes. Pour in the wine and bring to a boil, then remove from the heat.

★ Transfer the steaks to individual plates and spoon the mushrooms evenly over the top. Garnish with the tomatoes, onions and herb sprigs and serve immediately.

SERVES 4

1½ teaspoons honey
¼ cup (2 fl oz/60 ml) beef stock
¼ cup (2 fl oz/60 ml) heavy (double) cream

FOR THE STUFFING:

1 ear of corn, grilled and kernels cut from cob
pulp from 1 head roasted garlic (see glossary)
1 tablespoon lightly toasted pine nuts
1 tablespoon minced, reconstituted dry-packed sun-dried tomato
1 fresh poblano chili pepper, roasted, peeled, seeded and minced (see glossary)
1 tablespoon freshly grated Romano cheese
1 teaspoon minced fresh oregano

freshly cracked pepper
toasted pine nuts for garnish

★ Place the filets mignons in a shallow dish. In a small bowl, whisk together the olive oil, vinegar, minced garlic and cumin until well mixed. Pour over the steaks and turn to coat them on both sides. Let stand for 1 hour.

H e a r t   o f   T e x a s

MIXED GRILLED VEGETABLES WITH CHIMICHURRI SAUCE

Grilling vegetables brings out their tremendous flavors, textures and colors, plus they take on the heady aromas of the wood smoke. The secret to success for this dish is selecting the very freshest vegetables. Grill whatever seasonal vegetables you prefer; some suggestions appear here. Baste and serve with the chimichurri *sauce, a popular Argentine marinade and grilling sauce. To add even more flavor while basting, snip 8–10 fresh herb sprigs—rosemary, thyme, oregano, marjoram—each 5–8 inches (13–20 centimeters) long and tie together with kitchen twine. Use the herb brush for basting the sauce onto the vegetables, and then toss the brush onto the hot coals to release a wonderful smoke flavor onto the food. Cilantro pesto (see glossary) can be drizzled over the grilled vegetables as well. Offer crunchy French bread so no one misses a chance to mop up the delicious juices. Or tuck the vegetables into pita bread with alfalfa sprouts.*

FOR THE *CHIMICHURRI* SAUCE:

6–8 cloves garlic
2 cups (3 oz/90 g) chopped fresh parsley
½ cup (¾ oz/20 g) chopped fresh cilantro (fresh coriander)
2 teaspoons dried oregano
2 teaspoons dried thyme
2 teaspoons fresh rosemary leaves
½ teaspoon red pepper flakes
¾ cup (6 fl oz/180 ml) white wine vinegar
¾ cup (6 fl oz/180 ml) olive oil
salt

2½–3 lb (1.25–1.5 kg) assorted mixed vegetables, such as stemmed shiitake mushrooms, bell pepper (capsicum) quarters, red (Spanish) onion quarters, corn on the cob, asparagus spears, small new potatoes, eggplant wedges or slices, whole green (spring) onions, tomato halves and/or zucchini (courgette) or other summer squash halves or quarters, in any combination

Grilled Salmon with Chipotle Butter and Basil-Garlic Bread

★ To make the *chimichurri* sauce, in a food processor fitted with the metal blade, mince the garlic. Add the parsley, cilantro, oregano, thyme, rosemary, red pepper flakes and vinegar and process to blend. With the motor running, add the oil in a slow, steady stream, processing until well mixed. Set aside.
★ Prepare an indirect-heat fire in a charcoal grill and oil the grill rack.
★ Brush the vegetables on all sides with the sauce and place on the grill rack. Grill, turning as needed and basting with more sauce, until tender. The timing will depend upon the types of vegetables being grilled.
★ Serve the vegetables on a warmed platter with any remaining sauce on the side.

SERVES 6–8   *Photograph page 12*

S a n   A n t o n i o

GRILLED SALMON WITH CHIPOTLE BUTTER AND BASIL-GARLIC BREAD

This butter is so good you will want to pass extra. The perfect springtime accompaniments would be roasted baby new potatoes skewered on fresh rosemary branches, asparagus spears and yellow and red tomato halves. Serve the salmon on a bed of mixed spring greens, if desired. Boneless grilled chicken breasts or thin fillets of quickly grilled beef are equally delicious with the chipotle butter. Try a fruity soft Pinot Noir or your best Chardonnay.

FOR THE BASIL-GARLIC BREAD:

½ cup (4 fl oz/125 ml) olive oil
¼ cup (⅓ oz/10 g) minced fresh basil
1 teaspoon minced fresh thyme
2 teaspoons minced fresh oregano
3 cloves garlic, minced
1 French baguette, split horizontally

FOR THE CHIPOTLE BUTTER:

1 or 2 canned chipotle chilies in adobo (see glossary)
½ cup (¾ oz/20 g) chopped fresh cilantro (fresh coriander)
½ cup (4 oz/125 g) butter, at room temperature
3 cloves garlic, minced
juice of ½ lime
1 tablespoon tequila
salt

4 salmon fillets, each about 6 oz (185 g) and 1–1½ in (2.5–4 cm) thick
⅓ cup (1½ oz/45 g) freshly grated Parmesan cheese

★ To make the basil-garlic bread, in a small bowl, whisk together the olive oil, basil, thyme, oregano and garlic. Let stand for 1–2 hours to blend the flavors. Brush the oil mixture evenly over the cut sides of the bread. Set aside.
★ Prepare a direct-heat fire in a charcoal grill and oil the grill rack.
★ To make the chipotle butter, in a blender or in a food processor fitted with the metal blade, combine all the ingredients, including salt to taste, and process until smooth. Transfer to a small bowl and set aside.
★ Rub the fish fillets on both sides with some of the chipotle butter and place on the grill rack. Grill, turning once, just until the fish flakes easily, 4–5 minutes on each side. At the same time, place the prepared bread, cut side down, on the grill rack until browned, 2–3 minutes. Turn the bread right side up, sprinkle with the Parmesan cheese and grill until lightly toasted, 1–3 minutes longer.
★ Transfer the fillets to warmed individual plates. Cut each bread half into slices on the diagonal and serve alongside. Pass any remaining chipotle butter for guests to top their fish.

SERVES 4

Chicken Fajitas with Guacamole

CHICKEN FAJITAS WITH GUACAMOLE

Here is a true South Texas inspiration. If you like, serve mango-jalapeño salsa (see chorizo-stuffed poblanos, recipe page 142) in place of the guacamole.

3 tablespoons white wine
6 tablespoons (3 oz/90 g) butter
1 tablespoon soy sauce
4 cloves garlic, minced
1 teaspoon freshly ground pepper
2 lb (1 kg) boneless, skinless chicken breasts
  or thighs
grilled red (Spanish) onions and green bell pepper
  (capsicum) strips
16–20 flour tortillas, warmed
guacamole (see glossary)

pico de gallo (optional; see glossary)
sour cream (optional)

★ Prepare an indirect-heat fire in a charcoal grill and oil the grill rack.

★ In a small frying pan over medium heat, warm the wine for 1–2 minutes to burn off the alcohol. Add the butter and, once it melts, stir in the soy sauce, garlic and pepper. Cook for about 1 minute, then remove from the heat.

★ Dip the chicken pieces into the wine sauce, turning to coat. Place the chicken on the grill rack and grill, turning once, until opaque throughout when cut into with a knife, 4–5 minutes on each side.

★ Transfer the chicken to a cutting board and cut into finger-length strips. Serve the chicken strips, red onions and bell pepper strips on a warmed platter. Place the tortillas in a basket and the guacamole and the sour cream and *pico de gallo,* if using, in bowls. Let guests assemble their own fajita-filled tortillas, adding the condiments as desired.

SERVES 6–8

127

HEART OF TEXAS

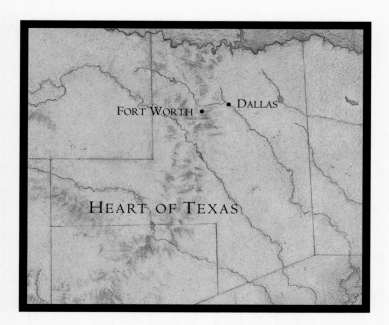

FORT WORTH • • DALLAS

HEART OF TEXAS

HEART OF TEXAS

The "denim and diamonds" mystique popular around the world, the reputation for growing beautiful women and handsome men, and the aggressive, innovative and self-assured impact of the state's leading chefs on contemporary cuisine are no more prominent than they are in Dallas. Dallasites have never been timid about spending money, whether for erecting sparkling contemporary buildings or refurbishing beautiful historic structures. Oil, deal making and huge fashion, home and electronic trade centers form the nucleus of the modern economy. Sports and international business also fuel this cosmopolitan city that looks to the future while building on the past. And Dallasites have been trailblazers in forging contemporary trends in food, sometimes building on traditions and at other times amazing everyone with their originality.

Perhaps the state's best-known food doyenne is Helen Corbitt, who for years directed Neiman Marcus's famous Zodiac tearoom in Dallas. She is credited with inventing poppy-seed dressing, tamale pie and Prairie Fire bean dip, and later went on to oversee the Greenhouse Health Spa, where she revised, modified and developed foods for wealthy, health-conscious eaters.

Also building on tried-and-true traditions is back-to-basics Dallas entrepreneur Paula Lambert, who has made her name as a manufacturer of Italian-style mozzarella

Previous pages: The rich black soil of the prairies near Waco has attracted farmers since the beginning of the nineteenth century. Left: The juxtaposition of old and new architecture in Fort Worth documents the city's transition from a Wild West cowtown to a modern metropolis.

131

Until the Civil War, the cotton industry was the backbone of the Texas economy.

cheeses. Upon returning to Texas after living in Italy, she missed fresh mozzarella so much she established her own company to make it. Today, the award-winning cheese—still made by hand the old-fashioned way—is shipped to restaurants and gourmet stores across the nation, and there is a long list of specialty cheeses in addition to the now-famous mozzarella.

Creative, innovative and, at times, just plain way-out, the ice creams and sorbets from Out of a Flower could be the inspiration for new songs, new sonnets and new works of art, so beautiful and delicious are this Dallas-based company's creations. Edible flowers and fresh herbs are artfully blended into taste sensations that include rosemary ice cream, and rose geranium, red rose, opal basil, nasturtium and cinnamon basil sorbets. And on the more practical side, Dallas's Take Stock, Inc. produces the all-important flavors associated with an old-fashioned, honest-to-goodness, back-of-the-stove stockpot and ships the concentrates to customers.

Dallas chefs Dean Fearing, Lori Finkelman and Stephen Pyles and the food editors of the region's newspapers are leading the way in setting new trends and in raising the quality of food to a level that merits it being dubbed Texas cuisine. Each year, the *Dallas Morning News,* in conjunction with the Texas Department of Agriculture and the Texas Hill Country Wine & Food Festival, presents the Who's Who in Food and Wine awards in Austin, which honor the state's culinary movers and shakers.

Fifty miles (eighty kilometers) south of Dallas, in Corsicana, Collin Street Bakery is producing 4 million pounds (2 million kilograms) of fruitcakes each season and shipping them throughout the United States and to nearly two hundred countries. Collin Street Bakery, established in 1896, is the oldest fruitcake bakery in the country, and it takes its business seriously. This product of German baking skills and Texas pecans began as an ordinary part of rooming-house fare. But a booming mail-

order business was born when John Ringling and his circus troupe passed through many decades ago, and now the product is so well known that letters addressed to Fruit-cake, Texas, are delivered right to the bakery in Corsicana.

Nearby Fort Worth is content to take a slower pace, to boast of brick-paved streets and to be known affection-ately as Cowtown. Gaslights and the famous Stockyards tell of the days of cattle barons, cowboys and a different kind of stock market. The city fathers tout Fort Worth as "the way you want Texas to be." Billy Bob's, a legendary modern-day version of a dance hall and saloon, several outstanding museums—the Kimbell Art Museum to name just one—and, of course, the Stockyards, built in 1907, are all found in this most Texan of Texas cities. It is under-stood that cowboy skills are considered an art form here, and in a state where steak has always been a main event, Fort Worth holds pride of place for simply prepared, first-rate cuts of meat. The nation's oldest continuing livestock event, Fort Worth's Southwestern Exposition and Live-stock Show, takes up one hundred acres (forty hectares) and lasts for seventeen days, drawing more than eight hundred thousand visitors from every state and many foreign countries.

But new things are happening here, for this is the headquarters of the American Ostrich Association. Ostrich and emu ranchers will provide meat for tables across the nation and even the hemisphere in the near future, say the determined farmers, who are as competi-tive as the University of Texas and Oklahoma football teams. The red meat has a flavor and protein content similar to beef but contains half the calories and is extremely low in fat and cholesterol. Not only are the birds in demand for their low-fat meat, but their feathers and hides play important roles in the world of fashion.

The pleasures and hardships of early Texas settlers are remembered at a contemporary re-creation of pioneer life.

According to Native American legend, the Texas state flower originated when warriors fighting in the Happy Hunting Grounds knocked chunks of the sky to the ground, where they turned into bluebonnets.

The Texas wine industry is growing in this part of the state as well. Grapevine, an historic community near the Dallas–Fort Worth Airport, is home to at least two wineries—Preston Trail Winery and Delaney Vineyards—in addition to the annual September GrapeFest and the New Vintage Festival, which takes place in late April. Three more wineries are slated to open in the area. Preston Trail produces a proprietary dessert wine called Tiffany, as well as a popular French Colombard and Merlot Blanc; a sparkling wine is planned for the future.

Texas A&M University plays an important role in the agricultural industry of Texas. Scientists there develop new varieties of fruits, vegetables and other crops that will withstand local growing conditions. One of the most successful ventures is the 1015 Supersweet onion. This grapefruit-sized onion is billed as "the biggest, the sweetest and the juiciest onion on God's green earth!" And it can be eaten like an apple. This onion is so specialized that the inventor decided that it should be planted on a particular day: October 15. Thus the name 1015 Supersweet.

The tiny town of Brenham was established in the republic era and serves as the commercial center for some of the state's most historic counties. The town was a center for commerce in the mid-1800s, when steamboats plied the Brazos River, and it has continued to prosper. In the early 1900s, city fathers began what is believed to be the oldest county fair in the state; they also commissioned Alfred Finn, designer of the San Jacinto Monument, to create a country club and golf course in the 1920s. This showplace, refurbished and known today as The Citadel, featured the first swimming pool in Texas, as well as a knobless back door through which ladies could escape with their inebriated escorts.

The inside scoop on the ice cream industry proclaims that the Brenham Creamery Company began producing its famous ice cream in 1911, and not much has changed at the company over the years, except the amount made. The company's old-fashioned flavors are churned from milk produced the day before. Given its name in 1930 in honor of the East Texas wildflower, Blue Bell Creameries uses only homegrown ingredients in their ice creams, except for vanilla and chocolate, which are not produced in the state. The result is ice cream that tastes as if it was made on a front porch with a hand-cranked machine.

Food fads may come and go, but two things are certain: steaks will remain popular, and talented chefs and other food professionals living in the heart of the state will continue to make their mark on culinary history.

MILD TO WILD

In a land where beef reigns supreme on menus, it is not surprising that livestock outnumber people.

MILD TO WILD

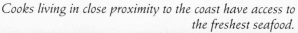

In the great days of the French court, famous chefs were as highly honored as artists, and at the chef's request, the finest ingredients were sought out. Large numbers of servants provided the labor needed to produce the exotic dishes demanded by the households. The processions of courses resembled miniature stage settings, and elaborately decorated foods remained popular until the fifteenth century, when the discovery of the New World forever changed art and cooking.

Columbus's search for spices altered the way food looked and tasted, forging the first bond between the Old World and the New World as he transported fruit, spice and vegetable plants in both directions on his voyages. Corn, tomatoes, turkey, peppers, chocolate, pineapples, yams, strawberries and new varieties of seafood were taken back to Europe. Out of the trials and errors of these early explorers and the settlers who followed came regional cooking as it is known today. Fortunately, animals and fish that existed in great numbers in Texas in those early times continue to be plentiful.

Cooks within easy reach of the Texas shore have the enviable opportunity to choose freshly caught shrimp and oysters from stands along the bay roads. Restaurants across the state serve delicious seafood dishes sparked with exotic Greek, flavorful Italian and spicy Eastern seasonings, as well as fillets or gigantic shrimp and oysters cloaked in popular southern batters and deep-fried. Chefs such as Michael Bomberg, Ann Clark, Ernest Torres and

Anne Greer have developed successful techniques and adapted new ingredients for seafood that have helped to create innovative recipes that are part of the new Texas cuisine.

Game is again on menus, but none of the venison harvested by the Texas Wild Game Cooperative for upscale restaurants is native to North America. Most of the species—nilgai antelope, axis deer, black buck ante-

Cooks living in close proximity to the coast have access to the freshest seafood.

Previous pages: Farmer's Seafood Boil (recipe page 172–173)

German communities preserve a bit of their heritage by making traditional wurst.

lope—are native to Asia and have been raised on Hill Country ranches. The popularity of venison is attributed in part to its leanness, which puts it into the category now called "sensible elegance" or "healthy gourmet" food.

But beef is still king. The process of "upbreeding" Texas cattle began in the 1870s, when Bob Kleberg, son-in-law of legendary King Ranch founder Richard King, developed the Santa Gertrudis, a cross of the Brahman and British shorthorn. The result was a breed that could withstand the sweltering South Texas heat. In 1940, the Santa Gertrudis was named the first American beef breed, and America's passion for a perfectly cooked steak, a traditional Sunday pot roast or a grilled hamburger began in earnest.

Meat and seafood, the basis of main dishes in homes as well as restaurants, perhaps reflect the trends present in the new Texas cuisine more than any other menu components. New informal dining establishments feature regional food stylishly prepared with European techniques. And dining, no longer a prelude to the evening's entertainment, is the main event, so that now where people choose to dine is as important as the food itself. Gone for many of the youngish set are hushed, candlelit food shrines staffed with hovering waiters. Instead, the new restaurants are more like European cafes crossed with architecture from the year 2001, or they boast a bistrolike atmosphere typical of southern France where perfectly prepared food, engaging conversation and happy clatter prevail.

The 1990s approach to preparing fine food no longer focuses on truffles, foie gras and out-of-season fruits and vegetables. Instead, fresh tuna, mackerel, snapper, poultry, farm-raised fish and shrimp, lean beef and local game are the order of the day, and seasonal produce reigns supreme. Thanks to large grocery chains that purchase foods from all over the world, Texans are learning to savor an international offering of food at the height of its season. But at the same time that Texans are sampling the newest trends at the table, they take comfort in knowing that their old-time favorites are available, too.

Heart of Texas

STEAK VERDE WITH CRISPY PEPPER-FRIED ONION SHREDS

This dish showcases beef, the food that made Texas famous. The timing is important here. You will need to begin coating the onions for frying not long before the meat is removed from the oven. Serve with roasted tiny new potatoes flavored with rosemary and an oak-aged Cabernet Sauvignon.

FOR THE CRISPY PEPPER-FRIED ONION SHREDS:

2 large sweet onions, preferably Texas 1015 Supersweet
2 cups (16 fl oz/500 ml) buttermilk
1 cup (5 oz/155 g) all-purpose (plain) flour
3 tablespoons yellow cornmeal
1 teaspoon paprika
¼ teaspoon ground cumin
¼ teaspoon cayenne pepper
⅛ teaspoon freshly ground black pepper
1 tablespoon chili powder
salt
vegetable oil for deep-frying

1 whole beef fillet, 4–5 lb (2–2.5 kg)
coarsely cracked peppercorns
¼ cup (2 fl oz/60 ml) olive oil or (2 oz/60 g) butter
¼–½ cup (1½–3 oz/45–60 g) roasted garlic, mashed
  (see glossary)
1 red (Spanish) onion, thinly sliced
3 cups (12 oz/375 g) shredded pepper Jack cheese
  (see glossary)
2 cups (10 oz/315 g) chopped, roasted green poblano chili
  peppers (see glossary)
2 tablespoons fresh rosemary leaves
2 tablespoons fresh oregano leaves

★ To make the onion shreds, using a mandoline or a food processor fitted with the fine slicing blade, thinly slice the onions. Separate into rings and place in a bowl. Add the buttermilk and let soak for 1 hour.
★ Turn to preparing the beef. Preheat an oven to 500°F (260°C).
★ Trim off all fat and sinews from the fillet. Season to taste with cracked peppercorns. In a heavy frying pan over high heat, warm the olive oil or melt the butter. Add the fillet and brown on all sides, 6–8 minutes total. Remove the meat to a plate and let cool slightly.
★ Using a sharp knife, make 6 deep cuts crosswise every 2 in (5 cm) along the length of the fillet to create pockets about 1½ in (4 cm) deep. Spread each pocket with an equal amount of the roasted garlic paste. Then, using half of the red onion slices and half of the cheese, chilies, rosemary and oregano, fill the pockets.
★ Place the fillet on a rack in a roasting pan and place in the oven. Immediately reduce the heat to 350°F (180°C). Roast until done to your taste, about 30 minutes for rare, or until an instant-read thermometer inserted into the fillet registers 125°F (52°C).
★ Remove from the oven. Preheat the broiler (griller). Top the fillet with the remaining red onion slices, cheese, chilies, rosemary and oregano. Place under the broiler until the cheese melts, just a few minutes. Remove from the broiler, cover loosely with aluminum foil and let rest for 10 minutes.
★ Return to preparing the onion shreds. Drain the onion rings. In a plastic bag, combine the flour, cornmeal, paprika, cumin, cayenne pepper, black pepper, chili powder and salt to taste. Shake to mix well. Add the onion rings and shake to coat.
★ In a deep frying pan or saucepan, pour in vegetable oil to a depth of 2 in (5 cm). Heat to 365°F (185°C) on a deep-fat thermometer, or until a tiny bit of bread begins to brown within a few moments of being dropped in the oil. Working in batches, add the onion rings and fry, stirring frequently, until golden brown, 2–3 minutes. Using a slotted spoon, transfer to paper towels to drain briefly, then sprinkle to taste with salt.
★ Transfer the fillet to a platter and top with the onion shreds. Serve immediately.

SERVES 6

The Panhandle

OVEN-DRIED VENISON JERKY

In the days before refrigeration, the best way to preserve beef was by drying it. The cowboys and pioneers would cut the meat into thin strips, dry it in the sun and carry it with them in their saddle-bags on cattle drives and wagon trains. Later, clotheslines hung with drying strips of meat were common sights on ranches, and the resulting jerky would help sustain the family through the cold winter. Today, jerky is widely sold and is eaten primarily as a snack. Sometimes, though, it is boiled, drained, shredded and then added to scrambled eggs with chopped onion, jalapeños, garlic and tomatoes for serving in warm flour tortillas. Although this recipe calls for venison, beef or nilgai (antelope) can also be used.

1 whole venison fillet, 2½ lb (1.25 kg)
1–2 tablespoons kosher salt
1 tablespoon sugar
1 teaspoon onion powder
1–2 tablespoons freshly ground black pepper
½ teaspoon cayenne pepper (optional)
¼ teaspoon ground cumin (optional)

★ Preheat an oven to 140°F (108°C).
★ Cut the meat with the grain into long, paper-thin strips. (It is helpful to freeze the meat partially to ease the slicing.) Spread the meat in a single layer on 3 ungreased baking sheets.
★ In a small bowl, stir together the salt, sugar, onion powder, black and cayenne peppers and cumin. Sprinkle the spice mixture evenly over both sides of each meat strip. Bake, turning once, until dried and dark brown, about 4 hours.
★ Turn off the oven and leave the meat in the oven for 24 hours to dry further. Transfer the jerky to 1 or more airtight containers and store for up to 1 month in the refrigerator or at cool room temperature.

SERVES 10

Cotulla

VENISON BURGERS WITH BRANDIED APPLE-MUSTARD SAUCE

Serve this full-bodied, lean and healthful fall venison dish with rice or couscous. Lean ground beef may be substituted for the venison. A barrel-aged Cabernet or Zinfandel is always a good match with game dishes.

1 lb (500 g) ground (minced) venison
⅓ lb (5 oz/155 g) bacon, finely chopped
1 small yellow onion, finely chopped
1 egg
½ teaspoon grated lemon zest
⅛ teaspoon thyme
⅛ teaspoon marjoram

Clockwise from bottom left: Steak Verde with Crispy Pepper-Fried Onion Shreds, Oven-Dried Venison Jerky, Venison Burgers with Brandied Apple-Mustard Sauce

salt and freshly ground pepper
about ½ cup (1 oz/30 g) fresh bread crumbs
vegetable oil and/or butter for cooking

FOR THE BRANDIED APPLE-MUSTARD SAUCE:

3 green (spring) onions, including tender green tops, minced
1 cup (8 fl oz/250 ml) apple juice
½ cup (4 fl oz/125 ml) beef stock
½ teaspoon minced fresh thyme
2 tablespoons butter
1 tablespoon Dijon-style mustard
½ cup (4 fl oz/125 ml) milk
1 apple, unpeeled, cored and finely chopped
⅓ cup (3 fl oz/80 ml) brandy
fresh thyme sprigs and thin lemon slices for garnish

★ In a bowl, combine the venison, bacon, onion, egg, lemon zest, thyme, marjoram and salt and pepper to taste. Stir to mix until all the ingredients are evenly distributed; then add bread crumbs as needed to form a mixture that holds together but is not dry. Form the mixture into 6 patties, each about 1 in (2.5 cm) thick.
★ In a large, nonstick frying pan over medium heat, warm enough oil or butter to coat the bottom of the pan lightly. Add the patties and sauté, turning once, until golden brown on both sides, about 5 minutes total. Do not overcook or the venison will become tough. Transfer the patties to a baking dish in which they fit in a single layer. Reserve the drippings in the frying pan.
★ Preheat an oven to 350°F (180°C).
★ To make the sauce, pour off all but 2 tablespoons of the drippings and place the pan over medium heat. Add the green onions and sauté until softened, 2–3 minutes. Pour in the apple juice and deglaze the pan by stirring up any browned-on bits. Cook over medium heat until reduced by one-half.
★ Add the stock, thyme, butter, mustard, milk, apple and brandy and stir well. Simmer, uncovered, over medium heat until thickened, about 15 minutes. Taste and adjust the seasoning.
★ Pour the sauce over the venison patties and cover with aluminum foil. Bake for 10 minutes. Uncover and bake until browned, bubbly and further reduced, 10 minutes longer.
★ Transfer the patties to warmed individual plates and spoon some of the sauce over each serving. Garnish with thyme sprigs and lemon slices and serve at once.

SERVES 4–6

Top to bottom: Roast Chicken with Achiote and Mustard, Chicken Breasts with Bread-Crumb Pesto, Prairie Chicken

South Texas

ROAST CHICKEN WITH ACHIOTE AND MUSTARD

Achiote paste is made from achiote seeds, also known as annatto seeds; they can be found in Latin American markets. Serve the chicken on a bed of bulgur pilaf with fresh asparagus and cherry tomatoes alongside. Offer a light amber beer or a Chardonnay, Pinot Noir or any fine red wine.

1 cup (8 oz/250 g) whole-grain mustard
1–2 tablespoons ground cumin
3 tablespoons achiote paste or Hungarian paprika
2 tablespoons dry mustard
½ cup (4 oz/125 g) butter or margarine, at room temperature
1 cup (1 oz/30 g) fresh parsley leaves
salt
2 chickens, 1½–2 lb (750 g–1 kg) each, cut in half
¼ cup (2 fl oz/60 ml) olive oil
3 tablespoons fresh lime juice

★ In a food processor fitted with the metal blade, combine the whole-grain mustard, cumin, achiote paste or paprika and dry mustard. Process briefly to mix. Add the butter or margarine, parsley and salt to taste and process until smooth and all the ingredients are evenly distributed.
★ Preheat an oven to 400°F (200°C).
★ Using your fingertips, gently loosen the skin covering each chicken breast, being careful not to tear the skin or fully detach it. Rub the mustard butter onto the meat under the skin. Pat the skin gently in place.
★ Place the chicken halves on a rack in a roasting pan and drizzle the olive oil evenly over the tops. Roast until the meat is opaque throughout when pierced with a knife and the juices run clear, 45–55 minutes.
★ Transfer the chicken halves to warmed individual plates and immediately sprinkle with the fresh lime juice. Serve at once.

SERVES 4–6

Heart of Texas

CHICKEN BREASTS WITH BREAD-CRUMB PESTO

Boneless chicken breasts are stuffed with a light bread-crumb pesto, lightly floured, sautéed and then served on a bed of wilted spinach. The pesto is lower in calories than more traditional pestos, which include nuts and cheese. This recipe makes more pesto than you will need for stuffing the breasts. Place leftover pesto in a jar, top with a film of olive oil, cover and refrigerate for up to 6 months. Use as a topping for fish fillets, toss with freshly cooked pasta or spoon into mushroom caps.

FOR THE BREAD-CRUMB PESTO:

4 cloves garlic
1 cup (1½ oz/45 g) tightly packed fresh basil leaves
1½ cups (6 oz/185 g) whole-wheat (wholemeal) bread crumbs
1 teaspoon salt
¾ teaspoon freshly cracked pepper
3 tablespoons apple cider vinegar
¾ cup (6 fl oz/180 ml) olive oil

4 boneless, skinless chicken breast halves, 5–6 oz
    (155–185 g) each
all-purpose (plain) flour, seasoned to taste with salt, freshly
    ground pepper and dried thyme
¼ cup (2 fl oz/60 ml) vegetable oil
slightly wilted spinach leaves, cherry tomatoes and lemon
    wedges for garnish

★ To make the pesto, in a food processor fitted with the metal blade, add the garlic and process to mince. Add the basil leaves and chop completely. Add the bread crumbs, salt, pepper and vinegar and pulse to combine, scraping down the sides of the bowl as necessary. With the motor running, add the olive oil in a thin, steady stream, processing until emulsified.
★ Preheat an oven to 350°F (180°C).
★ Make a small slit in the side of each chicken breast, working the knife back and forth to form a pocket. Spread about 2 tablespoons of the pesto in each pocket. (Reserve the remaining pesto for another use.) Press the opening closed. Place the seasoned flour in a paper bag or plastic bag. Carefully add the breasts, one at a time, and toss to coat.
★ In a large frying pan or sauté pan over high heat, warm the vegetable oil. When a droplet of water sputters in the oil, add the chicken breasts and sauté, turning once, until golden brown on both sides, about 4 minutes total. Transfer the breasts to a baking dish in which they will fit in a single layer. Bake until the chicken is opaque throughout when pierced, 15–20 minutes.
★ Arrange a bed of lightly wilted spinach on each plate and top with a chicken breast. Place the cherry tomatoes and lemon wedges alongside and serve at once.

SERVES 4

South Texas

PRAIRIE CHICKEN

Boudro's, on the famed San Antonio Riverwalk, claims this recipe for small chickens marinated in tequila and lime. The marinade moves San Antonio's favorite cocktail, the margarita, from the bar to the table. If you can't find poussins (young chickens weighing less than 1 pound (500 grams), Cornish hens will also work well. This same marinade can be used on jumbo shrimp (prawns).

4 poussins, about 1½ lb (750 g) each
½ cup (4 fl oz/125 ml) fresh lime juice
½ cup (4 fl oz/125 ml) gold tequila
⅓ cup (3 fl oz/80 ml) olive oil
¼ cup (2 fl oz/60 ml) Grand Marnier or orange-flavored
    liqueur
2 teaspoons minced fresh cilantro (fresh coriander)
2 cloves garlic, minced
¼ teaspoon salt
½ teaspoon freshly ground pepper
⅓ cup (3 fl oz/80 ml) heavy (double) cream
1 tablespoon butter
½ cup (2½ oz/75 g) minced red bell pepper (capsicum)
½ cup (2½ oz/75 g) minced green bell pepper (capsicum)

★ Using a knife or poultry shears, split each bird lengthwise along one side of the backbone. Carefully remove the backbone. Place each bird, skin side up, on a flat work surface and press firmly until the birds are reasonably flattened.
★ In a large bowl, combine the lime juice, tequila, olive oil, liqueur, cilantro and garlic. Add the chickens and turn to coat evenly. Cover and refrigerate for at least 2½ hours or as long as overnight.
★ Preheat an oven to 400°F (200°C).
★ Remove the chickens from the marinade, reserving the marinade. Arrange the chickens in a shallow baking pan, skin side up. Season with the salt and pepper and place on the top rack of the oven. Bake, basting generously with the marinade, until the skin is golden and the juices run clear when a thigh is pierced at its thickest point, 25–30 minutes.
★ Transfer the chickens to warmed individual plates. Place the baking pan on the stove top over high heat. Add the cream and butter and stir to dislodge any browned-on bits. Stir in the red and green bell pepper and cook until the sauce is reduced by one-third, 1–2 minutes.
★ Spoon the sauce over the chickens and serve at once.

SERVES 4–6

South Texas

CHORIZO-STUFFED POBLANOS WITH MANGO SALSA

The flavorful blend of seasonings in this homemade sausage can be used in any recipe calling for Mexican chorizo. Paired with fresh spinach and mushrooms, it is a winning combination. Papaya, pineapple, peach or nectarine can be substituted for the mango in the salsa.

FOR THE CHORIZO:

1 lb (500 g) lean ground pork
1 teaspoon salt
2 teaspoons chili powder
3 cloves garlic, minced
2 teaspoons white wine vinegar
1 teaspoon dried oregano
1 teaspoon paprika
¼ teaspoon ground cinnamon
½–1 teaspoon red pepper flakes, or to taste
½ teaspoon ground cumin
1 teaspoon cumin seeds
1 tablespoon tequila (optional)

FOR THE STUFFING:

2 lb (1 kg) spinach, stems removed and coarsely chopped
½ lb (250 g) fresh mushrooms, coarsely chopped
⅓ cup (1½ oz/45 g) pine nuts or pecans, lightly toasted
1½ cups (3 oz/90 g) fresh bread crumbs
¾ cup (3 oz/90 g) shredded pepper Jack cheese (see glossary)
1 egg, lightly beaten
salt

12 fresh anaheim or fresh poblano chili peppers (see glossary)

FOR THE MANGO SALSA:

¾ cup (4 oz/125 g) diced, peeled mango
¼ cup (¾ oz/20 g) minced green (spring) onion, including tender green tops
¼ cup (1½ oz/45 g) diced red bell pepper (capsicum)
1 fresh jalapeño chili pepper, seeded, if desired, and minced
2 tablespoons minced fresh cilantro (fresh coriander)
2 teaspoons chopped fresh basil
1 tablespoon fresh lime juice
½ teaspoon grated lime zest
1 tablespoon olive oil
1 small avocado, peeled, halved, pitted and diced

★ To make the chorizo, in a bowl, combine all the ingredients, stirring to mix well. Cover and refrigerate for several hours or as long as overnight to blend the flavors.
★ To make the stuffing, in a large frying pan over medium-high heat, crumble the chorizo mixture. Sauté, stirring, until browned, about 10 minutes. Add the spinach and mushrooms and cook, stirring, until the liquid evaporates, about 10 minutes longer.
★ Remove from the heat and stir in the pine nuts or pecans, bread crumbs, cheese and egg, mixing well. Season to taste with salt.
★ Preheat an oven to 400°F (200°C).
★ Leave the stems on the chilies and slit each lengthwise. Remove the seeds and ribs. Divide the stuffing evenly among the chilies, being careful not to tear them. Place seam side up in a single layer in a baking dish.
★ Bake until soft and light brown, about 25 minutes.
★ While the chilies are baking, make the mango salsa. In a bowl, gently stir together all the ingredients. Cover and refrigerate until ready to use.
★ Transfer the chilies to individual plates and serve the mango salsa on the side.

SERVES 12

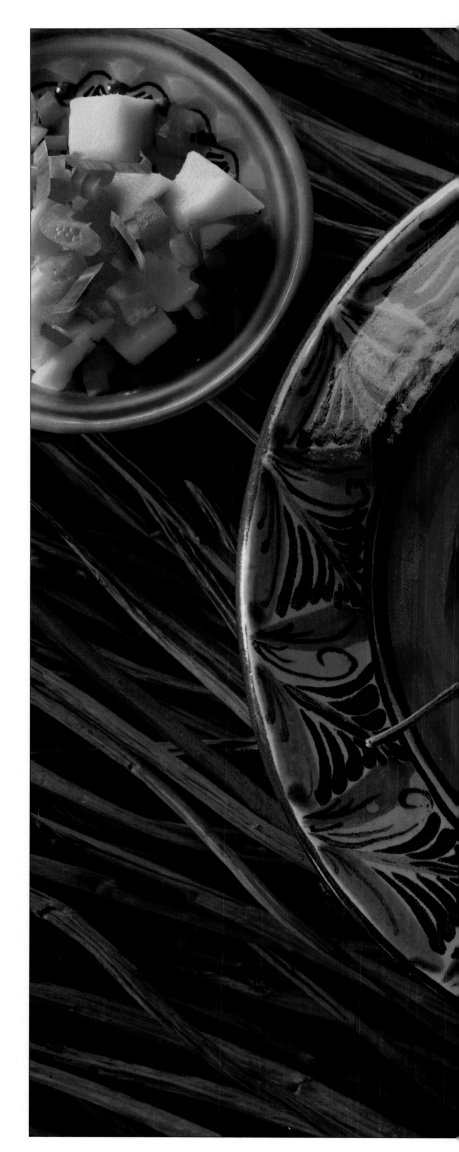

Chorizo-Stuffed Poblanos with Mango Salsa

Left to right: Pipian Verde, Chicken and Corn Enchiladas with Tomatillo-Corn Salsa, Chicken Enchiladas with Pueblo-Style Mole Sauce

El Paso

CHICKEN ENCHILADAS WITH PUEBLO-STYLE MOLE SAUCE

This variation on mole poblano, the spicy Mexican sauce that includes chocolate, comes from El Paso's Park Kerr. He simplifies the preparation by using prepared mole poblano paste, which is available under several brand names, among them Doña Maria and Rogelio Bueno. This is a good way to use up leftover cooked chicken. If you have none on hand, see the recipe for chicken and corn enchiladas with tomatillo-corn salsa on page 145 for directions on how to boil chicken for using here. The chicken enchiladas are traditionally served with refried black or pinto beans (see glossary) sprinkled with a sharp cheese.

2 jars (8¾ oz/270 g each) mole poblano paste
¼ cup (2½ oz/75 g) peanut butter
about 3½ cups (28 fl oz/875 ml) chicken stock
corn oil, as needed
12 corn tortillas, each 6 in (15 cm) in diameter
5 oz (155 g) Monterey Jack cheese, shredded
5 oz (155 g) mozzarella cheese, shredded
4 cups (1½ lb/750 g) shredded, cooked chicken
salt
¾ cup (4 oz/125 g) minced yellow onion
½ cup (4 fl oz/125 ml) crème fraîche (see glossary)
2 tablespoons sesame seeds, lightly toasted in a dry pan

★ Preheat an oven to 375°F (190°C).
★ In a heavy frying pan over low heat, combine the mole poblano paste and the peanut butter and cook, mashing, until almost melted. Gradually whisk in enough of the stock to make a smooth, medium-thick sauce. Reduce the heat to low and keep hot.
★ In another frying pan over medium heat, pour in corn oil to a depth of ½ in (12 mm). Using tongs, slip the tortillas, one at a time, into the hot oil for 3–5 seconds to soften; turn and heat for 3–5 seconds and then transfer to paper towels to drain.
★ Spread ¾ cup (6 fl oz/180 ml) of the mole sauce on the bottom of a shallow 9-by-13-in (23-by-33-cm) baking dish or 4 individual baking dishes. In a bowl, toss together the cheeses.
★ Using tongs, dip the tortillas, one at a time, into the hot mole sauce and place on a plate. Spread about ⅓ cup (2 oz/60 g) of the shredded chicken across the lower one-third of the first tortilla and season lightly with salt. Sprinkle with about 1 tablespoon of the onion and top with about 2 tablespoons of the mixed cheeses. Roll up the tortilla and lay it, seam side down, in the baking dish. Repeat with the remaining tortillas until all the ingredients are used. Drizzle the remaining mole over the top and sprinkle with the remaining mixed cheeses.
★ Cover loosely with aluminum foil. Bake until heated through and the cheese is bubbly, about 12 minutes. Remove from the oven and serve with the crème fraîche on the side. Sprinkle with the toasted sesame seeds and serve at once directly from the dish.

SERVES 4

PIPIAN VERDE

Cookbook author James Peyton, in his El Norte: The Cuisine of Northern Mexico, *has discovered the heart and soul of northern Mexican cuisine in recipes such as pipian verde (also often called* mole verde*)—dishes that form the basis for much of today's popular Southwest cooking. This exquisite sauce is delicious served over chicken and rice or chicken enchiladas.*

4 boneless, skinless chicken breast halves, 5–6 oz
   (155–185 g) each
1 lb (500 g) tomatillos, brown husks removed
2 fresh serrano chili peppers (see glossary)
vegetable oil for frying
⅓ cup (1½ oz/45 g) unsalted pumpkin seeds
¼ cup (1½ oz/45 g) slivered, blanched almonds
1 white onion, minced
2 cloves garlic, minced
1 corn tortilla
¼ cup (¼ oz/7 g) fresh cilantro (fresh coriander) leaves,
   minced
1 fresh poblano chili pepper, roasted, peeled and coarsely
   chopped (see glossary)
¾ teaspoon salt, or to taste
2 teaspoons distilled white vinegar
1 teaspoon sugar

★ Place the chicken breasts in a saucepan and add water to cover. Bring to a simmer over low heat and cook very slowly until just barely cooked through, about 10 minutes. Using tongs, transfer the chicken breasts to a plate; reserve the cooking liquid.
★ Place the tomatillos and serranos in another saucepan and add water to cover. Bring to a boil over high heat, reduce the heat to medium and simmer until soft, 5–10 minutes. Transfer to a blender and process for 30 seconds. Using a food mill, strain the tomatillo mixture to remove any seeds and return it to the blender.
★ In a small, heavy frying pan over medium heat, warm a little oil. Add the pumpkin seeds and fry, stirring, until they puff, 1–3 minutes. Be careful, as they will dance about and sometimes splatter hot oil. Using a slotted spoon, transfer the seeds to the blender.
★ Add a little more oil to the pan, if necessary, and add the almonds. Fry over medium heat, stirring, until they just begin to turn brown, 1–3 minutes. Using the slotted spoon, transfer to the blender. Add the onion and garlic and sauté until soft but not browned, about 3 minutes. Using the slotted spoon, add to the blender as well.
★ In the same frying pan over medium to medium-high heat, pour in vegetable oil to a depth of ½ in (12 mm). When the oil is hot, add the tortilla and fry until just starting to crisp, about 10 seconds. Turn and fry on the second side about 10 seconds longer. Using tongs, transfer to paper towels to drain briefly, then break up and add to blender.
★ Add the cilantro, poblano chili and salt to the blender and process for 30 seconds. Add enough of the cooking liquid from the chicken to make a total of 4 cups (32 fl oz/1 l) and process until smooth, about 15 seconds.
★ In a saucepan over medium heat, warm ¼ cup (2 fl oz/ 60 ml) vegetable oil. Add the tomatillo mixture and cook uncovered, stirring occasionally, until the mixture is the consistency of a thick milkshake, 15–20 minutes. Stir in the vinegar and sugar.
★ Add the chicken breasts to the pan and heat through, 2–3 minutes. Transfer to a warmed serving dish or individual plates and serve at once.

SERVES 4

CHICKEN AND CORN ENCHILADAS WITH TOMATILLO-CORN SALSA

San Antonio restaurateur Arthur Cerna developed these enchiladas for his popular restaurant, El Jarro. The combination of different textures, colors and tastes makes them one of the most requested items on the menu. Use corn cut fresh from the cob, if possible. It adds a wonderful crunch that is a perfect foil for the creamy tomatillo sauce and melted cheese. If you have difficulty finding fresh tomatillos, canned ones may be used.

1 chicken, about 3 lb (1.5 kg)
1 bay leaf
salt and freshly ground pepper
2 white onions, finely chopped
1 green bell pepper (capsicum), seeded and finely
   chopped
2 large tomatoes, diced
2 tablespoons olive oil
3 lb (1.5 kg) tomatillos, brown husks removed and
   halved
6 cloves garlic, minced
1 cup (8 fl oz/250 ml) water
salt
kernels from 2 ears of corn
12 corn tortillas, each about 6 in (15 cm) in diameter
1 cup (4 oz/125 g) shredded Monterey Jack cheese
fresh cilantro (fresh coriander) sprigs and avocado slices
   for garnish

★ Place the chicken in a large pot and add the bay leaf, salt and pepper to taste and water to cover by 2 in (5 cm). Bring to a boil over medium-high heat. Cover partially, reduce the heat to low and simmer until opaque throughout and the juices run clear when the thigh joint is pierced, about 1 hour. Remove from the cooking liquid, reserving the liquid, and let cool. Skin and bone the chicken and chop the meat into medium dice.
★ Place the chicken in a bowl and add 1 of the onions, the bell pepper, the tomatoes and the olive oil. Stir gently to combine. Add ¼ cup (2 fl oz/60 ml) of the stock to moisten, mix well and set aside.
★ In a saucepan over medium heat, combine the tomatillos, the remaining onion, the garlic and the water. Bring to a simmer and cook until the tomatillos are tender, about 15 minutes. Transfer to a blender or a food processor fitted with the metal blade and purée until smooth. Season to taste with salt. Pour the sauce into a frying pan and heat gently; keep warm.
★ Preheat an oven to 375°F (190°C).
★ Pour half of the sauce into a small saucepan and add the corn. Place over medium heat and cook gently until the corn is just tender, about 3 minutes. Set aside.
★ To soften the tortillas, pass them, one at a time, through the tomatillo sauce remaining in the frying pan. Place an equal amount of the chicken mixture in the center of each tortilla and roll up. Place side by side in a baking dish in a single layer. Spoon the tomatillo sauce remaining in the frying pan evenly over the top. Then strew with the cheese and top with the corn mixture.
★ Bake until heated through and the cheese melts and is bubbly, about 12 minutes.
★ Garnish the enchiladas with cilantro sprigs and avocado slices and serve at once.

SERVES 6

Swordfish Steaks with Asian Searing Sauce

This is another indication of the Asian influence on Texas Gulf Coast cooking. Shrimp (prawns), scallops or cubed shark fillets can be used in place of the swordfish or tuna; reduce the marinating time to 1 hour. Serve with fluffy white rice and crispy stir-fried snow peas (mangetouts) or broccoli steamed with just a hint of Chinese five-spice powder.

¼ cup (2 oz/60 g) firmly packed brown sugar
¼ cup (2 fl oz/60 ml) rice wine vinegar
2 cloves garlic, minced
1 tablespoon minced, peeled fresh ginger
½ teaspoon freshly cracked pepper
2 tablespoons Asian sesame oil
2 tablespoons soy sauce
1 fresh jalapeño or serrano chili pepper
⠀⠀(see glossary), minced
2 green (spring) onions, including tender green tops, minced
2 swordfish or tuna steaks, each 7 oz (220 g) and ¾ in
⠀⠀(2 cm) thick

★ In a small saucepan, combine the brown sugar and rice wine vinegar. Bring to a boil, stirring until the sugar is dissolved. Remove from the heat and stir in the garlic, ginger, pepper, sesame oil, soy sauce, chili pepper and green onions. Let cool.
★ Place the fish steaks in a single layer in a shallow glass or ceramic dish and pour the cooled vinegar-sugar mixture evenly over them. Cover and refrigerate for 2 hours.
★ Remove the fish from the marinade and pat dry. Heat a heavy frying pan, preferably cast iron, over medium-high heat. When the pan is hot, add the fish steaks and sear, turning once, until nicely browned on both sides and the flesh flakes when pierced with a fork, 4–5 minutes on each side.
★ Transfer the steaks to warmed individual plates and serve immediately.

SERVES 2

Mustard-Rubbed Tuna with Tomato-Mint Relish

Native-born chef Helen Duran created this flavorful tuna dish and suggests serving it with couscous and steamed asparagus.

½ teaspoon cumin seeds
2–3 tablespoons Dijon-style mustard, or to taste
½ teaspoon honey
½ teaspoon dried thyme leaves
½ teaspoon chopped fresh mint
6 tuna steaks, 5–6 oz (155–185 g) each

FOR THE TOMATO-MINT RELISH:

6 plum (Roma) tomatoes
½ teaspoon chopped fresh mint
½ teaspoon chopped fresh parsley
½ teaspoon fresh lemon juice
1 tablespoon extra-virgin olive oil
¼ teaspoon grated lemon zest

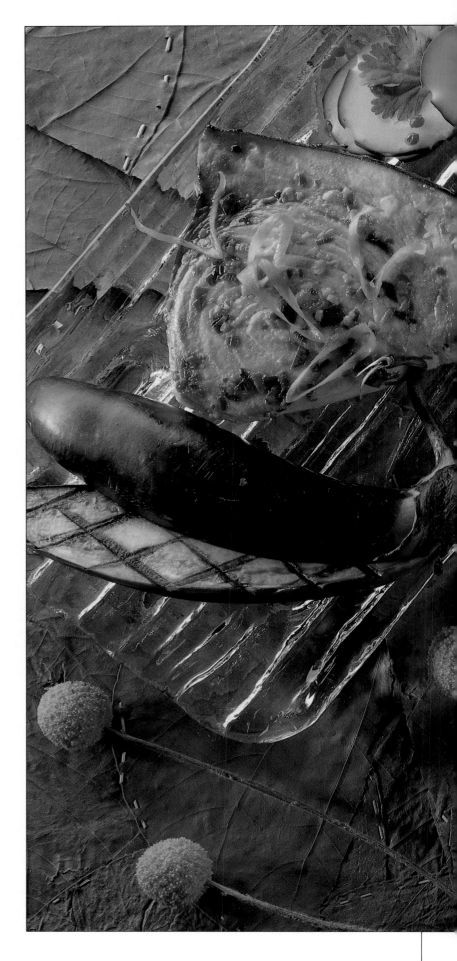

½ teaspoon kosher salt
½ teaspoon freshly ground pepper
¼ cup (1½ oz/45 g) pine nuts, lightly toasted

olive oil for cooking
salt and freshly ground pepper

★ In a small, dry sauté pan over medium heat, toast the cumin seeds until fragrant, about 3 minutes. Pour into a small bowl and add the mustard, honey, thyme and mint; mix well.

Left to right: Swordfish Steaks with Asian Searing Sauce,
Mustard-Rubbed Tuna with Tomato-Mint Relish

★ Place the tuna steaks in a single layer in a shallow glass or ceramic dish and rub on both sides with the mustard mixture. Cover and refrigerate for several hours.

★ To make the relish, quarter the tomatoes and remove the seeds. Dice the tomato quarters into ¼-in (6-mm) pieces. Place in a bowl and add all the remaining ingredients, except the nuts. Let stand for 1–2 hours. Stir in the pine nuts just before serving.

★ Place a large nonstick frying pan (or 2 pans) over high heat and heat until almost smoking. Add just enough olive oil to cover the bottom of the pan. Sprinkle the tuna steaks with salt and pepper to taste and add to the hot pan. Sear on one side until just brown; turn and sear on the second side. Total cooking time should be 6–8 minutes. There should be a very thin pink line around the sides of the steaks, which means the fish is medium to medium-rare. If cooked longer, the tuna will be dried out.

★ Transfer to warmed individual plates and serve immediately. Accompany with the tomato-mint relish.

SERVES 6

Gulf Coast

TEXAS HOT-PEPPER SHRIMP WITH AVOCADO SALSA

Absolutely delicious and fiery hot, these peel-your-own shrimp beg for ice-cold tea or beer as a cooling accompaniment.

FOR THE AVOCADO SALSA:

2 avocados, halved, pitted, peeled and cut into ½-in
   (12-mm) cubes
¼ cup (⅓ oz/10 g) minced fresh cilantro (fresh coriander)
3 green (spring) onions, minced
2 cloves garlic, minced

¾ cup (6 fl oz/180 ml) olive oil
⅓ cup (3 fl oz/80 ml) fresh lime juice
salt and freshly ground pepper

½ teaspoon red pepper flakes
1 teaspoon cayenne pepper, or to taste
1 teaspoon freshly ground black pepper, or to taste
1 tablespoon dried thyme
1 tablespoon dried rosemary
2 teaspoons dried oregano
½ cup (4 oz/125 g) butter or margarine
4 cloves garlic, minced
1 teaspoon Worcestershire sauce
2 lb (1 kg) shrimp in the shell

148

sauce and seasoning mixture and stir well. Immediately add the shrimp and sauté over high heat for 2 minutes.

★ Add the beer and continue to sauté until the shrimp curl, turn pink and are cooked through, 3–4 minutes longer. Serve directly from the cast-iron pan or transfer to a serving platter. Accompany with the avocado salsa and with French bread, if desired.

SERVES 6–8

Clockwise from left: Texas Hot-Pepper Shrimp with Avocado Salsa, Lone Star Pasta Salad with Shrimp and Peppers, Blue Cornmeal Shrimp with Marinated Tomatoes (recipe page 150)

½ cup (4 fl oz/125 ml) beer
French bread slices for serving (optional)

★ To make the salsa, in a bowl, gently stir together all the ingredients, including salt and pepper to taste, until well mixed. Cover and refrigerate until chilled before serving.
★ In a small bowl, stir together the red pepper flakes, cayenne pepper, black pepper, thyme, rosemary and oregano. Set the seasoning mixture aside.
★ In a large frying pan, preferably cast iron, over high heat, melt the butter or margarine. Add the garlic, Worcestershire

Houston

LONE STAR PASTA SALAD WITH SHRIMP AND PEPPERS

Houston is arguably one of America's most exciting cities, a place where you will find everything from ranch-kitchen to big-city cuisine. This salad has all the colors and flavors of summertime. The Texas-shaped or wagon-wheel pasta makes it clear where the recipe originated.

8 large tomatoes
1 ripe Haas avocado, halved, pitted, peeled and
    cut up
3 tablespoons fresh lime juice
¾ cup (6 fl oz/180 ml) chicken stock
½ cup (4 fl oz/125 ml) sour cream or plain nonfat yogurt
salt
¼ cup (1½ oz/45 g) chopped white onion
½ teaspoon ground cumin
Tabasco or other hot-pepper sauce
1 lb (500 g) Texas-shaped or wagon wheel–shaped pasta
1 or 2 fresh jalapeño chili peppers, seeded and minced
½ small red bell pepper (capsicum), seeded and diced
½ small yellow bell pepper (capsicum), seeded
    and diced
½ small green bell pepper (capsicum), seeded
    and diced
1 lb (500 g) shrimp (prawns), cooked in boiling water,
    drained, peeled and deveined
lettuce leaves and fresh cilantro (fresh coriander) sprigs
    for garnish
corn tortilla chips (see glossary)

★ Cut off the tops of the 8 large tomatoes and, using a spoon, scoop out the pulp, forming tomato bowls with sides ¼ in (6 mm) thick. Place upside down to drain. Dice enough of the pulp to measure 1½ cups (9 oz/280 g) and set aside; reserve the remaining pulp for another use.
★ Fill a large pot three-fourths full of water and bring to a boil.
★ Meanwhile, in a food processor fitted with the metal blade or in a blender, combine the avocado and lime juice. Process until smooth. Add the stock, sour cream or yogurt, salt to taste, onion, cumin and hot-pepper sauce to taste. Process until well blended. Transfer to a large bowl.
★ Add the pasta to the boiling water and cook until al dente, 8–10 minutes or according to package directions. Drain and rinse in cold water until cool. Drain again, shaking to remove all moisture, then add to the bowl holding the avocado mixture. Add the jalapeño pepper, reserved tomato pulp, red, yellow and green bell pepper and shrimp and mix well.
★ Line individual plates with the lettuce leaves. Spoon the pasta mixture into the hollowed-out tomatoes and set each on a lettuce-lined plate. The pasta salad will spill over the edges. Garnish with the cilantro and serve with the tortilla chips on the side.

SERVES 8

CORNISH HENS WITH TWO GLAZES

Deliciously quick and easy to prepare, these elegant glazes are also wonderful with chicken, quail, duck or pheasant. Serve with wild rice and steamed asparagus. Pinot Noir will complement the fruity flavors of the glazes.

4 Cornish hens

FOR THE APRICOT GLAZE:

1 cup (10 oz/315 g) apricot preserves
1 cup (8 fl oz/250 ml) undiluted orange juice concentrate

FOR THE GUAVA GLAZE:

1 cup (10 oz/315 g) guava jelly
1 cup (8 fl oz/250 ml) undiluted lime juice concentrate

★ Preheat an oven to 375°F (190°C). Line with aluminum foil a baking dish in which the birds will fit comfortably. Place the birds, breast side up, in the pan.
★ To make the apricot glaze, in a saucepan over medium heat, combine the apricot preserves and orange juice concentrate. Heat, stirring constantly, until melted and well combined.
★ To make the guava glaze, in a saucepan over medium heat, combine the guava jelly and lime juice concentrate. Heat, stirring constantly, until melted and well combined.
★ Brush 2 hens with the apricot glaze and the remaining 2 hens with the guava glaze. Roast, basting frequently with the glazes, until the juices run clear when a thigh is pierced at its thickest point, about 45 minutes.
★ Transfer the birds to serving plates. Cut the hens in half, and place 2 halves on each of 4 warmed individual plates. Pass any leftover glazes at the table.

SERVES 4

ROSEMARY–RED SERRANO ROASTED PORK LOIN

This recipe won first place in the Best Tasting category in the statewide Herb Competition sponsored by the Texas Herb Marketers and Growers Association. San Antonio chef Jay McCarthy developed it by taking a Jamaican jerk barbecue recipe and substituting serrano for habanero chilies and fresh rosemary for the thyme. It is delicious with garlic-flavored mashed potatoes or cumin-flavored spaetzle (recipe page 190).

½ cup (4 fl oz/125 ml) soy sauce
½ cup (½ oz/15 g) fresh rosemary leaves, chopped
6–8 fresh red serrano chili peppers, cut up (see glossary)
⅓ cup (1½ oz/45 g) garlic cloves, minced
¼ cup (1 oz/30 g) freshly cracked pepper
⅓ cup (3 fl oz/80 ml) peanut oil
½ cup (2 oz/60 g) toasted fine dried bread crumbs
1 boneless center-cut pork loin roast, 4 lb (2 kg)
salt

★ Preheat an oven to 350°F (180°C).
★ In a blender, combine the soy sauce, rosemary, serranos, garlic and cracked black pepper. Blend to mix. With the motor running, add the peanut oil in a slow, thin stream and blend until emulsified. Add the bread crumbs and blend until the mixture becomes very thick.
★ Season the pork loin with salt to taste. Pack the rosemary-serrano paste evenly over the entire surface of the loin. Place in a roasting pan and roast until the meat is cooked through and no longer pink, 45–60 minutes, or until an instant-read thermometer registers 155°F (68°C).
★ Transfer to a serving platter and let rest for about 10 minutes before serving. Then cut into slices and serve.

SERVES 8–10

BLUE CORNMEAL SHRIMP WITH MARINATED TOMATOES

Here, jumbo shrimp are breaded with seasoned blue cornmeal, gently fried, tossed with marinated tomatoes and then topped with a Mexican white cheese. If you cannot find Chihuahua cheese, Monterey Jack can be substituted, or look for queso quesadilla, a white cheese similar to mozzarella that melts very well.

FOR THE MARINATED TOMATOES:

⅓ cup (3 fl oz/80 ml) balsamic vinegar
1 green (spring) onion, minced
freshly ground pepper
¼ teaspoon dried oregano
1 teaspoon Dijon-style mustard
½ cup (4 fl oz/125 ml) olive oil
6–8 plum (Roma) tomatoes, quartered lengthwise

1 cup (5 oz/155 g) blue or yellow cornmeal
1 tablespoon blackened seasoning mix (see glossary)
1 cup (5 oz/155 g) all-purpose (plain) flour
1 egg white
3 tablespoons olive oil
1 lb (500 g) shrimp (prawns), peeled and deveined
½ cup (2 oz/60 g) shredded Chihuahua (see glossary)
   or Monterey Jack cheese
minced fresh chives or green (spring) onion tops
   for garnish

★ To make the marinated tomatoes, in a small bowl, stir together the vinegar, green onion, pepper to taste, oregano and mustard. Slowly whisk in the olive oil. Place the tomatoes in a bowl and pour the oil mixture over them. Let stand at room temperature for 30 minutes.
★ Preheat a broiler (griller).
★ In a shallow bowl, stir together the cornmeal and blackened seasoning mix. In another shallow bowl, place the flour, and in a third, lightly beat the egg white.
★ In a large frying pan or sauté pan over medium-high heat, warm the olive oil. Working in batches, dip the shrimp in the flour, then in the egg white and finally in the cornmeal. Add to the hot oil and sauté quickly until golden brown, 2–3 minutes. Using a slotted spoon, transfer to paper towels to drain briefly, then place in a bowl.
★ Using the slotted spoon, remove the tomatoes from their marinade and add to the shrimp. Toss well and divide among 4 individual gratin dishes or place in a single baking dish. Sprinkle with the shredded cheese and place under the broiler until the cheese melts, just a few minutes.
★ Garnish with chives or green onion tops and serve immediately.

SERVES 4   *Photograph pages 148–149*

Left to right: Cornish Hens with Two Glazes, Rosemary–Red Serrano Roasted Pork Loin

Left to right: Tortilla-Crusted Gulf Snapper,
Sesame-Seed Catfish Nuggets

TORTILLA-CRUSTED GULF SNAPPER

Here is a delicious variation on a tortilla crust preparation by chef Terry Conlan for the Lake Austin Spa Resort.

½ cup (2½ oz/75 g) all-purpose (plain) flour
2 egg whites
2 tablespoons buttermilk
4 red snapper fillets, each about ¼ lb (125 g) and ⅓ in (9 mm) thick
4 corn tortillas, cut into long, very narrow strips
nonstick vegetable cooking spray
2 teaspoons olive oil
chipotle mayonnaise (recipe page 117)

★ Place the flour in a shallow bowl. In another bowl, lightly beat the egg whites with the buttermilk until blended. Dip the fish fillets in the flour, coating evenly, and then in the egg whites. Then coat the fish fillets evenly with the tortilla strips, pressing them on firmly with your fingertips. Spray the coated fish with the vegetable spray.
★ In a nonstick frying pan over medium heat, warm the olive oil. Add the fish fillets and sauté, turning as needed so that the tortillas become crisp but do not burn, until the fish flakes easily with a fork, 5–6 minutes total.
★ Transfer to warmed individual plates and serve immediately with chipotle mayonnaise on the side.

SERVES 4

SESAME-SEED CATFISH NUGGETS

Some old-time anglers who fish Texas rivers are convinced that the only way to prepare catfish is to cut it into strips, roll it in seasoned white cornmeal and deep-fry it to a light golden brown. But now that catfish is farmed and thus more readily available, a wealth of sophisticated preparations can be found on Texas tables. Typically East Texan, this recipe is mild and flavorful. Serve the fish over mustard or collard greens that have been quickly sautéed with bacon, onion, vinegar and a dash of sugar or honey.

1 cup (2 oz/60 g) fresh bread crumbs
⅓ cup (1½ oz/45 g) sesame seeds, preferably a mixture of black and white, lightly toasted in a dry pan
3 tablespoons minced fresh parsley
all-purpose (plain) flour for dusting
2 eggs
1½ lb (750 g) catfish fillets with skin intact, cut into 1-in (2.5-cm) nuggets
¼ cup (2 fl oz/60 ml) vegetable oil
1½ teaspoons Asian sesame oil

★ In a shallow bowl, combine the bread crumbs, sesame seeds and parsley. In another bowl, place some flour. In a third bowl, beat the eggs until blended. Coat the catfish nuggets with the flour, shaking off the excess. Dip in the beaten egg and then in the crumb mixture, pressing it on with your fingertips to adhere.
★ In a frying pan or sauté pan over medium-high heat, warm the vegetable oil and sesame oil. Add the nuggets, skin side down, and cook, turning once, until golden, 4–5 minutes on each side.
★ Transfer to a warmed platter and serve at once.

SERVES 4

Mustang Island

SAND DOLLAR FLOUNDER

The Gulf of Mexico is the source of a generous harvest of seafood, from Port Arthur, Galveston and Port Aransas to Padre Island and Brownsville. Principal catches include flounder, drum, redfish, kingfish, sea trout and red snapper. Serve this special-occasion main course with buttered tiny new potatoes and steamed broccoli spears with lemon wedges. Offer a barrel-aged Chardonnay.

½ cup (2½ oz/75 g) all-purpose (plain) flour, seasoned to taste with salt and pepper
4 small or 2 large flounder fillets, 1½–2 lb (750 g–1 kg) total weight
3 tablespoons butter
1 tablespoon olive oil
¼–⅓ cup (2–3 fl oz/60–80 ml) Cognac
2 cloves garlic, minced
2 tablespoons minced fresh parsley
½ cup (4 fl oz/125 ml) heavy (double) cream
½ cup (3 oz/90 g) fresh-cooked crab or lobster meat, picked over for cartilage and shell fragments and flaked or coarsely chopped
2 tablespoons freshly grated Parmesan cheese

★ Preheat a broiler (griller).
★ Spread the seasoned flour on a plate. Coat the fish fillets evenly with the flour mixture, shaking off the excess. In a frying pan or sauté pan over medium-high heat, melt the butter with the olive oil. When the mixture foams, add the fish and cook gently, turning once, until the fish flakes easily with a fork, 2–3 minutes on each side. Transfer to a warmed flameproof platter.
★ Pour the Cognac into the frying pan and place over high heat. Deglaze by stirring up any browned-on bits. Reduce the Cognac slightly, then add the garlic, parsley and cream. Cook, stirring, until slightly thickened, 2–3 minutes. Reduce the heat to medium-low, add the crab or lobster meat and heat gently.
★ Using a slotted spoon, top the fillets with the warmed crab or lobster meat and then spoon the sauce over the top. Dust lightly with the Parmesan cheese and slip under the broiler for 15 seconds to glaze the top. Serve immediately.

SERVES 4

Gulf Coast

JALAPEÑO PESTO–COATED OYSTERS ON ANGEL-HAIR PILLOWS

This recipe, created by chef Camille Mays, is a perfect way to use Gulf Coast oysters and the Hill Country's incomparable pecans. Peeled and deveined jumbo shrimp (prawns) can be used in place of the oysters. Any leftover pesto is superb spread on tomato halves and broiled, or mixed with mayonnaise for a sandwich spread.

2–4 fresh jalapeño chili peppers, seeded, if desired, and cut up
4 cloves garlic, chopped
¾ cup (3 oz/90 g) pecan halves
¼ lb Parmesan cheese, grated
¼ cup (¼ oz/7 g) fresh basil leaves
½ cup (½ oz/15 g) fresh flat-leaf (Italian) parsley
¼ cup (¼ oz/7 g) fresh cilantro (fresh coriander) leaves
⅓–½ cup (3–4 fl oz/80–125 ml) olive oil
rock salt
12 oysters in the shell
½ lb (250 g) fresh angel hair pasta
unsalted butter

★ Preheat an oven to 400°F (200°C). Fill a large pot three-fourths full of water and bring to a boil.
★ Meanwhile, in a food processor fitted with the metal blade or in a blender, combine the jalapeños, garlic, pecans and Parmesan. Process until minced. Add the basil, parsley and cilantro and again process until minced. With the motor running, pour in the olive oil in a slow, thin stream, adding as much as is needed to form a smooth paste. Set aside.
★ Make a bed of rock salt in a baking dish large enough to accommodate the oysters in a single layer. Holding an oyster rounded side down, insert the tip of an oyster knife or other sturdy knife blade between the shells near the hinge and twist to open. Pull off and discard the top shell and slide the knife blade under the flesh to sever the muscle, leaving the oyster in the bottom shell. Nest the oyster in the rock salt and repeat with the remaining oysters. Top each with a dollop of the pesto. Place in the oven until hot and bubbly, 8–10 minutes.
★ When the oysters are almost ready, add the angel hair pasta to the boiling water and cook until al dente, 1–2 minutes. Drain and toss with a little butter.
★ Divide the pasta among 4 individual plates. Carefully remove the oysters from the shells and place 3 oysters on each serving.

SERVES 4

Gulf Coast

ESCABECHE DE PESCADO

In this colorful variation on a Latin American dish, lightly sautéed fish fillets are marinated in orange juice, olive oil, red and green peppers and orange zest. Scallops or shrimp (prawns) may be substituted for the fish, if desired. The French wine makers at Ste. Geneviève in Fort Stockton produce a crisp, fragrant Sauvignon Blanc that goes well with this dish. Accompany with crusty French bread.

3 tablespoons plus ¼ cup (2 fl oz/60 ml) olive oil
2 lb (1 kg) flounder or tilapia fillets
½ cup (4 fl oz/125 ml) fresh orange juice
3–4 tablespoons (1½–2 fl oz/45–60 ml) Mexican marigold mint (see glossary), rosemary or tarragon vinegar
2 bay leaves
1 teaspoon salt, or to taste
zest of 2 oranges, cut into narrow strips
1 green bell pepper (capsicum), seeded and cut into strips
1 red bell pepper (capsicum), seeded and cut into strips
1 fresh jalapeño chili pepper, seeded, if desired, and cut into rings
2 tablespoons finely minced green (spring) onion, including tender green tops
2 cloves garlic, minced
1 small red (Spanish) onion, thinly sliced
¼ cup (⅓ oz/10 g) minced fresh cilantro (fresh coriander)

★ In a large, heavy frying pan over medium heat, warm the 3 tablespoons olive oil. Add the fillets and sauté, turning once, until just cooked through, 3–4 minutes on each side; do not overcook. Transfer the fillets to a shallow glass dish.
★ In a bowl, stir together all the remaining ingredients until well mixed. Pour over the fillets, turning them as needed to coat evenly. Cover tightly and refrigerate for at least 12 hours or as long as 2 days.
★ Transfer the fish fillets to a platter and serve chilled.

SERVES 6–8

Clockwise from top left: Sand Dollar Flounder, Jalapeño Pesto–Coated Oysters on Angel-Hair Pillows, Escabeche de Pescado

Pecan-Crusted Crab Cakes with Mango Slaw and Chipotle-Lime Aioli

Every coastal region of the South boasts its own special version of crab cakes. This recipe comes from chef Jay McCarthy, who developed it for The Cascabel in San Antonio. He serves his crab cakes with chipotle-lime aioli and a cactus butter. Here, San Antonio chef Bruce Auden's mango slaw replaces the butter. Crisp fried tortilla shreds are an attractive garnish for the cakes.

FOR THE MANGO SLAW:

1 cup (3 oz/90 g) finely shredded red cabbage
1 cup (6 oz/185 g) chopped, peeled mango
1 tomato, chopped
1 fresh serrano chili pepper, finely chopped (see glossary)
1 green (spring) onion, including tender green tops, chopped
⅓ cup (½ oz/15 g) chopped fresh cilantro (fresh coriander)
3 tablespoons fresh lime juice
1 teaspoon olive oil
⅛ teaspoon salt
⅛ teaspoon freshly ground pepper

FOR THE CHIPOTLE-LIME AIOLI:

2 chipotle chilies in adobo, drained (see glossary)
zest and juice of 2 limes
¼ cup (1½ oz/45 g) roasted garlic (see glossary)
1 tablespoon mustard
2 egg yolks
¼–½ cup (2–4 fl oz/60–125 ml) olive oil

FOR THE CRAB CAKES:

1 egg
zest and juice of 2 limes
1 green (spring) onion, chopped
1 tablespoon minced fresh serrano chili pepper (see glossary)
1 tablespoon minced fresh cilantro (fresh coriander)
1 teaspoon Worcestershire sauce
1 lb (500 g) fresh-cooked lump crab meat, picked over for cartilage and shell fragments and flaked
¼ cup (1½ oz/45 g) minced red bell pepper (capsicum)
2 cups (8 oz/250 g) fine dried bread crumbs
¾ cup (3 oz/90 g) minced toasted pecans
2 tablespoons butter
fresh cilantro (fresh coriander) leaves for garnish

*Top to bottom: Rio Grande Pizzas with Pepper-and-Corn Salsa,
Pecan-Crusted Crab Cakes with Mango
Slaw and Chipotle-Lime Aioli*

★ To serve, spoon an equal amount of the aioli and slaw on individual plates. Place the crab cakes alongside and garnish with cilantro leaves. Serve at once.

SERVES 6

Texas

RIO GRANDE PIZZAS WITH PEPPER-AND-CORN SALSA

Rio Grande pizzas use the bounty of the summer months—vine-ripened tomatoes, robust chilies, aromatic herbs. They are great with 1 tablespoon cilantro pesto (see glossary) brushed on the tortillas before topping with the remaining ingredients. Serve as an appetizer, sit-down first course, or low-calorie lunch or supper main course. The colorful salsa is a wonderful addition, but the pizzas are also delicious without it. Pita bread rounds may be substituted for the tortillas.

FOR THE PEPPER-AND-CORN SALSA:

2 ears of corn, husks intact
3 red bell peppers (capsicums), roasted and peeled (see glossary)
⅓ cup (2 oz/60 g) drained, cooked black beans (see glossary)
1 fresh jalapeño chili pepper, minced
½ cup (2½ oz/75 g) chopped red (Spanish) onion
½ cup (¾ oz/20 g) chopped fresh cilantro (fresh coriander)
dash of sugar
juice of ½ lime
dash of salt

FOR THE PIZZAS:

2 whole-wheat (wholemeal) flour tortillas
2 teaspoons olive oil
1 small tomato, thinly sliced
1 small green bell pepper (capsicum), seeded and thinly sliced crosswise
1 fresh jalapeño chili pepper, seeded and thinly sliced
½ cup (3 oz/90 g) shredded, cooked chicken
2 tomatillos, brown husks removed and sliced
2 tablespoons sliced black or green olives
½ cup (2 oz/60 g) shredded low-fat mozzarella cheese
2 tablespoons freshly grated Parmesan cheese
shredded fresh basil leaves
fresh rosemary leaves
3 tablespoons pine nuts, lightly toasted

★ To make the mango slaw, in a bowl, combine all the ingredients and stir gently to mix well. Cover and chill for at least 2 hours or for up to 1 day before serving.
★ To make the aioli, in a blender, combine the chipotle chilies, lime zest and juice, roasted garlic, mustard and egg yolks. Purée until smooth. With the motor running, slowly add the olive oil in a thin stream, blending until emulsified. Use only as much of the oil as is needed to form a good thick consistency. Transfer to a bowl, cover and refrigerate until serving.
★ To make the crab cakes, in a bowl, beat the egg until fluffy. Add the lime zest and juice and fold in the green onion, serrano chili, minced cilantro and Worcestershire sauce. Gently fold in the crab meat and bell pepper. Add the bread crumbs and mix gently to distribute evenly. Form into 6 cakes each 2½ in (6 cm) in diameter and ½ in (12 mm) thick.
★ Spread the pecans on a plate and coat the crab cakes evenly with the pecans. Place on a plate, cover and freeze overnight.
★ Preheat an oven to 400°F (200°C).
★ In an ovenproof frying pan over medium to medium-high heat, melt the butter. Add the frozen crab cakes and cook, turning once, until the cakes are lightly browned on both sides, 4–5 minutes on each side. Transfer the pan to the oven and bake until the crab cakes are cooked through, about 10 minutes longer.

★ To make the salsa, prepare a fire in a charcoal grill. Place the unhusked corn in a bowl and add cold water to cover.
★ When the coals are ready, remove the corn from the water and place on the grill rack. Grill, turning often, until the husks are brown and charred and the corn is tender, 15–20 minutes. Remove from the grill rack and, when cool enough to handle, remove the husks and cut the kernels from the ears. Alternatively, do not grill the corn; simply husk it and cut the raw kernels from the ears.
★ In a mixing bowl, combine the corn with all the remaining salsa ingredients, stirring to mix well. Set aside at room temperature.
★ Preheat an oven to 450°F (230°C).
★ To make the pizzas, brush both sides of each tortilla with olive oil. Place on a baking sheet. Arrange the tomato, green bell pepper, jalapeño, chicken, tomatillos and olives on the tortillas. Sprinkle with the mozzarella and Parmesan cheeses.
★ Bake until the cheese melts and is bubbly, about 6 minutes. Remove from the oven and sprinkle with basil and rosemary leaves and toasted pine nuts. Cut into quarters and serve immediately, with the salsa on the side.

SERVES 2

SALPICON

This shredded beef salad with chipotle dressing epitomizes the cuisine and culture of El Paso, according to author and chef Park Kerr, who includes this recipe in his book, The El Paso Chile Company's Texas Border Cookbook. *This genuine local specialty is smoky and tart, cool and spicy, meaty and light. It can be served rolled up in warm corn or flour tortillas and garnished with wedges of avocado. For a more festive presentation, serve roasted long green chilies stuffed with guacamole (see glossary). A smooth, fruity Beaujolais-style wine will set off the mild meat and the bright, fresh chili and herb flavors.*

1 top-cut brisket of beef, 5 lb (2.5 kg)
2 large white onions, sliced
4 cups (32 fl oz/1 l) beef stock
1 can (7 oz/220 g) chipotle chilies in adobo, puréed
   (see glossary)
⅔ cup (5 fl oz/150 ml) olive oil
½ cup (4 fl oz/125 ml) fresh lime juice
⅓ cup (3 fl oz/80 ml) white wine vinegar
1½ teaspoons salt
2 cloves garlic, minced
½ lb (250 g) Monterey Jack cheese, cut into ¼-in
   (6-mm) dice
1 cup (5 oz/155 g) diced red (Spanish) onion
¾ cup (1¼ oz/37 g) minced fresh cilantro
   (fresh coriander)
4 fresh poblano chili peppers, roasted, peeled and cut
   into long strips ¼ in (6 mm) wide (see glossary)
1 head romaine (cos) lettuce, tomato wedges and sliced
   radishes for garnish
corn or flour tortillas, warmed

★ Lay the brisket, fat side up, in a 6-qt (6-l) pot. Scatter the onion slices over the meat. Pour in the beef stock and then add water to cover by 3 in (7.5 cm). Place over medium heat and bring to a boil.

★ Reduce the heat to low, cover and simmer, adding additional boiling water as needed to maintain original level and turning the brisket at about the halfway point, until the brisket is tender enough to shred easily at its thickest point, about 4 hours.

★ Remove from the heat, uncover and let stand in the liquid until cool enough to handle.

★ Remove the brisket from the pot. Strain the liquid, measure out 1½ cups (12 fl oz/375 ml) and reserve the remainder for another use.

★ Trim off the fat from the brisket. Then, holding a fork in each hand, thoroughly shred the meat with the tines, using a downward pulling motion. The resulting shreds should be almost fluffy.

★ In a bowl, combine the shredded beef and the 1½ cups (12 fl oz/375 ml) cooking liquid. Cover and let stand at room temperature while you ready the remaining ingredients. (The meat can be prepared up to this point 2 hours in advance; do not refrigerate.)

★ In a large bowl, whisk together the puréed chipotles, olive oil, lime juice, vinegar, salt and garlic. Drain the shredded meat, pressing hard with a spoon to extract any liquid that has not been absorbed. Add the beef to the chipotle mixture, along with the diced cheese, and toss well. Add the red onion, cilantro and roasted chili strips and toss again. Taste and adjust the seasoning. It should be tart, smoky and fairly piquant.

★ Line a large platter with the romaine leaves. Mound the meat mixture on the lettuce. Garnish with the tomato wedges and scatter the radish slices over all.

★ Serve the salad accompanied with warmed tortillas.

SERVES 12 AS A MAIN COURSE, 20 OR MORE AS AN APPETIZER

TOUCHDOWN BEEF WITH PICKLED RED ONIONS

Cooking beef al carbon (over charcoal) is a Texas tradition. The meat is typically marinated and grilled, and then coarsely diced and folded into warm corn or flour tortillas. Guacamole (see glossary), salsa and grilled green onions are offered alongside. In this version, the flank steak is thinly sliced against the grain and served with pickled red onions and French bread. Texas is equally well known for football and this is perfect tailgate fare. The hearty, rich flavors of a red Zinfandel can stand up to the rough-and-tumble flavors of this dish.

FOR THE STEAK:

1 lb (500 g) flank steak
1 teaspoon sugar
1 teaspoon salt
¼ cup (1 oz/30 g) minced green (spring) onion, including
   tender green tops
½ teaspoon dry mustard

Left to right: Salpicon, Touchdown Beef with Pickled Red Onions

½ teaspoon fresh rosemary
½ teaspoon ground ginger
1 teaspoon whole peppercorns
¾ cup (6 fl oz/180 ml) fresh lime juice
½ cup (4 fl oz/125 ml) olive oil
2 cloves garlic, minced

FOR THE PICKLED RED ONIONS:

½ cup (4 fl oz/125 ml) red wine vinegar
2 green (spring) onions, including tender green
    tops, sliced
3 cloves garlic, minced
1 tablespoon sugar
1 teaspoon paprika
1 teaspoon dry mustard
½ teaspoon dried thyme
½ teaspoon oregano
salt and freshly ground pepper
1 cup (8 fl oz/250 ml) vegetable oil
1 lb (500 g) red (Spanish) onions, thinly sliced

sliced French bread

★ To prepare the steak for grilling, place it in a shallow glass or ceramic dish. In a small bowl, stir together all the remaining ingredients until well mixed. Pour over the steak, cover and refrigerate for 3–4 hours or as long as overnight; turn the meat occasionally.

★ To make the pickled red onions, in a bowl, whisk together the vinegar, green onions, garlic, sugar, paprika, mustard, thyme, oregano and salt and pepper to taste. Using a wire whisk, beat in the vegetable oil in a slow, steady stream. Add the red onions, tossing to coat. Cover and refrigerate until serving. (The pickled onions will keep in the refrigerator for up to 1 week.)

★ Prepare a fire in a charcoal grill, or preheat a broiler (griller). Remove the meat from the marinade, reserving the marinade, and place on the grill rack or on a rack in a broiler pan. Broil or grill, turning once and basting with the marinade, until done to your taste, 4–5 minutes on each side for medium-rare. Remove to a cutting board and cut into slices very thinly on the diagonal. Arrange on a platter and serve with French bread and the red onions alongside.

SERVES 4

Top to bottom: Crispy Chicken with Peppered Pan Gravy, Country-Fried Catfish

H e a r t   o f   T e x a s

TEXAS RIB-EYE WITH FRESH HERB MARINADE

Absolutely delightful in its simplicity, this recipe is a variation on a dish developed by chef Daniel Hammer. Serve with mashed potatoes flavored with garlic or grilled rosemary potatoes. If desired, top the steaks with pico de gallo *(see glossary) to which pesticide-free edible flowers—nasturtiums, violas—have been added just before serving.*

2 large fresh thyme sprigs
2 large fresh oregano sprigs
2 large fresh basil sprigs
1 large fresh marjoram sprig
4 cloves garlic, minced
½ cup (4 fl oz/125 ml) olive oil
¼ cup (2 fl oz/60 ml) balsamic vinegar
salt and freshly ground pepper
4 rib-eye steaks, each 6–8 oz (185–250 g) and ½ in (12 mm) thick, trimmed of excess fat

★ In a small food processor fitted with the metal blade or in a blender, place all the herbs and the garlic. Process until finely chopped. Add the olive oil and vinegar and process to mince finely. Season to taste with salt and pepper.
★ Place the steaks in a single layer in a shallow glass or ceramic baking dish. Pour the herb mixture evenly over the steaks, turning the steaks as needed to coat evenly. Cover and refrigerate for 2–3 hours.
★ Prepare a fire in a charcoal grill.
★ When the coals are ready, remove the steaks from the marinade and place on the grill rack. Grill, turning once, until done to your taste, 3–4 minutes on each side for medium-rare.
★ Transfer to a warmed platter or individual plates and serve at once.

SERVES 4 — *Photograph page 12*

E l   P a s o

CRISPY CHICKEN WITH PEPPERED PAN GRAVY

The chili powder and black pepper added to the flour in this variation on a recipe from Park Kerr's The El Paso Chile Company's Texas Border Cookbook *fire up the chicken just enough. The gravy, which is delicious spooned over mashed potatoes and biscuits as well as the chicken, turns out slightly spicy, and the crust on the chicken is crunchy and delicious. Served cold, the chicken makes great picnic fare.*

1 cup (8 fl oz/250 ml) buttermilk
1½ teaspoons Tabasco or other hot-pepper sauce
1 frying chicken, about 3½ lb (1.75 kg), cut into serving pieces
1½ cups (7½ oz/235 g) all-purpose (plain) flour
1 teaspoon chili powder, or to taste
¼ teaspoon ground cumin
2 teaspoons salt, plus salt to taste
about 2 cups (1 lb/500 g) vegetable shortening
2–2½ cups (16–20 fl oz/500–625 ml) milk
½ teaspoon freshly ground pepper

★ In a bowl, whisk together the buttermilk and hot-pepper sauce. Place the chicken pieces in a deep bowl and pour the buttermilk mixture over them. Cover and refrigerate for 2 hours, stirring once or twice.
★ In a pie plate, stir together 1¼ cups (6½ oz/200 g) of the flour, the chili powder, the cumin and the 2 teaspoons salt. Using a slotted spoon, lift the chicken pieces from the buttermilk, letting the excess drip back into the bowl. Coat the chicken pieces with the seasoned flour, shaking off any excess. Place the floured chicken on a rack and let stand for 30 minutes to firm up the coating.
★ In a large, deep frying pan, preferably cast iron, over high heat, melt enough shortening so that it will reach about halfway up the sides of the chicken pieces. When it registers 360°F (182°C) on a deep-fat thermometer (or when a tiny bit of bread begins to turn brown within moments of being dropped into the pan), add the chicken pieces, skin side down. Cook, uncovered, for 12 minutes. Turn and continue to cook until crispy and a deep reddish brown on both sides, 12–15 minutes longer. Using a slotted spatula or spoon, transfer to paper towels to drain briefly. Transfer to a platter and cover loosely to keep warm.
★ Pour off most of the drippings, reserving ¼ cup (2 fl oz/60 ml) in the pan. Place over low heat and whisk in the remaining ¼ cup (1 oz/35 g) flour. Cook, stirring often, for 5 minutes. Slowly whisk in enough of the milk to form a smooth gravy. Bring to a simmer over medium heat and cook, stirring often, until thickened, 5–7 minutes. Season to taste with salt and add the pepper.
★ Taste and adjust the seasoning. Serve the chicken with the gravy alongside.

SERVES 4–6

E a s t   T e x a s

COUNTRY-FRIED CATFISH

Serve these crispy catfish piping hot from the pan on warmed plates. Small individual containers or seashells of seafood jalapeño tartar sauce (recipe pages 172–173) and a flavorful coleslaw are musts. Complete the menu with fried okra salad (page 52). As a delicious alternative, serve the fried catfish fillets on soft sandwich rolls spread with the tartar sauce.

6 pan-dressed whole catfish or catfish fillets, about 8 oz (250 g) each
1 egg
1 cup (8 fl oz/250 ml) buttermilk
½ cup (2½ oz/75 g) self-rising flour
¼ teaspoon salt
freshly ground black pepper
dash of cayenne pepper or blackened seasoning mix (see glossary)
1½ cups (7½ oz/235 g) yellow cornmeal
vegetable shortening or oil for deep-frying
small bunch fresh parsley sprigs, well dried, and lemon wedges for garnish

★ Pat the fish dry with paper towels. In one shallow bowl, lightly beat the egg and then whisk in the buttermilk. In a second shallow bowl, combine the flour, salt, black pepper to taste and cayenne pepper or blackened seasoning mix. In a third bowl, place the cornmeal. Dip the fish first into the buttermilk-egg mixture, then into the flour mixture and finally into the cornmeal, coating evenly at each step.
★ Preheat an oven to 200°F (93°C).
★ In a heavy frying pan, preferably cast iron, over high heat, melt enough shortening or warm enough oil to reach a depth of 2 in (5 cm). When it registers about 365°F (185°C) on a deep-fat thermometer (or a tiny bit of bread begins to turn brown within moments of being dropped into the pan), add 2 or 3 of the whole fish or fish fillets. Fry until they flake when tested with a fork or toothpick, 5–7 minutes. Using a slotted spatula or tongs, transfer to paper towels to drain, then keep them warm in the oven while frying the remaining fish.
★ For the garnish, drop the parsley sprigs into the hot oil and fry until crisp, about 1 minute. Using a slotted spoon, transfer to paper towels to drain.
★ Place the catfish on a warmed platter or individual plates and garnish with the parsley and lemon wedges. Serve at once.

SERVES 6

East Texas

CRAYFISH ÉTOUFFÉE

At the turn of the century, Jefferson County, located in East Texas, possessed the state's only rice crop and mill and irrigation canals. Today, Texas ranks third among rice-growing states and is the nation's number one rice-milling center. This popular East Texas recipe is traditionally served over plain fluffy white rice and is perfect accompanied with French bread and a mixed green salad. Shrimp (prawns) can be used in place of the crayfish, if the latter are unavailable. A melon-flavored Chenin Blanc from College Station's Messina Hof Winery will provide a cool, refreshing foil for the Cajun spice of the étouffée.

¼ cup (2 fl oz/60 ml) vegetable oil
¼ cup (1¼ oz/37 g) all-purpose (plain) flour
1 cup (5 oz/155 g) chopped white onion
1 green bell pepper (capsicum), seeded and chopped
2 celery stalks, chopped
4 cloves garlic, minced
2 teaspoons Cajun-style hot sauce or cayenne pepper, or
   to taste
½ teaspoon dried thyme
freshly ground black pepper
2 cups (16 fl oz/500 ml) chicken stock
2 lb (1 kg) crayfish tail meat (see glossary)
2–3 cups (10–15 oz/310–465 g) freshly steamed long-grain
   white rice
minced green (spring) onions, including tender green tops,
   for garnish

★ In a frying pan over medium heat, warm the vegetable oil. Add the flour and stir constantly until the mixture turns a copper brown, 20–25 minutes; do not allow to burn. (This mixture is called a roux.)
★ Add the white onion, bell pepper, celery and garlic and cook gently, stirring occasionally, until slightly softened, about 15 minutes. Stir in the hot sauce or cayenne, thyme and black pepper to taste and pour in the chicken stock. Bring to a boil, reduce the heat to medium and add the crayfish. Cook until the crayfish is slightly firm, 5–6 minutes.
★ To serve, place a mound of rice on each individual plate and spoon some of the crayfish mixture alongside. Sprinkle with green onions and serve at once.

SERVES 4–6

Beaumont

CRAYFISH POLENTA LASAGNA

The Doguet Crayfish Farm in China, close to Beaumont, proves that more than beef is raised in Texas. Here each January crayfish season begins and continues through the first of July. The operation farms 500 acres (200 hectares) of crayfish with an average yield of 650 pounds (295 kilograms) of crayfish per acre. Some 95 percent is sold live throughout the United States and 5 percent is sold as "tail" meat, processed ready for cooking. In addition to farming crayfish, the Doguet family raises beef and grows and mills 30 million pounds (13.5 million kilograms) of rice in this small community in Jefferson County.

This deliciously different and hearty dish, created by San Antonio executive chef Kim Swendson-Cameron, utilizes the classic East Texas ingredients of cornmeal and crayfish. Try any light-bodied crisp white wine to contrast with its heartiness.

FOR THE POLENTA:

2 cups (16 fl oz/500 ml) milk
2 cups (16 fl oz/500 ml) chicken stock

1½ teaspoons salt
½ teaspoon dried thyme
½ teaspoon freshly cracked pepper
1½ cups (7½ oz/235 g) yellow cornmeal
2 tablespoons butter

FOR THE FILLING:

2 tablespoons olive oil
1½ cups (7½ oz/235 g) diced yellow onion
1 cup (5 oz/155 g) diced green bell pepper (capsicum)
4 cloves garlic, minced
2 cups (12 oz/375 g) corn kernels
3 cups (18 oz/560 g) seeded, diced tomatoes
½ cup (1½ oz/45 g) minced green (spring) onion, including
   tender green tops
1 lb (500 g) crayfish tail meat, cooked (see glossary)
1 teaspoon drained capers (optional)
3 tablespoons fresh lemon juice
1½ teaspoons salt
½ teaspoon freshly ground pepper
1 teaspoon Tabasco or other hot-pepper sauce

Left to right: Crayfish Étouffée, Crayfish Polenta Lasagna

1 teaspoon Creole seasoning blend
1 teaspoon herbes de Provence
¼ cup (2 fl oz/60 ml) tomato juice
1½ cups (6 oz/185 g) shredded mozzarella cheese
1½ cups (6 oz/185 g) shredded Monterey Jack cheese

★ To make the polenta, in a heavy-bottomed saucepan, combine the milk, stock, salt, thyme and pepper. Bring to a boil over high heat. Slowly whisk in the cornmeal, stirring constantly and beating as necessary to remove any lumps. Reduce the heat to medium-low and continue to stir until the polenta begins to pull away from the pan sides and a steam pocket forms underneath the polenta, about 15 minutes. Add the butter and stir to melt.

★ Remove from the heat and pour onto a greased jelly-roll (Swiss-roll) pan or baking sheet with sides and smooth the surface. Let cool, cover and refrigerate to chill thoroughly.

★ To make the filling, in a frying pan over high heat, warm the olive oil. Add the onion and sauté until translucent, 5–7 minutes. Add the bell pepper, garlic and corn and cook, stirring occasionally, 4–5 minutes. Add the tomatoes, green onions and crayfish tails and sauté for 3 minutes. Add the capers (if using), lemon juice, salt, ground pepper, hot-pepper sauce, Creole seasoning, herbes de Provence and tomato juice. Simmer over medium heat for 15 minutes. Taste and adjust the seasoning. Remove from the heat and let cool.

★ Preheat an oven to 350°F (180°C).

★ To assemble, oil a 9-in (23-cm) square baking dish or similar-sized oblong dish. Invert the pan of polenta onto a work surface and cut into 2 pieces as close to the dimensions of the prepared baking dish as possible. Reserve any trimmed edges. Place 1 polenta layer in the dish, patching if necessary with trimmings to line the dish fully. Spread half of the crayfish mixture on top and top with half each of the mozzarella and Monterey Jack cheeses. Place the second polenta sheet on top, again patching if necessary, and spread with the remaining crayfish mixture. Sprinkle with the remaining cheeses.

★ Bake until hot and bubbly, 35–40 minutes. Remove from the oven and let sit for a few minutes, then cut into squares and serve directly from the dish.

SERVES 6–8

SHRIMP VERACRUZ

Brownsville, which has a reputation as an international seaport with a sizable shrimp fleet, is known as the Shrimp Capital of the World. Dishes such as this are frequently found on Texas menus and are reminders of how many recipes have come here from coastal Mexico. The rich tomato sauce is traditionally served over whole red snappers or snapper fillets. Accompany the shrimp with crusty French bread for mopping up the excess sauce and with

steamed white rice tossed with minced green (spring) onion, green bell pepper (capsicum) and pimiento. Pour a Sauvignon Blanc or Chardonnay.

3 tablespoons olive oil
1 small yellow or white onion, chopped
3 cloves garlic, minced
1 or 2 fresh serrano chili peppers, minced (see glossary)
1 green bell pepper (capsicum), seeded and diced

½ teaspoon dried oregano, crumbled
¼ cup (2 fl oz/60 ml) white wine
salt and freshly ground pepper
1 tablespoon butter
24 jumbo fresh shrimp (prawns), peeled and deveined

★ In a frying pan or sauté pan over medium-high heat, warm the olive oil. Add the onion, garlic, serranos and bell pepper and sauté until softened, 3–4 minutes. Add the tomatoes, minced cilantro, capers, green olives, jalapeños, oregano and white wine, and season to taste with salt and pepper. Simmer over medium-low heat, stirring occasionally, until thickened, 10–15 minutes. Keep warm.
★ In another frying pan or sauté pan over high heat, melt the butter. Add the shrimp and sauté until the shrimp curl and turn pink, 6–7 minutes.
★ Divide the shrimp among warmed individual plates. Spoon the sauce over the top and serve at once.

SERVES 4

Gulf Coast

SHRIMP BOATS WITH TOMATILLO SALSA

The sun and surf of the Texas Gulf Coast draw people from other parts of the state and beyond. Once there they find interesting foods that reflect the innovative spirit that pervades the area. This recipe is an excellent example of the fare offered along the coast.

1½ cups (7½ oz/220 g) yellow cornmeal
½ cup (2½ oz/75 g) all-purpose (plain) flour
1 teaspoon salt
1 teaspoon sugar
3 teaspoons baking powder
¾ cup (6 fl oz/180 ml) beer
2 eggs, beaten
1 ear of corn, husks intact
¼ cup (¾ oz/20 g) minced green (spring) onions, including
    tender green tops
2 or 3 fresh jalapeño chili peppers, minced
1 lb (500 g) shrimp (prawns), cooked in boiling water,
    drained, peeled and deveined
½ cup (3½ oz/105 g) drained, cooked black beans
    (see glossary)
vegetable oil for deep-frying
double recipe tomatillo salsa (see page 166)
¼ cup (1½ oz/45 g) minced red bell pepper (capsicum)

★ In a bowl, combine the cornmeal, flour, salt, sugar and baking powder, mixing well. Stir in the beer and eggs to form a batter.
★ Remove the husks from the corn and reserve. Using a sharp knife, cut the kernels off the cob. Add them to the batter, along with the green onions, jalapeños, shrimp and black beans.
★ In a deep frying pan or a saucepan, pour in vegetable oil to a depth of 2 in (5 cm) and heat to 375°F (190°C), or until a tiny bit of bread begins to brown within a few moments of being dropped in the oil. Using a teaspoon, drop the batter by rounded oval spoonfuls into the hot oil, being careful not to crowd the pan. Fry until golden brown and cooked through, about 1 minute. Using a slotted spoon, transfer to paper towels to drain briefly.
★ Line a serving platter or individual plates with the reserved corn husks and spoon the tomatillo salsa on top of the husks. Arrange the shrimp fritters on top of the salsa and serve hot.

SERVES 12–15 AS APPETIZERS

Left to right: Shrimp Veracruz, Shrimp Boats with Tomatillo Salsa

4 large ripe tomatoes, peeled and chopped
¼ cup (⅓ oz/10 g) minced fresh cilantro
    (fresh coriander)
2 tablespoons drained capers
2 tablespoons pimiento-stuffed green olives, rinsed
    and sliced
2 pickled jalapeño chili peppers, minced
    (see glossary)

CHICKEN-FRIED STEAK WITH PICO DE GALLO

Texas chef Stephen Pyles reports in his cookbook, The New Texas Cuisine, *that the Texas Restaurant Association estimates a mind-boggling 800,000 chicken-fried steaks are consumed daily in the state. As with Texas chili, there is much debate as to the best way to prepare it. Flour, soda cracker crumbs and crushed pretzels are but a few of the breadings. This is by no means an authentic recipe, but it is delicious nonetheless.*

½ cup (2½ oz/75 g) *masa harina* (see glossary)
¼ cup (1¼ oz/37 g) all-purpose (plain) flour
½ teaspoon ground cumin
½ teaspoon dried oregano
½ teaspoon garlic powder
¼ teaspoon salt
2 eggs
2 tablespoons butter
2 tablespoons vegetable oil
2 beef cube steaks or tenderized (pounded) boneless round
   steaks, about ½ lb (250 g) each
pico de gallo (see glossary)

★ In a shallow plate, combine the *masa harina,* flour, cumin, oregano, garlic powder and salt. Lightly beat the eggs in another shallow plate until blended.
★ In a sauté pan or frying pan over high heat, melt the butter with the oil. Dip each cube steak into the flour mixture, coating evenly. Then dip into the beaten egg and then back into flour mixture. Add to the pan and cook, turning once, until browned on both sides and tender and pink in the center, about 3 minutes on each side.
★ Place the steaks on warmed individual plates and top with a generous helping of *pico de gallo.* Serve at once.

SERVES 2

BARBECUED PORK

Here is a variation on a typical East Texas barbecue recipe that appears in Texas Barbecue, *by Paris Permenter and John Bigley. A light, fruity but dry red would be the wine to serve.*

2 teaspoons butter
¼ cup (1½ oz/45 g) coarsely chopped white onion
1 clove garlic, minced
¾ cup (6 fl oz/180 ml) bottled chili sauce
1 tablespoon firmly packed brown sugar
1 tablespoon white wine vinegar
1 tablespoon light or dark molasses
1 tablespoon water
1 teaspoon fresh lemon juice
1 teaspoon mustard
¼ teaspoon liquid smoke (optional)
⅛ teaspoon cayenne pepper
⅛ teaspoon salt
¾ lb (750 g) cooked boneless pork loin, thinly sliced
4 onion rolls, split and toasted

★ In a saucepan, over medium-high heat, melt the butter. Add the onion and garlic and sauté until translucent, 4–5 minutes. Stir in the chili sauce, sugar, vinegar, molasses, water, lemon juice, mustard, liquid smoke (if using), cayenne pepper and salt. Bring to a boil over high heat, reduce the heat to low and simmer, uncovered, for about 15 minutes. Add the pork slices, stirring gently to coat the meat with the sauce. Continue to simmer until the pork is heated through, about 5 minutes.

★ Serve the pork slices on toasted onion rolls, with any extra sauce in a bowl on the side.

SERVES 4   *Photograph page 168*

JALAPEÑO CHICKEN-FRIED STEAK WITH TOMATILLO SALSA AND CHEESE

A Texas tradition with a new slant. This mildly flavored steak is tenderized by the pickled jalapeño juice and the beer. The meat can also be served cut into 1-inch (2.5-cm) cubes, fried, threaded onto skewers and then dipped into the tomatillo salsa. The tart herbal qualities of a Texas Sauvignon Blanc would match the tanginess of the tomatillos.

1 venison, beef sirloin or round steak, 2 lb (1 kg) and
   ¼–½ in (6–12 mm) thick
10–12 pickled jalapeño chili peppers, with juice (see glossary)
1 white onion, thinly sliced
6 cloves garlic, minced
1 can (12 fl oz/375 ml) beer
1 tablespoon olive oil
salt

FOR THE TOMATILLO SALSA:

1⅓ cups (8 oz/250 g) chopped tomatillos
1 or 2 cloves garlic, minced
3 tablespoons chopped white onion
1 or 2 fresh serrano chili peppers, cut up (see glossary)
salt

2 eggs
all-purpose (plain) flour for dusting
dash of ground cumin
dash of cayenne pepper
vegetable oil, for frying
1 cup (5 oz/155 g) crumbled *queso fresco* (see glossary)
deep-fried tortilla strips (optional) and minced green bell
   pepper (capsicum) for garnish

★ Place the steak in a shallow glass or ceramic dish. Top the steak with the jalapeños, onion, garlic, beer, olive oil and salt to taste. Cover and refrigerate for 4–5 hours.
★ To make the tomatillo salsa, in a food processor fitted with a metal blade or in a blender, combine all the ingredients, including salt to taste. Process until smooth. Transfer to a saucepan and place over medium heat. Bring to a simmer and cook, stirring occasionally, until the mixture no longer has a raw taste, 5–8 minutes. Remove from the heat and let cool to room temperature. Set aside.
★ Preheat a broiler (griller).
★ In a large shallow bowl, place the eggs and beat until blended. In another large shallow bowl, combine the flour, cumin and cayenne and stir to mix. Remove the steak from the marinade and pat dry. Dip first in the egg and then coat evenly with the flour, dusting lightly.
★ In a flameproof frying pan over medium-high heat, pour in oil to a depth of ¾–1 in (2–2.5 cm). When hot, add the steak and fry, turning once, until nicely browned on both sides and cooked to desired doneness, 6–7 minutes total for medium-rare.
★ Top the steak with the tomatillo salsa and sprinkle with the crumbled *queso fresco.* Slip the pan under the broiler until the cheese melts and is bubbly, 2–3 minutes. Transfer to a warmed platter and sprinkle with the tortilla strips, if using, and bell pepper. Slice and serve immediately.

SERVES 4–6

Top to bottom: Jalapeño Chicken-Fried Steak with Tomatillo Salsa and Cheese, Chicken-Fried Steak with Pico de Gallo

Texas

TEXAS POT ROAST

I developed this recipe for the 150th birthday of Texas, and the out-of-this-world sauce is equally good with pork or chicken. The long, slow cooking yields a tender piece of beef, rich with sizzling Southwest flair. Serve with shredded lettuce topped with tomato slices and guacamole (see glossary).

7 tablespoons (3½ fl oz/105 ml) vegetable oil, plus vegetable oil for deep-frying
1 small white onion, quartered, plus 2 medium-sized white onions, sliced
3 cloves garlic
8 corn tortillas
3 cups (18 oz/560 g) canned tomatoes, drained
2 fresh jalapeño chili peppers, seeded and cut up
salt and freshly ground pepper
3 lb (1.5 kg) boneless chuck roast
shredded Cheddar cheese, minced green (spring) onions and fresh cilantro (fresh coriander) sprigs for garnish

★ Preheat an oven to 350°F (180°C).
★ In a small frying pan over medium heat, warm 3 table-spoons of the oil. Add the quartered onion and the garlic and sauté until translucent, about 5 minutes. Transfer to a food processor fitted with a metal blade or to a blender. Tear 2 of the corn tortillas into pieces and add to the processor or blender, along with the tomatoes and jalapeños. Process until smooth. Season to taste with salt and pepper and set aside.
★ In a large frying pan over medium-high heat, warm the remaining 4 tablespoons (2 fl oz/60 ml) oil. Add the chuck roast and brown on all sides, 6–8 minutes. Transfer the meat to a 3–4 qt (3–4 l) baking dish. Heat the oil remaining in the frying pan over medium heat. Add the sliced onion and sauté until translucent, about 5 minutes. Place the onions on top of the meat, then pour the reserved sauce over all. Cover and bake until the meat is quite tender when cut into with a knife, 2–3 hours.
★ Cut the remaining 6 tortillas into strips ½ in (12 mm) wide. In a frying pan over medium-high heat, pour in vegetable oil to a depth of 1 in (12.5 cm). When the oil is hot, working in batches, add the tortilla strips and fry, turning as needed, until crisp, 3–4 minutes. Using a slotted spoon, transfer to paper towels to drain.
★ Transfer the pot roast to a cutting board and cut into thin strips. Arrange the meat strips on warmed individual plates. Top each serving with some of the crispy tortilla strips and garnish with Cheddar cheese, green onion and cilantro sprigs. Serve immediately.

SERVES 4–6

Top to bottom: Barbecued Pork (recipe page 166), Texas Pot Roast

South Texas

ROSEMARY AND GARLIC ROAST TURKEY WITH SOUTHWEST STUFFING

This turkey is made incredibly moist by frequent bastings with rosemary-garlic butter. The corn bread stuffing includes chayote, also known as mirliton or chocho, a squash native to Central America with creamy flesh and pale green skin. Serve the turkey and stuffing with garlic-laced mashed potatoes or baked sweet potatoes and green beans with toasted pine nuts. Pour a pleasantly smoky Pinot Noir.

FOR THE SOUTHWEST STUFFING:

¼ cup (2 oz/60 g) margarine or butter
1 cup (5 oz/155 g) chopped, peeled chayote or yellow squash
4 fresh jalapeño chili peppers, seeded and chopped
2 cloves garlic, minced
1 large white onion, minced
2 tablespoons chopped fresh cilantro (fresh coriander)
salt
½ teaspoon dried thyme
½ teaspoon dried rosemary leaves
½ teaspoon dried sage
1 tablespoon ground coriander
9 cups (18 oz/560 g) corn bread cubes
1–1½ cups (8–12 fl oz/250–375 ml) chicken stock
1 cup (4 oz/125 g) chopped pecans
2–4 pork tamales, corn husks removed and sliced into 1-in (2.5-cm) pieces, or 1 lb (500 g) chorizo sausage, crumbled, fried and drained

1 turkey, 12 lb (6 kg)
1 lb (500 g) butter
6 cloves garlic, minced
¼ cup (⅓ oz/10 g) fresh rosemary leaves, crushed
salt and freshly ground pepper

Rosemary and Garlic Roast Turkey with Southwest Stuffing

FOR THE CRANBERRY SALSA:

2 cups (8 oz/250 g) cranberries, coarsely chopped
1 navel orange, unpeeled, coarsely chopped
1–2 fresh jalapeño chili peppers, minced, or 2 small dried
  hot red chili peppers
1 tablespoon grated, peeled fresh ginger
2 tablespoons minced fresh cilantro (fresh coriander)
2 tablespoons Triple Sec or brandy
2 teaspoons fresh lime juice
¼ cup (2½ oz/75 g) honey

large fresh rosemary sprigs, crab apples or Lady apples and
  grapes for garnish

★ To make the stuffing, in a frying pan or sauté pan over medium-high heat, melt the margarine or butter. Add the chayote or yellow squash, chilies, garlic and onion and sauté until the vegetables are tender, 6–8 minutes. Stir in the cilantro, salt to taste, thyme, rosemary, sage and coriander until well blended. Then stir in about half of the corn bread cubes until well coated with the pan mixture.

★ Transfer the pan contents to a large bowl. Add 1 cup (8 fl oz/250 ml) of the stock, the remaining bread cubes, the pecans and the tamales or chorizo. Toss well to moisten the bread. Add more stock as needed to moisten.

★ Preheat an oven to 325°F (165°C).

★ Spoon the stuffing into the cavity of the bird; do not pack too tightly. Truss the bird closed. Spoon the remaining stuffing into a baking dish, cover and set aside.

★ Place the turkey, breast side up, on a rack in a shallow roasting pan. In a small saucepan, combine the butter, garlic, rosemary and salt and pepper to taste. Baste the bird with some of the butter mixture and place in the oven. Roast, basting frequently with the butter mixture until the turkey is done, 3–3½ hours or until a thermometer registers 180°F (82°C) when inserted into the thickest part away from the bone. During the final 45–60 minutes of roasting, place the baking dish holding the stuffing into the oven to cook alongside the bird.

★ Meanwhile, make the cranberry salsa. In a bowl, stir together all the ingredients and let stand at room temperature for at least 1 hour.

★ Transfer the turkey to a large serving platter and let stand for 15–20 minutes. Remove the stuffing from the cavity and place in a bowl. Surround the turkey with rosemary sprigs and tuck fresh polished crab apples or Lady apples and small grape clusters around it. Carve at the table and accompany with the stuffing (including the stuffing cooked in the baking dish) and cranberry salsa.

SERVES 10–12

Hill Country

PAPRIKA SCHNITZEL BLACK FOREST

The crispness of the fall air around Fredericksburg, in the Hill Country, is the perfect setting for this German specialty. This schnitzel is full of flavor; balance it with a dry Riesling.

3 tablespoons butter
1 tablespoon vegetable oil
2 lb (1 kg) boneless pork loin cutlets, each about ⅛ in (3 mm) thick
salt and freshly ground black pepper
1 tablespoon Hungarian sweet paprika, plus paprika to taste (optional)
2 teaspoons all-purpose (plain) flour
½ cup (4 fl oz/125 ml) heavy (double) cream, sour cream or plain yogurt
pinch of cayenne pepper
lemon wedges, dipped into finely minced fresh parsley, for garnish (optional)

★ In a frying pan or sauté pan over medium-high heat, melt the butter with the vegetable oil. Sprinkle the pork with salt and black pepper to taste and add to the pan. Sauté, turning once, until lightly browned on both sides and almost cooked through, 2–3 minutes on each side. Sprinkle both sides of the meat with the 1 tablespoon paprika and sauté for 30 seconds longer on each side. Transfer to a warmed platter.
★ Stir the flour into the drippings remaining in the pan and cook over medium heat, stirring, for 1–2 minutes. Then stir in the cream, sour cream or yogurt and add the cayenne pepper and additional paprika, if using.
★ When the sauce is smooth, pour it over the cutlets and garnish with parsley-coated lemon wedges, if using. Serve at once.

SERVES 4

Castroville

CHOUCROUTE GARNI

Castroville was founded in 1844, when Henri Castro led his Alsatian immigrants to this tranquil, tree-shaded area along the Medina River. Today, the town is a mixture of many cultures, including French, German, English, Alsatian and Spanish.

In Castroville, the sausages are often cooked separately from the famed Alsatian choucroute garni and combined with additional potatoes on a large serving platter. This is a flexible dish and the ingredients can be varied endlessly, but the slow cooking of the sauerkraut with the apples and wine is essential. Match the choucroute with a Johannisberg Riesling, just as the Alsatians do.

1 lb (500 g) pork ribs or chops
1 jar (15 oz/470 g) sauerkraut, drained
2 tart green cooking apples, halved, cored and sliced
1 white onion, sliced
2 potatoes, unpeeled, cut into 2-in (5-cm) chunks
1 bay leaf
2 cloves garlic (optional)
4 whole cloves
2 teaspoons juniper berries or 1 tablespoon gin
Johannisberg Riesling wine, to cover
1 lb (500 g) fully cooked knockwurst or bratwurst

★ Preheat an oven to 350°F (180°C).
★ In a sauté pan over high heat, add the pork ribs or chops and

brown well on both sides, turning once; this should take 5–6 minutes total. Remove from the heat.
★ In a large pot, layer half of the sauerkraut, apple slices and onion slices. Top with the potatoes, bay leaf, garlic cloves (if using), whole cloves and juniper berries or gin. Arrange the remaining sauerkraut, apples and onions on top and then the

170

Left to right: Paprika Schnitzel Black Forest, Choucroute Garni

browned pork. Pour in wine just to cover completely.

★ Bake until the potatoes and pork are tender and most of the liquid has been absorbed, about 2 hours.

★ Meanwhile, place the sausages in a saucepan and add water to cover. Bring to a boil, reduce the heat to medium-low and simmer until the sausages are heated through, about 15 minutes. Drain. Alternatively, add the sausages to the pot holding the sauerkraut and other ingredients during the last 20 minutes of cooking and heat through.

★ To serve, transfer the sauerkraut mixture to a large platter and pile the pork and sausages in the center. Serve at once.

SERVES 4–6

SEARED LAMB LOIN WITH CORIANDER SEED PASTE

Coriander seeds are an enormously fragrant addition to lamb. Grilled figs and grilled artichoke hearts would make delicious accompaniments. Roast lamb calls for a classic Cabernet, such as that produced by Pheasant Ridge in Lubbock, the oldest Cabernet vineyard in Texas.

3 tablespoons coriander seeds
1½ teaspoons whole peppercorns
5 cloves garlic
4½ teaspoons Asian fish sauce
5 teaspoons soy sauce
2 tablespoons fresh lime juice
1 lamb loin, 1½ lb (750 g)
chives and chive blossoms for garnish (optional)

★ In a blender, combine the coriander seeds, peppercorns, garlic, fish sauce, soy sauce and lime juice and process until the seeds are fully crushed.
★ Place the lamb loin in a shallow glass or ceramic dish and spread the coriander seed mixture over its entire surface. Cover and refrigerate for at least 6 hours or for up to 24 hours.

★ Preheat an oven to 350°F (180°C). Place a dry frying pan over medium-high heat. When it is hot, add the lamb and sear, turning as needed to brown richly on all sides. Transfer to a roasting pan and place in the oven. Roast until done to your taste, 20–25 minutes for medium-rare, or until an instant-read thermometer inserted at the thickest point registers 130°–140°F (54°–60°C).
★ Transfer to a cutting board and let rest for 5 minutes. Using a sharp knife, cut into thick medallions and arrange on a warmed platter. Garnish with chives and chive blossoms, if desired.

SERVES 4

FARMER'S SEAFOOD BOIL

A peel-'em-and-eat-'em seafood boil may be found at such butcher paper–covered table-top operations as Rockport's Boiling Pot and Port Aransas's Crazy Cajun. Rockport red sauce and seafood jalapeño tartar sauce are the traditional accompaniments. When blue crabs, stone crabs or crayfish are in season, they are added to the pot. You can also boil the shrimp in beer to cover for a true taste of the Texas Gulf Coast. If you don't have time to assemble

Left to right: Seared Lamb Loin with Coriander Seed Paste, Lamb Sauté with Brandied Peach Cream

2 tablespoons whole allspice
1 tablespoon ground cloves
3 or 4 dried hot red chili peppers, crushed
3 bay leaves, crumbled

FOR THE BOIL:

4 qt (4 l) water, or to cover
1 tablespoon salt
12–14 red new potatoes, unpeeled
4 white onions, quartered
1 lb (500 g) hot link sausages, cut into 2-in (5-cm) lengths
2 lb (1 kg) shrimp (prawns) in the shell
4 ears of corn, quartered

★ To make the Rockport red sauce, in a bowl, stir together all ingredients, mixing well. Cover and refrigerate until serving.
★ To make the tartar sauce, in a bowl, stir together all ingredients, mixing well. Cover and refrigerate until serving.
★ To make the seasoning mix, combine all the ingredients and set aside.
★ To assemble the boil, in a large stockpot, combine the water, seasoning mix and salt and bring to a boil. Add the potatoes and simmer for 10 minutes.
★ Add the onions and sausages and boil for 5 minutes. Add the shrimp and corn and boil until the shrimp turn pink and curl, about 5 minutes longer.
★ Using a large slotted spoon, lift out the seafood and vegetables, draining well, and arrange on a platter. Place the Rockport and tartar sauces alongside and serve at once.

SERVES 6   *Photograph pages 134–135*

Heart of Texas

LAMB SAUTÉ WITH BRANDIED PEACH CREAM

This elegant dish is easy to prepare. Each rosemary-scented lamb chop is topped with a brandy-flavored peach half and then with the sauce. Serve with green beans or petite peas and roasted potatoes.

8 loin lamb chops, about 1 in (2.5 cm) thick, trimmed of
    excess fat
freshly ground pepper
1 teaspoon minced fresh rosemary
5 tablespoons (2½ oz/75 g) unsalted butter
2 cloves garlic, minced
4 peaches, halved, pitted and peeled
¼ cup (2 fl oz/60 ml) brandy, warmed
1¼ cups (10 fl oz/310 ml) heavy (double) cream

★ Season the lamb chops with pepper to taste and the rosemary. In a large, heavy frying pan or sauté pan over medium-high heat, melt 3 tablespoons of the butter with the garlic. As the butter melts, the garlic will flavor it. When the butter has melted, add the chops and sauté quickly, turning once, until nicely browned on both sides and the centers are still slightly pink, 3–4 minutes on each side. Transfer the chops to a warmed platter and keep warm. Pour off any drippings in the pan.
★ In the same pan over medium heat, melt the remaining 2 tablespoons butter. Add the peach halves and cook, turning to warm all sides. Pour the warmed brandy over the peaches and, using a long match, ignite the brandy. When the flames subside, add the cream and heat slowly until the peaches and cream are warm.
★ Top each lamb chop with a peach half and spoon the cream sauce over the top. Serve at once.

SERVES 4

the ingredients for the seasoning mix, use two 3-ounce (90-gram) packages of crab and shrimp boil. This is an adaptation of a recipe developed by seafood consumer education specialist Annette Reddell Hegen for the Texas Marine Advisory Service.

FOR THE ROCKPORT RED SAUCE:

1 cup (8 fl oz/250 ml) bottled chili sauce or ketchup
3 tablespoons fresh lemon juice
1 tablespoon prepared horseradish
3–5 drops Tabasco or other hot-pepper sauce

FOR THE SEAFOOD JALAPEÑO TARTAR SAUCE:

3 green (spring) onions, including tender green tops, minced
2 cups (16 fl oz/500 ml) mayonnaise
2 teaspoons fresh lemon or lime juice
1 teaspoon finely minced fresh dill or 2 tablespoons minced
    dill pickles
2 tablespoons minced fresh parsley
1 teaspoon drained capers, minced
1 hard-cooked egg, chopped (optional)
1 fresh jalapeño chili pepper, minced (optional)

FOR THE SEASONING MIX:

¼ cup (1½ oz/45 g) yellow mustard seeds
¼ cup (1½ oz/45 g) coriander seeds
2 tablespoons dill seed

EAST TEXAS

EAST TEXAS

The Piney Woods, once home to towering, wide-spaced virgin pines that merged into a tangle of vines and plants at the western edges of the Louisiana swamplands, has been transformed into a patchwork quilt of small farms. One of these farms, Dunsavage, is known for the rich, delectable cheesecake produced there, a dessert to rival its most formidable New York competition. Based on a family Pennsylvania Dutch recipe, Lyn's New York Cheesecake has been a success almost from its beginning in 1986, when Lyn sold 10 cakes the first week, 35 the second week and 135 the third week. At peak times today, more than 1,000 cakes are baked daily in ten home-style ovens.

Lyn's New York Cheesecake and Laura's Cheesecake of nearby Daingerfield both have earned the coveted Taste of Texas endorsement from the Texas Department of Agriculture. Laura adds a dash of showmanship to the eating experience and gives a history lesson at the same time, for she cooks in the Main Street Bakery, located in a refurbished 1890s building that, by turns, has been a mercantile shop, clothier, barber shop and post office. Although best eaten in either of the two charming dining rooms of the respective bakers, both cheesecakes are available in some of the state's top restaurants and by mail order. They are excellent examples of how far Texas tastes have evolved from the early days of simple sweets made from pumpkin and molasses.

Previous pages: Before the water was diverted, Caddo Lake was an important waterway for steamboat traffic from New Orleans.
Left: Despite the difficulties of penetrating the dense forests of what is now the Davy Crockett National Forest, early settlers prevailed.

East Texas towns with names like Mineola, Nacogdoches and Angelina combine plantation hospitality with French Creole and Cajun influences. Stately mansions, once home to southern aristocrats who migrated west, now provide exceptional bed-and-breakfast accommodations for twentieth-century travelers, including generous meals that feature such contemporary favorites as peppered bacon and fluffy biscuits, chocolate praline cake, blackberry cobbler and rich, dark espresso—all too tempting to resist. One hundred years ago, the kitchens of these mansions turned out quail, partridges and plover served with gravy flavored with currant jelly, deep-dish pies cooked in earthenware dishes and fresh oysters in season. The oysters were shipped in salt water to keep them alive, and some houses even built special pits or added salt water to their basements to create oyster "beds."

These nineteenth-century households also served bushels of crabs and blackbird and wild duck pies, and it was typical to see pork ribs, pig's feet, veal, beef, chicken, venison, dried meat and, if the home happened to be near a river or creek, fish prepared in several different ways all on the table at the same time. This lavish array of dishes was prepared in hopes of appealing to the varied tastes of guests, and it was the ultimate expression of hospitality.

A slow, unhurried way of life permeates the rural communities of East Texas.

Refreshment tables were heavily laden with Champagne, juleps, brandy and fine liqueurs. Many plantation owners made their own beer, wine and corn liquor and imported large quantities of whiskey, brandy and fine wines.

Of course, not all meals were this varied. Early writings often lament the simple diet of corn bread, fat pork and greens typical of people who eked out only the barest subsistence and lived in the tiny cabins and shanties that dotted the landscape.

Corn was an important crop to early settlers as well as to the Native Americans. Fresh corn was roasted or boiled; dried corn was ground to make cornmeal. To make ashcakes, the meal was mixed with cold water and a little salt, and then covered with hot ashes to cook. Johnnycake was made by spooning the mixture, sometimes with milk, eggs and a little sugar added, into a greased skillet that was set over the hot coals. Placed on a hoe blade by workers cooking their midday meal in the fields, the simple combination of water, salt and cornmeal became a hoecake. And it was called cornpone or corn dodgers when cooked in a spider, a long-legged cooking pot that was placed over the coals; sweet syrups were sometimes poured over the bread to make a dessert. Because imported flour was expensive, sometimes costing as much as seventy-five dollars a barrel, breads and cakes made of flour were luxury items enjoyed only by the wealthy or on special occasions.

Hominy, too, was important. The corn grains were cooked in a weak solution of lye water until they swelled and shed their skins. After repeated washings to remove the skins, the kernels were boiled in two or three changes of water, then baked, boiled with meat or fat, or fried. Dried hominy was ground into grits, which were boiled into a mush and served plain or with butter or red-eye (ham) gravy.

Meats were frequently cut into small roasts and smoked, and whole animals and huge haunches were roasted over glowing coals. Sometimes the old ways are best left unchanged. Mineola's Cap Ranch has acquired a national reputation for the use of original Texas smokehouse techniques to produce the succulent meats slow-smoked over sweet East Texas hickory. Many barbecue "experts" claim that East Texas barbecue is the only barbecue worth driving a long distance to enjoy. Its secret is the sweet, molasses-based sauces, or "mops," that are slathered on after the smoking.

Many East Texas cooks prefer pork barbecue, which lends itself to the sweet sauces popular in this part of the state. But beef holds its own, as do chicken and Cajun-inspired sausage. Today, one of the most sought-after longhorn sires in the state lives for six months of the year on the Circle K Ranch in Van Zandt County, twenty miles west of Tyler. This cosseted bovine resides in Colorado the other half of the year to escape the long, hot summer. There is nothing but the best for this reigning monarch, for raising beef is big business.

The farms and ranches that occupy this part of the state were carved out of huge trees that could have come straight from Paul Bunyan's tall tales. The trees were cut in wholesale fashion, and loggers and their oxen dragged the mammoth giants to the sawmills, disturbing the soil in the process and changing the native plant

Daingerfield State Park, surrounding a picturesque lake, offers a quiet refuge for hikers, birders and nature lovers.

life forever. Underbrush and shrubs sprang up in the spaces that received sunlight because the tree canopy no longer existed, and farmers laid claim to the new acreage.

The face of the land continued to change. Ditches and fence rows provided ideal settings for the rapid growth of brambles, weeds, many kinds of trees, wildflowers and large numbers of quail that heretofore had been rare or nonexistent. By the 1940s, the farmers were moving to the city or working in oil refineries, and their farms evolved into cattle ranches and pine plantations. The result is that East Texas claims most of the state's Christmas tree farms today. This part of the state also has a new, successful blueberry industry and is awaiting the outcome of the emerging truffle industry. Here, too, is Piney Woods Country Wines, located in Orange, which produces wines made from locally grown fruits, berries and muscadine grapes.

The rivers are slow-flowing today, just as they were two hundred years ago, and stands of stately cypresses tower to the skies. Native redbud and dogwood trees lend glorious vistas in the spring, and the loblolly and shortleaf pines still provide "green cathedrals." Here you will find the Caddoan Mounds, mute testimony to the ancient Caddo Indians who first farmed the land, and cities such as Tyler, which claims to grow more roses than any other city in the United States. The swamps are enormously tranquil, with a heartbeat of their own, and the rest of the countryside continues to change as more homes are built on what was once virgin timberland.

THE TEXAS PANTRY

The farmer's market in Dallas is among the largest urban markets in the country.

THE TEXAS PANTRY

Of the many tastes, temptations and traditions associated with Texas foods, perhaps the most comforting are those rich recipes made with farm fresh eggs and rich cheese, ingredients essential to the Texas pantry. Artworks, books, movies and television programs that have romanticized the Lone Star lifestyle often focus on the meat-and-potatoes aspect of Texas menus. Little is heard about the rich ice creams made with country fresh eggs that are shipped by private plane to points north, south, east and west, or the bountiful quantities of cheese that appear in markets from coast to coast. Little is heard about other staples of the Texas pantry, the huge amounts of wheat, rice and winter vegetables that are grown annually and shipped to the far corners of the world.

These ingredients enjoy a pride of place, but lighter, healthier versions of traditional recipes, which heretofore incorporated large amounts of dairy products and eggs, have taken center stage in recent years. Although egg-rich recipes, heavy cheese sauces and cream-based gravies are sometimes replaced with Parmesan-rich sun-dried tomato and spinach pestos, goat cheeses and Italian-style low-fat mozzarella, many old-fashioned recipes continue to find their way to the table.

Mexican cheeses are popular and are readily available in all parts of the state. Specialty food and cheese shops throughout the state stock an array of farm-fresh cheeses made in Old World style. Locally produced goat cheese is considered to be a match for the best French *chèvre,* and

buffalo's milk mozzarella, mushroom and bleu-flecked Bries and Camembert are all widely marketed. But low-fat, low-sodium cheeses are replacing some exotic triple crèmes, and these handmade cheeses are more flavorful, and therefore more popular, than mass-produced cheeses. Some foods are considered to be pleasurable necessities, and cheese is one of them. Tidbits of delight, enjoyed in moderation, cheese is here to stay. Consumption of cheese has doubled in the past thirty years nationwide, and Texas has kept pace by eating its fair share.

Regional and local cooperative farmer's markets and individual small farmers are contributing a treasure trove of fresh vegetables to Texas pantries. Some vegetables are grown year-round; others appear in markets only for a brief time. Farmer's markets pop up in spring and summer. Word of the best "pick your own" fields of okra, corn and peas spreads from family to family. Weekends may be spent canning, freezing or just snacking on freshly harvested fruits and vegetables.

Corn-shucking contests, where competitors try to shuck the most ears of corn in an allotted time, are common. So are county fair competitions for the best recipes for German-style cabbage, apple pie, strawberry wine and even watermelon pickles. More and more home cooks, taking a cue from professional chefs, have learned to grow and to prepare vegetables in season. Many plant tomatoes, bell peppers (capsicums) and hot peppers, zucchini (courgettes), green (spring) onions,

Previous pages, clockwise from top: Whole Roasted Onions (recipe page 190), Twice-Baked Jalapeño Potatoes Au Gratin (recipe page 189), Fried Camembert with Four-Pepper Glaze (recipe page 186), Herb-Marinated Mozzarella (recipe page 186), Avocado Pilaf (recipe page 192)

spinach, brussels sprouts, cabbages and eggplants (aubergines) amid the zinnias, marigolds and petunias in their backyards.

Vegetables are prepared on the grill and are deep-fried, steamed or baked. Skewers of vegetables add color and interest as well as nutrition to weekend cookouts. Gourmet pizzas with vegetable toppings are becoming as popular as pizzas with meat toppings. Fresh vegetables prepared with cheese toppings or fried in egg batters set taste buds tingling. Some lend themselves to such unexpected presentations as fried okra salad and black-eyed pea caviar. Commercially grown baby vegetables appear in home recipes and on more and more menus in restaurants large and small.

Rice fields abound in the southeastern portion of the state and produce interesting varieties: Indian-style basmati; tender, long-grained Texmati; a pecan-scented rice, which has a rich but light, slightly wild but earthy essence; and jasmine rice, which has pleasing, faint floral overtones. Among the trends in Texas cuisine is the incorporation of these distinctive rice varieties into menus as replacements for plain white or brown rice. Traditional Mexican-spiced, tomato-based white rice continues be be popular, and Cajun-style dirty rice appears on menus from time to time.

The High Plains is a source of mammoth amounts of garden crops, notably potatoes, and also wheat and corn. Intensive irrigation systems in the High Plains produce greater quantities of high-quality grains than are grown in

Some fruits and vegetables are grown year-round in Texas; others appear in markets seasonally.

the fields of South Texas, most of which rely on natural rainfall. Corn kernels are smaller in the southern part of the state, due to weather and soil conditions. Much of the corn produced here is ground into cornmeal and made into tamales and tortillas.

The Texas pantry, decidedly different from the days when a sack of dried beans, a barrel of flour and a keg of syrup were the most common staples, overflows with fresh vegetables produced by a long growing season, locally made cheeses created in various international styles and grains transplanted from many lands.

The modern Texas pantry overflows with specialty cheeses, a variety of grains and fresh-from-the-field vegetables—much of it produced within the state.

*Clockwise from bottom left: Whole-Wheat Tortilla Pizza with
Four Mexican Cheeses, Queso Fundido, Chili con Queso*

184

S o u t h   T e x a s

QUESO FUNDIDO

San Antonio executive chef Michael Bomberg created this variation on a popular antojito *(appetizer) served in Mexican restaurants. They are Monterrey-style tacos filled with spicy chorizo sausage, cubed potatoes,* rajas *(roasted chili strips), nopalitos (cactus) and cheese. For an interesting twist, fill the tortillas with Italian sausage, mozzarella cheese and bell pepper (capsicum) strips. Although they are most authentic when grilled over charcoal, the stove top works equally well.*

3 chorizo sausages, about 1½ lb (750 g) total, removed from casings
½ cup (4 oz/125 g) diced, cooked potato (½-in/12-mm dice)
½ cup (4 oz/125 g) julienne-cut roasted red, yellow and/or green bell peppers (capsicums) (see glossary)
¼ cup (2 oz/60 g) julienne-cut roasted anaheim or poblano chili peppers (optional; see glossary)
¼ cup (2 oz/60 g) chopped pickled *nopalitos,* rinsed and drained (see glossary)
2 oz (60 g) Monterey Jack or pepper Jack cheese (see glossary), cut into ¼-in (6-mm) dice
8–10 whole-wheat (wholemeal) flour tortillas, warmed
fresh tomato salsa, chopped fresh cilantro (fresh coriander) and/or avocado slices for garnish

★ In a frying pan or sauté pan over medium heat, crumble the chorizo. Sauté, stirring, until almost cooked through, about 5 minutes. Pour off all but 1 teaspoon of the drippings.
★ Add the potato, bell pepper, anaheim or poblano chili and *nopalitos* and cook, stirring occasionally, until heated through, 1–2 minutes. Add the cheese to the chorizo mixture and stir once more before removing the pan from the heat; the cheese will continue to melt.
★ Spoon the chorizo mixture onto the warmed tortillas, fold in half and place on warmed individual plates. Top with the salsa, cilantro and/or avocado. Serve immediately.

SERVES 4 OR 5

H e a r t   o f   T e x a s

WHOLE-WHEAT TORTILLA PIZZA WITH FOUR MEXICAN CHEESES

Mexican cheeses are becoming more and more popular with cooks who demand authentic ingredients for their Southwest and Mexican recipes. In addition to those given in the recipe, cheeses particularly appropriate for this pizza include Chihuahua and Oaxaca. A Spanish cheese, Idiazabal, is especially interesting in this dish. If such cheeses cannot be found, use a variety of flavored Jack cheeses. A white flour tortilla or a prepared pizza crust can be used in place of the whole-wheat tortilla; if you have a pizza stone, use that as well.

1 burrito-sized whole-wheat (wholemeal) tortilla, about 12 in (30 cm) in diameter
1–2 teaspoons olive oil
1 fresh poblano chili pepper, cut into long, thin strips (see glossary)
¼ cup (1 oz/30 g) each shredded *asadero, anejo, queso fresco* and pepper Jack cheese (see glossary)
½ teaspoon fresh oregano leaves

2 cloves roasted garlic (see glossary)
1 tablespoon salted, roasted pumpkin seeds or toasted pine nuts
¼ cup (1¼ oz/37 g) julienne-cut red bell pepper (capsicum)
¼ teaspoon fresh thyme leaves, plus thyme sprigs for garnish
¼ teaspoon whole pink pepperberries (see glossary)
⅛ teaspoon crushed red pepper flakes

★ Preheat an oven to 350°F (180°C).
★ Lightly brush both sides of the tortilla with the olive oil. Place the tortilla on a baking sheet and slip the sheet into the oven for 5 minutes.
★ Remove the baking sheet from the oven. Raise the oven temperature to 400°F (200°C). Divide the tortilla into pie-shaped quarters by using the poblano chili strips. In each quarter, place 1 of the cheeses. Sprinkle the *asadero* cheese with the oregano and roasted garlic. Sprinkle the *anejo* cheese with the pumpkin seeds or pine nuts and red bell pepper. Sprinkle the *queso fresco* with the thyme and pepperberries, and the pepper Jack with the red pepper flakes.
★ Return the baking sheet to the oven and bake until the cheeses melt and the edges of the tortilla are golden, 2–4 minutes. Transfer to a serving platter and garnish with thyme sprigs. Cut into wedges and serve at once.

SERVES 4–6 AS AN APPETIZER

T e x a s

CHILI CON QUESO

Few Texans can resist this creamy "chili with cheese." You'll find that there are as many variations on this dish as there are on salsa, chicken-fried steak and chili. In its simplest form, melted processed yellow cheese is used in combination with canned picante sauce or with tomatoes and green chilies. Cheddar or Monterey Jack cheese, or a combination, can be used in place of the pepper Jack. Serve the spicy melted cheese spooned over crispy tortilla chips (see glossary) or as a dip in a chafing dish with tortilla chips or French bread on the side. Or layer hot flour tortillas with the melted cheese and then sprinkle toasted pumpkin seeds over the top. Flaked crab meat can be added to dress up the mixture with delicious results.

2 tablespoons vegetable oil
1 large white or yellow onion, minced
2 cloves garlic, minced
2–4 fresh jalapeño chili peppers, minced
4–6 fresh anaheim chili peppers, roasted, peeled and chopped (see glossary)
2 cups (12 oz/375 g) diced, drained tomatoes
1 can (5 fl oz/150 ml) evaporated milk (optional)
6 cups (1½ lb/750 g) shredded pepper Jack cheese (see glossary)

★ In a saucepan over medium heat, warm the vegetable oil. Add the onion and sauté until softened but not browned, 3–5 minutes. Add the garlic, jalapeño and anaheim chilies, and tomatoes and cook, stirring, until fragrant, about 1 minute longer.
★ Stir in the evaporated milk, if using, and bring to a boil. (If you are not using the milk, bring the tomato mixture to a simmer.) Remove from the heat and stir in the cheese. Cover and let stand, stirring occasionally, until melted, 8–10 minutes.
★ Serve at once, as described in note.

SERVES 8–10

Fried Camembert with Four-Pepper Glaze

Texas chef Jay McCarthy developed this exceptional recipe, which tops a wheel of warm Camembert with a complex pepper glaze. If you are short of time, use a commercial pepper jelly, melting it in a small saucepan over low heat and stirring in 1 teaspoon grated, peeled fresh ginger before spooning it over the cheese. The cheese can also be prepared as directed and baked in an oven preheated to 400°F (200°C) for about 15 minutes and then topped with glaze.

¼ cup (1¼ oz/37 g) all-purpose (plain) flour
1 egg, beaten
¼ cup (1 oz/30 g) fine dried bread crumbs
1 wheel (8 oz/250 g) Camembert cheese
2 tablespoons butter
¾–1 cup (8–10 oz/250–310 ml) four-pepper jelly
  (see glossary)

★ Spread the flour on a dinner plate. In a shallow bowl large enough to accommodate the cheese wheel, beat the egg until blended. Spread the bread crumbs on another plate.
★ Dip the Camembert wheel first into the flour, coating both sides, and then into the egg, again coating both sides. Finally dip the cheese into the bread crumbs, coating evenly.
★ In a frying pan over medium heat, melt the butter. Add the cheese and cook, carefully turning once, until golden brown and crusty on both sides, about 5 minutes total.
★ Transfer the cheese to a serving plate and spoon the jelly over the top. It will melt into a glaze from the heat of the cheese. Serve at once.

SERVES 6–8   *Photograph pages 180–181*

Herb-Marinated Mozzarella

Serve this savory cheese with toasted slices of Italian or French bread or coriander bolillos (recipe page 79). It can also be cubed for adding to salads, or set out with toothpicks and offered as an appetizer. If desired, add 2 tablespoons slivered sun-dried tomatoes to the marinade. Once the cheese is eaten, the remaining oil can be used as a marinade or combined with balsamic vinegar for a salad dressing.

1 lb (500 g) whole-milk or part-skim mozzarella, chilled,
  sliced ¼ in (6 mm) thick
8–10 tablespoons (4–5 fl oz/125–150 ml) olive oil
½ teaspoon red pepper flakes
3 tablespoons minced fresh parsley
8 whole black peppercorns
8 whole green peppercorns
8 whole pink pepperberries (optional; see glossary)
1 tablespoon chopped fresh basil
1 tablespoon fresh thyme leaves
1 tablespoon fresh rosemary leaves
1 teaspoon minced fresh chives
3 cloves garlic, minced
2 bay leaves
fresh herb leaves and blossoms for garnish

★ In a wide, clear glass serving dish, slightly overlap the cheese slices. In a small bowl, stir together all the remaining ingredients until well mixed. Drizzle the mixture evenly over the cheese slices.
★ Let stand for 2 hours at room temperature before serving.

SERVES 8   *Photograph pages 180–181*

Arroz a la Mexicana

A staple on typical Tex-Mex plates, this rice is full of flavor and color. If you like, mix in a little chopped bell pepper (capsicum) with the onion and garlic, or toss in cooked green peas and strips of pimiento just before serving.

1 tomato, quartered
1 white onion, quartered
1 clove garlic
¼ cup (2 fl oz/60 ml) vegetable oil
1 cup (7 oz/220 g) long-grain white rice
3 tablespoons minced fresh parsley
1 fresh jalapeño chili pepper, minced
2½ cups (20 fl oz/625 ml) chicken stock
½ teaspoon salt, or to taste

★ In a food processor fitted with the metal blade or in a blender, combine the tomato, onion and garlic. Purée until smooth.
★ In a heavy saucepan over medium heat, warm the vegetable oil. Add the rice and cook, stirring constantly, until the rice is golden, about 5 minutes. Add the puréed vegetables and cook, stirring, for 5 minutes longer.
★ Stir in the parsley, jalapeño, stock and salt. Reduce the heat to low, cover and simmer until the liquid is absorbed, about 25 minutes.
★ Remove from the heat and let stand, covered, for 10 minutes before serving.

SERVES 4–6

Fresh Corn Tamales

Tamales are a Christmas tradition in South Texas. This is an adaptation of Chef Stephan Pyles's recipe for corn tamales found in his book, The New Texas Cuisine. *It is a basic tamale that is usually served as an accompaniment to grilled meats or as an appetizer; it is also the foundation for tamales that are stuffed with various fillings, from shrimp, chicken and chorizo to venison, turkey and lobster. They may be assembled in advance, steamed and then allowed to cool and refrigerated for up to 2 days or frozen for up to 3 months; place in a steamer to reheat until warmed through. Cap Rock Brut or another classic* méthode champenoise *sparkling wine is perfect with the smooth, mellow flavors of this quintessential comfort food.*

1½ cups (9 oz/280 g) corn kernels
½ cup (4 oz/125 g) vegetable shortening, at room temperature
1 cup (5 oz/155 g) *masa harina* (see glossary)
⅔ cup (3½ oz/105 g) yellow cornmeal
¼ teaspoon cayenne pepper
1 teaspoon salt
¼ teaspoon ground cumin
1 teaspoon baking powder
¾ cup (6 fl oz/180 ml) warm water or chicken stock
1 cup (4 oz/125 g) shredded Monterey Jack cheese
  (optional)
¼ cup (¾ oz/20 g) minced green (spring) onion, including
  tender green tops (optional)
1 fresh green poblano chili pepper, roasted, peeled and
  chopped (optional; see glossary)
14 dried corn husks, soaked in warm water to cover for 30
  minutes to soften (see glossary)

★ In a food processor fitted with the metal blade, place ¾ cup (4½ oz/140 g) of the corn kernels and grind until quite smooth. In a bowl, using an electric mixer set on medium-high speed, beat the shortening until light and fluffy. In a second bowl, stir

Top to bottom: Arroz a la Mexicana, Fresh Corn Tamales, Tomatillo Rice

together the *masa harina,* cornmeal, cayenne pepper, salt, cumin and baking powder. Gradually stir in the warm water or chicken stock until a thick dough forms. Then add the dough to the whipped shortening, mixing until well blended. Stir in the ground corn, the remaining ¾ cup (4½ oz/140 g) whole corn kernels and the cheese, green onion and chili, if using. Combine thoroughly; the mixture will be quite sticky.
★ Drain the corn husks and pat dry. Tear 2 of the husks lengthwise into 6 strips each, to use for tying the tamales. On a flat work surface, arrange the remaining 12 husks in pairs, with their large ends overlapping by about 2 in (5 cm).
★ Divide the tamale dough evenly among the 6 pairs of husks, spreading it in the center and leaving about 1 in (2.5 cm) at each end uncovered. Roll the corn husks around the dough to enclose completely. Twist each end and then tie with the reserved corn husk strips.
★ Place the tamales on a steamer rack over boiling water, cover and steam until heated through and the dough separates easily from the husk, about 30 minutes.
★ Transfer the tamales to individual plates for diners to open at the table.

MAKES SIX 4-IN (10-CM) TAMALES; SERVES 6

TOMATILLO RICE

Chef Dean Fearing created this fresh-tasting and colorful recipe. It is a perfect accompaniment to seafood.

8 tomatillos, about 1 lb (500 g), brown husks removed and cut up
3 cloves garlic, minced
2 fresh serrano chili peppers, minced (see glossary)
½ cup (¾ oz/20 g) chopped fresh cilantro (fresh coriander)
5 large spinach leaves, chopped
salt
fresh lime juice
4 cups (28 oz/875 g) hot cooked long-grain white rice

★ In a blender or in a food processor fitted with the metal blade, combine the tomatillos, garlic, serranos, cilantro and spinach. Purée until smooth. Season to taste with salt and lime juice.
★ Toss the tomatillo mixture with the hot rice, mixing thoroughly. Serve immediately.

SERVES 4–6

TWO-CHEESE GARDEN POTATOES

The perfect accompaniment to grilled meats or Texas barbecue, this preparation allows the flavor of the potatoes to shine. The addition of avocado, sour cream and cilantro gives the potatoes a true Texas accent.

¼ cup (2 oz/60 g) butter
3 russet potatoes, about 1½ lb (750 g), baked, cooled, peeled and diced
1 cup (4 oz/125 g) shredded pepper Jack cheese (see glossary)
1 cup (4 oz/125 g) shredded Cheddar cheese
2 tomatoes, peeled, seeded and chopped
¼ cup (1¼ oz/37 g) minced red onion
2 green (spring) onions, including tender green tops, minced
1 fresh jalapeño chili pepper, minced
1 teaspoon salt, or to taste
1 avocado, halved, pitted, peeled and sliced; minced fresh cilantro (fresh coriander) and ½ cup (4 fl oz/125 ml) sour cream for garnish

★ In a large, heavy frying pan over medium-high heat, melt the butter. Add the potatoes and cook, stirring occasionally, until lightly browned and crispy, 5–6 minutes.
★ Reduce the heat to low and stir in the cheeses, tomatoes, red and green onions and jalapeño; toss gently to melt the cheeses. Season with the salt and transfer to a warmed serving dish.
★ Garnish with the avocado slices and a sprinkling of cilantro. Serve immediately. Pass the sour cream for guests to top their servings as desired.

SERVES 4–6

TORTAS DE VERDURAS

These delicious vegetable pancakes from Mexico can be made from nearly any combination of vegetables. Try a mix of diced zucchini (courgette), yellow squash, green (spring) onion, jalapeño chili pepper, garlic and green bell pepper (capsicum), or a mix of avocado, fresh cilantro (fresh coriander), green onion, green bell pepper, jalapeño chili pepper and tomato. To turn this recipe into a main dish, add a little crispy bacon, minced ham or chopped cooked shrimp.

3 eggs
½ cup (2½ oz/75 g) all-purpose (plain) flour
1 teaspoon baking powder
½ teaspoon salt, or to taste
¼ teaspoon freshly ground pepper, or to taste
1 lb (500 g) assorted vegetables, diced (see note)
1 tablespoon butter
1 tablespoon vegetable oil
fresh oregano sprigs for garnish

★ Preheat an oven to 250°F (120°C).
★ In a bowl, whisk the eggs until blended. Add the flour, baking powder, salt and pepper and whisk until smooth. Stir in your choice of vegetables.
★ On a griddle over medium heat (or use a frying pan), melt 1 teaspoon of the butter with 1 teaspoon of the oil. To form each pancake, drop a tablespoonful of the batter onto the griddle, being careful not to crowd them. Cook, turning once, until well browned on both sides, 3–4 minutes total.
★ Using a slotted spatula, transfer to paper towels to drain briefly, then keep warm in the oven. Repeat with the remaining batter, adding the remaining butter and oil as needed.
★ Transfer to a warmed platter and garnish with oregano sprigs. Serve immediately.

MAKES 24 PANCAKES; SERVES 4–6

HORSERADISH POTATOES

Dallas chef Richard Chamberlain suggests serving this with smoked prime rib, but these delicious potatoes also complement a Texas T-bone to perfection.

4 large russet potatoes, 1½–2 lb (750 g–1 kg) total weight, peeled and quartered
¼ cup (2 oz/60 g) butter
½ cup (4 fl oz/125 ml) heavy (double) cream
2 tablespoons grated, peeled fresh horseradish root or 1½ teaspoons prepared horseradish
2 teaspoons salt
½ teaspoon white pepper

★ In a large saucepan, combine the potatoes with water to cover by 2 in (5 cm). Bring to a boil and boil until tender when pierced with a fork, 25–30 minutes. Drain and place in a large bowl.
★ Meanwhile, in a small saucepan over low heat, combine the butter and cream and warm gently only until the butter is soft and the mixture is slightly warm.
★ Add the mixture and the horseradish to the bowl holding the potatoes. Using an electric mixer set on high speed, whip until smooth.
★ Add the salt and pepper and serve at once.

SERVES 6–8

TWICE-BAKED JALAPEÑO POTATOES AU GRATIN

San Antonio chef Steve Peterson created this spicy version of a traditional potato recipe.

¾ lb (375 g) russet potatoes, peeled and cut into ½-in (12-mm) dice
6–8 oz (185–250 g) sliced bacon
2 cups (16 fl oz/500 ml) milk
¼ cup (2 oz/60 g) butter
½ cup (2½ oz/75 g) all-purpose (plain) flour
¾ lb (375 g) pepper Jack cheese, grated (see glossary)
1–2 tablespoons minced fresh jalapeño chili pepper
salt and freshly ground pepper

★ In a saucepan, combine the potatoes with salted water to cover by about 2 in (5 cm). Bring to a boil and cook until barely tender, 3–4 minutes. Drain and rinse in cold water to halt the cooking. Drain again and set aside.
★ While the potatoes are cooking, in a frying pan over medium heat, fry the bacon until crisp, 5–7 minutes. Using tongs or a slotted spatula, transfer to paper towels to drain. Crumble and set aside.
★ Preheat an oven to 350°F (180°C).
★ Pour the milk into a saucepan and place over medium heat; heat to just below boiling. Meanwhile, in a saucepan over medium-low heat, melt the butter. Stir in the flour and cook, stirring, until well blended, 1–3 minutes. Slowly add the milk to the butter-flour mixture, whisking vigorously to prevent lumps. Stir in the cheese, incorporating completely. Add the jalapeño and reserved bacon and potatoes, mixing well. Season to taste with salt and pepper, if needed. Spoon into eight ½-cup (4–fl oz/125-ml) gratin dishes.
★ Bake until bubbly hot, 10–15 minutes. Remove from oven and let stand for 5 minutes before serving.

SERVES 8   *Photograph pages 180–181*

WHOLE ROASTED ONIONS

Use Texas 1015 Supersweet onions, if possible, for this recipe. These grapefruit-sized onions are harvested in what is known as the Winter Garden area, which spreads from just south of San Antonio to the Rio Grande Valley, and they are in the markets from mid-April through May. The onions can also be roasted over a charcoal fire; plan on about the same timing.

6 large onions, about 3 in (7.5 cm) in diameter, unpeeled
6 teaspoons butter
blackened seasoning mix (see glossary)
6 teaspoons balsamic vinegar

★ Preheat an oven to 375°F (190°C).
★ Using a sharp knife, cut a thin slice off the stem end of each onion. Score the tops in a crisscross pattern and then top each onion with 1 teaspoon butter. Sprinkle the tops to taste with blackened seasoning mix. Place each onion on a large square of heavy-duty aluminum foil and enclose them so that each package is airtight. Place the packets on a baking sheet.
★ Bake until the onions feel soft when pressed with your fingertips, 30–40 minutes. Remove from the oven and unwrap the onions. Place on a platter or individual plates and drizzle each with 1 teaspoon vinegar. Alternatively, cut each onion in half and drizzle each half with ½ teaspoon vinegar.
★ Serve hot, warm or at room temperature.

SERVES 6 OR 12   *Photograph pages 180–181*

Left to right: Grandma's German Red Cabbage, Spaetzle

GRANDMA'S GERMAN RED CABBAGE

Serve this cabbage alongside sausages, schnitzel or wild game. A Johannisberg Riesling from the Fredericksburg-based Bell Mountain will complete the German theme.

3 tablespoons butter
1 large yellow onion, chopped
1 red cabbage, about 2½ lb (1.25 kg), thinly sliced
1 bay leaf
4 whole cloves
2 tablespoons apple cider vinegar
½ cup (4 fl oz/125 ml) water
4 tart cooking apples, about 1½ lb (750 g) total weight, halved, cored and thinly sliced lengthwise
1 teaspoon salt
1 tablespoon sugar
¼ cup (2 fl oz/60 ml) dry red wine

★ In a 5-qt (5-l) heavy-bottomed saucepan over medium heat, melt the butter. Add the onion and cook, stirring, until golden, about 5 minutes. Add the cabbage and stir until it is wilted, 5–7 minutes. Add the bay leaf, cloves, vinegar, water, apples and salt and stir well. Reduce the heat to medium-low, cover and simmer until most of the liquid has been absorbed and the cabbage is very tender, about 45 minutes.
★ Add the sugar and wine and simmer for 5 minutes longer. Discard the bay leaf and cloves and transfer to a warmed serving bowl. Serve hot.

SERVES 8–10

SPAETZLE

These tiny dumplings are a delicious accompaniment to paprika schnitzel (recipe page 170). If you like, add 1½ teaspoons ground cumin and 1 teaspoon grated lemon zest to the dough and serve with grilled chicken. The spaetzle can be boiled up to 3 days in advance, cooled, covered and refrigerated, and then reheated in the butter just before serving.

3 eggs
½ teaspoon salt, plus salt to taste
½ cup (4 fl oz/125 ml) water
1¾ cups (9 oz/280 g) all-purpose (plain) flour
2 tablespoons butter
freshly ground pepper

★ In a large bowl, using a whisk, beat together the eggs, the ½ teaspoon salt and water. Beat in the flour until well blended.
★ Select a colander with holes ⅛ in (3 mm) or larger (or use a spaetzle maker). Fill a large saucepan three-fourths full of salted water and bring to a boil. Place the colander over the boiling water. Using a rubber spatula, force small batches of the batter through the colander into the water. (The batter will fall in droplets.) When the dumplings float to the surface, after 15–30 seconds, cook for an additional 10 seconds. Using a slotted spoon, remove from the water and set aside.
★ When all of the batter has been cooked, in a large frying pan over medium heat, melt the butter. Add the spaetzle and cook, stirring and tossing, until heated through, about 2 minutes. Season to taste with salt and pepper.
★ Spoon into a warmed serving dish and serve immediately.

SERVES 4–6

Fried Green Tomatoes with Bacon

FRIED GREEN TOMATOES WITH BACON

Serve this old-time brunch dish with hot homemade biscuits for dipping into the creamy sauce. It is equally delicious made with red tomatoes. For a more calorie-conscious dish, omit the cream sauce.

¼ lb (125 g) sliced bacon
4–6 firm green tomatoes (about 2 lb/1 kg)
¼ cup (1¼ oz/37 g) all-purpose (plain) flour
¼ cup (1¼ oz/37 g) yellow cornmeal
1½ teaspoons dried dill
2 eggs
2 tablespoons butter or margarine
salt and freshly ground pepper
1 cup (8 fl oz/250 ml) heavy (double) cream
3 tablespoons minced fresh chives

★ Preheat an oven to 250°F (120°C).
★ In a large frying pan over medium heat, fry the bacon until

crisp, 5–7 minutes. Using a slotted spatula, transfer to paper towels to drain. Reserve the drippings in the pan.
★ Core the tomatoes and slice about ¼ in (6 mm) thick. In a shallow bowl, stir together the flour, cornmeal and dill. In another bowl, beat the eggs just until blended. Dip the slices in the beaten eggs and then coat on both sides with the flour mixture.
★ In the same frying pan over medium-high heat, melt the butter or margarine with the bacon drippings. Working in batches, add the tomato slices and cook, turning once, until golden brown on both sides, 4–5 minutes total. Season to taste with salt and pepper. Transfer to an ovenproof plate and place in the oven to keep warm while you fry the remaining slices.
★ When all of the tomatoes have been fried, pour off all but 1 tablespoon of the drippings remaining in the pan. Stir the cream into the reserved drippings and cook over medium heat, stirring occasionally, until reduced by half, 5–6 minutes. Stir in the chives.
★ Ladle the reduced cream onto a warmed platter and arrange the tomatoes on top of the cream. Crumble the bacon and scatter over the tomatoes. Serve at once.

SERVES 4–6

FRIED POTATOES WITH CUMIN KETCHUP

The French technique of double frying is the best way to achieve crispy French-fried potatoes. These are a favorite with Texas beef.

¾ cup (6 fl oz/180 ml) bottled chili sauce or ketchup
1 teaspoon ground cumin
1½ teaspoons balsamic vinegar
3 large russet potatoes, about 1½ lb (750 g) total weight
vegetable oil for deep-frying
1 teaspoon salt
1 teaspoon chili powder

★ In a small bowl, stir together the chili sauce or ketchup, cumin and balsamic vinegar. Set aside to allow the flavors to blend.
★ Peel the potatoes and cut crosswise into ripple-cut slices ½ in (12 mm) thick. Dry thoroughly with paper towels.
★ In a large, deep saucepan or deep-fat fryer, pour in vegetable oil to a depth of 3 in (7.5 cm). Heat to 370°F (188°C). Working in batches so as not to crowd the pan, add the potatoes and fry until tender and barely cooked, 4–6 minutes. Using a slotted spoon, transfer to paper towels to drain. Set aside to cool completely. Leave the oil in the pan.
★ Reheat the oil to 400°F (200°C). Again working in batches, add the potatoes and fry until golden brown and crisp, 2–3 minutes. Using the slotted spoon, transfer to clean paper towels to drain briefly.
★ In a cup, stir together the salt and chili powder. Place the potatoes on a serving dish, sprinkle with the salt mixture and serve piping hot, with the ketchup on the side.

SERVES 3 OR 4

AVOCADO PILAF

Texmati rice is the Texas-grown version of the fragrant basmati from India. This rice is grown in some twenty counties on the coastal prairie of Texas. This colorful dish is a wonderful accompaniment to grilled meats.

4 tablespoons (2 oz/60 g) butter
1 small white onion, finely minced
1 cup (7 oz/220 g) Texmati rice or other long-grain white rice
5 tablespoons (3 fl oz/80 ml) dry white wine
2 cups (16 fl oz/500 ml) beef stock
salt
1 small green bell pepper (capsicum), seeded and diced
1 small red bell pepper (capsicum), seeded and diced
¼ lb (125 g) fresh mushrooms, sliced
2 cloves garlic, minced
¼ teaspoon dried oregano
2 tomatoes, peeled, seeded and chopped
freshly ground black pepper
1 avocado, halved, pitted, peeled and diced
¼ cup (⅓ oz/10 g) minced fresh parsley

★ Preheat an oven to 350°F (180°C).
★ In a flameproof baking dish over medium heat, melt 2 tablespoons of the butter. Add the onion and cook, stirring, until softened but not browned, about 2 minutes. Add the rice and cook, stirring, for 1 minute longer. Pour in the wine and beef stock, season to taste with salt and bring to a boil. Cover and transfer to the oven. Bake until the liquid is absorbed, 25–35 minutes.

★ Just before the rice is ready, in a frying pan over medium-high heat, melt the remaining 2 tablespoons butter. Add the green and red bell pepper and sauté until softened, about 1 minute. Add the mushrooms and garlic and sprinkle with the oregano. Cook, stirring, for 2 minutes. Add the tomatoes and cook just to heat through, about 1 minute longer. Season with freshly ground pepper.
★ Add the vegetable mixture to the cooked rice and toss and stir to mix. Then add the avocado and minced parsley and toss gently. Serve immediately.

SERVES 4–6   *Photograph pages 180–181*

OKRA FRITTERS

Texas is known for both its haute cuisine and its down-home cookin'. These crisp, flavorful fritters are in the down-home camp, but they are wonderful with anything from grilled steaks and burgers to the most formal menu.

6 oz (185 g) okra, thinly sliced
½ cup (2½ oz/75 g) minced white onion
½ cup (2½ oz/75 g) diced green bell pepper (capsicum)
½ cup (3 oz/90 g) minced, drained tomato
½ cup (2½ oz/75 g) self-rising flour
½ cup (2½ oz/75 g) yellow cornmeal
3 eggs, beaten
¼ teaspoon salt, or to taste
¼ teaspoon freshly ground black pepper, or to taste
vegetable oil for frying

★ In a bowl, combine the okra, onion, bell pepper and tomato. Add the flour and cornmeal, tossing to coat evenly. Stir in the eggs, salt and black pepper. Stir well until the mixture thickens.
★ Preheat an oven to 200°F (93°C).
★ In a frying pan, pour in vegetable oil to a depth of ½ in (12 mm). Heat to 360°F (182°C), or until a tiny bit of the fritter batter sizzles within a moment of being dropped in the oil. Working in batches, drop the batter by tablespoonfuls into the hot oil and fry, turning once, until golden brown, about 1 minute total. Using a slotted spatula, transfer to paper towels to drain briefly. Transfer to a warmed serving platter and keep warm in the oven while frying the remaining batter.
★ When all of the fritters are ready, serve at once.

MAKES ABOUT 30 FRITTERS; SERVES 6–8

BOCK-BATTERED ONION RINGS, POBLANO RINGS AND SWEET POTATOES

This is always a showstopper. The sweet, yet crispy onion and poblano rings are delightful and the sweet potatoes and cactus add good counterpoints in texture. Avocado cream (see glossary) can be used in place of the chipotle-flavored ketchup for dipping.

1 cup (8 fl oz/250 ml) ketchup
1 chipotle chili in adobo, cut up (see glossary)
vegetable oil for deep-frying
1 bottle (12 oz/375 ml) Shiner Bock or other bock beer
1 egg, beaten

Clockwise from bottom left: Fried Potatoes with Cumin Ketchup, Okra Fritters, Bock-Battered Onion Rings, Poblano Rings and Sweet Potatoes

1 tablespoon baking powder
dash of salt
1 teaspoon seasoned salt
1½ cups (7½ oz/235 g) all-purpose (plain) flour
1 large Texas 1015 Supersweet onion or other large sweet onion, sliced crosswise ½ in (12 mm) thick and separated into rings
1 fresh poblano chili pepper, sliced crosswise into rings ½–¾ in (12 mm–2 cm) wide (see glossary)
1 small sweet potato, peeled and thinly sliced
2 cactus paddles, cleaned, cooked, drained and sliced into strips ½ in (12 mm) wide (optional; see glossary)

★ In a blender, combine the ketchup and chipotle chili and purée until smooth. Pour into a small bowl and set aside.
★ Preheat an oven to 250°F (120°C).
★ In a heavy saucepan or deep-fat fryer, pour in vegetable oil to a depth of 3 in (7.5 cm). Heat to 375°F (190°C), or until the oil is almost smoking.
★ Meanwhile, in a large bowl, combine the beer, egg, baking powder and regular and seasoned salt. Stir with a fork until blended. Gradually stir in the flour to form a loose batter. Drop the onion and poblano rings, the sweet potato rounds and the cactus slices, if using, into the batter, coating well.
★ Working in batches, and using tongs or a slotted spoon, lift the vegetables out of the batter, draining off any excess. Drop them into the hot oil and fry, turning once, until golden brown, 3–4 minutes total. Using the tongs or slotted spoon, transfer to paper towels to drain, then place in the warm oven until all the vegetables have been fried.
★ Transfer to a warmed platter and serve with the chipotle ketchup in a bowl alongside.

SERVES 4

Brie with Roasted Garlic and Olives

BRIE WITH ROASTED GARLIC AND OLIVES

You can also prepare this rich appetizer by placing the Brie wheels in a shallow metal pan and placing it on a grill rack over a charcoal fire. The garlic becomes quite mellow and slightly sweet when roasted, and combines deliciously with the Brie and the olives. Match with a Texas-style Côtes du Rhône, such as Slaughter-Leftwich Austin Rouge.

1 whole head garlic
1 fresh rosemary sprig

¼ cup (2 fl oz/60 ml) olive oil
2 wheels (4 oz/125 g each) Brie cheese
2 tablespoons sliced spicy Greek olives
2 tablespoons sliced Kalamata olives
¼ cup (2 oz/60 g) sliced dry-packed sun-dried tomatoes, reconstituted in water to cover, drained and cut into julienne strips
2 tablespoons pine nuts, lightly toasted
2 tablespoons minced fresh parsley
2 tablespoons minced fresh basil
apple wedges and toasted baguette slices for serving

★ Preheat an oven to 375°F (190°C).
★ Remove any loose papery skin from the garlic head and

194

place the garlic in a small baking dish. Add the rosemary sprig and olive oil, then cover tightly with aluminum foil. Bake until the garlic is soft when the cloves are pierced with a knife, about 35 minutes. Remove from the oven and let cool.

★ Raise the oven temperature to 400°F (200°C).

★ Using a sharp knife, slice the thin rind off the top of each Brie wheel. Place the wheels on an ovenproof serving plate. Press the garlic cloves free from their skins and spread the garlic evenly on the trimmed surface of each Brie wheel. Top with the olives, sun-dried tomatoes and pine nuts. Bake, uncovered, until the Brie is warm and softened, about 12 minutes.

★ Transfer the Brie wheels to 1 or 2 serving plates and sprinkle with the parsley and basil. Serve immediately with apple wedges and bread.

SERVES 8–10

Heart of Texas

OATMEAL AND PECAN PANCAKES WITH HAM, BANANAS AND PINEAPPLE

The town of Oatmeal is located forty miles (sixty-five kilometers) south of Bertram. The annual Oatmeal Festival there draws people from all over the state to celebrate with oatmeal recipes and old-fashioned Texas fun. Oatmeal mixed with pecans from San Saba, which lies southwest of Fort Worth and is the self-proclaimed Pecan Capital of the World, results in a deliciously different pancake. A mixture of fresh berries can be used in place of the bananas and pineapple.

2 cups (16 fl oz/500 ml) buttermilk
1⅔ cups (5 oz/155 g) old-fashioned rolled oats
2 eggs
½ cup (2½ oz/75 g) all-purpose (plain) flour
4½ teaspoons sugar
1 teaspoon baking soda (bicarbonate of soda)
½ teaspoon salt
½ cup (2 oz/60 g) chopped pecans
vegetable oil or butter for cooking

FOR THE TOPPING:

¼ cup (3 oz/90 g) butter
1½ cups (9 oz/280 g) well-drained pineapple chunks
3 bananas, cut into slices on the diagonal ½ in (12 mm) thick
½ lb (250 g) baked ham, sliced paper-thin

★ In a bowl, stir together the buttermilk and oats and let stand for 5 minutes to soften. Stir in the eggs, flour, sugar, baking soda, salt and pecans.

★ Heat a griddle over medium to medium-high heat (or use a nonstick frying pan). Oil or butter the griddle lightly and ladle on about 2 tablespoons of the batter for each pancake; do not crowd the griddle. Turn the pancakes when bubbles appear on the tops of the cakes, 1–2 minutes. Cook until lightly browned on the second side, 1½–2 minutes longer. Remove from the griddle and keep warm while you cook the remaining batter.

★ At the same time, to make the topping, in a large frying pan over medium-high heat, melt the butter. Add the pineapple chunks and banana slices and sauté, turning once, until lightly golden on both sides, 6–7 minutes total.

★ Arrange the pancakes on a warmed platter and top with the sautéed banana and pineapple and the ham. Serve at once.

SERVES 4 OR 5 *Photograph page 196*

SUMMER GREEN BEANS AND TOMATOES

These small garden-fresh green beans will keep their bright color if they are immersed in ice water immediately after cooking.

1 lb (500 g) young haricots verts or other small, young green beans, trimmed
ice water
3 tablespoons olive oil
2 tablespoons balsamic vinegar
salt and freshly ground pepper
½ teaspoon Dijon-style mustard
1 large vine-ripened tomato, chopped
1 small white onion, chopped
2 tablespoons minced fresh parsley
2 teaspoon capers, rinsed and drained
1 egg, hard-cooked and chopped

★ Bring a large pot three-fourths full of salted water to a boil and add the beans. When the water returns to a rolling boil, cook until the beans are tender-crisp, 2–3 minutes. Drain and immediately cool in ice water to halt the cooking and maintain the color. Place in a bowl.

★ In another bowl, whisk together the olive oil and vinegar; whisk in salt and pepper to taste and the mustard. Pour over the beans and toss gently. Add the tomato, onion, parsley, capers and egg and again toss gently.

★ Cover and refrigerate for at least 2 hours or for up to 12 hours before serving.

SERVES 6–8

Summer Green Beans and Tomatoes

Clockwise from left: Cornmeal Pancakes with Herbal Impressions, Oatmeal and Pecan Pancakes with Ham, Bananas and Pineapple (recipe page 195), German Potato Latkes

New Braunfels

GERMAN POTATO LATKES

Each year, at the Wurstfest in New Braunfels, there are long lines for potato latkes just like these. Typically they are served with applesauce, sour cream and a sprinkling of cinnamon.

3 cups (about 1½ lb/750 g) grated russet potatoes
¼ cup (1¼ oz/37 g) minced white onion
¼ teaspoon freshly ground pepper
¼ teaspoon ground nutmeg
2 eggs, lightly beaten
¼ cup (1¼ oz/37 g) all-purpose (plain) flour
1 teaspoon baking powder
1 teaspoon salt
vegetable oil for frying
applesauce, sour cream and ground cinnamon for serving

★ Preheat an oven to 250°F (120°C).
★ Using your hands, squeeze all the moisture from the potatoes or pat them dry with paper towels. Place them in a bowl and add the onion, pepper, nutmeg and eggs. In another bowl, stir together the flour, baking powder and salt; stir the flour mixture into the potato mixture.
★ In a large frying pan, preferably nonstick, pour in enough vegetable oil to cover the bottom (2–3 tablespoons) and place over medium-high heat. Working in batches, drop the potato mixture by tablespoonfuls into the hot oil. Flatten each mound slightly with a spatula into a 4-in (10-cm) round and cook, turning once, until lightly golden on both sides, about 3 minutes total. Transfer to a platter and place in the oven.
★ Serve the latkes on warmed individual plates. Place the applesauce, sour cream and cinnamon alongside, for guests to add as desired.

SERVES 6

East Texas

CORNMEAL PANCAKES WITH HERBAL IMPRESSIONS

The addition of cilantro, oregano or flat-leaf parsley to the cornmeal batter adds a little flair to these delicious cornmeal pancakes. Serve for brunch or as a light supper.

½ cup (2½ oz/75 g) yellow cornmeal
½ cup (4 fl oz/125 ml) boiling water
½ cup (2½ oz/75 g) all-purpose (plain) flour
½ teaspoon salt
1½ teaspoons sugar
1 tablespoon baking powder
1 egg, beaten
¼ cup (2 oz/60 g) butter, melted
¼ cup (2 fl oz/60 ml) milk
vegetable oil or butter for cooking
fresh flat-leaf (Italian) parsley, cilantro (fresh coriander) or oregano leaves
thinly sliced baked ham, sour cream, corn kernels and/or slivered green (spring) onions for topping

★ In a bowl, stir together the cornmeal and boiling water, blending well. Add the flour, salt, sugar, baking powder, egg, melted butter and milk and mix to form a thick batter.
★ Heat a griddle over medium to medium-high heat (or use a nonstick frying pan). Oil or butter the griddle lightly and ladle on about 2 tablespoons of the batter for each pancake. Gently press the parsley, cilantro or oregano leaves onto the batter in interesting patterns. Turn the pancakes when bubbles appear on the tops of the cakes, 1–2 minutes. Cook until lightly browned on the second side, 1½–2 minutes longer.
★ Place the pancakes on warmed individual plates and top with the ham, dollops of sour cream, a scattering of corn kernels and/or a few green onions. Serve immediately.

SERVES 4

Austin

SPINACH-FILLED CORN CRÊPES WITH ROASTED RED BELL PEPPER SALSA

Chef Terry Conlan has an enormous talent for combining good health and good eating. This is just such an example from his book, Lean Star Cuisine. *A Sauvignon Blanc will complement the spinach-mushroom filling.*

FOR THE RED BELL PEPPER SALSA:

2 tomatoes
1 small white onion, thickly sliced
1 fresh serrano chili pepper, halved and seeded (see glossary)
1 large red bell pepper (capsicum), halved and seeded
3 cloves garlic, cut up
2 tablespoons fresh cilantro (fresh coriander) leaves
juice of ½ lime
1 teaspoon ground cumin

FOR THE CRÊPES:

1 egg
1–1⅓ cups (8–11 fl oz/250–330 ml) nonfat milk
¼ cup (1¼ oz/37 g) all-purpose (plain) flour
¼ cup (1¼ oz/37 g) stone-ground yellow cornmeal
½ cup (2½ oz/75 g) *masa harina* (see glossary)
vegetable nonstick cooking spray

FOR THE FILLING:

½ teaspoon olive oil
1 cup (3 oz/90 g) sliced fresh mushrooms
¾ lb (375 g) spinach, stems removed and carefully washed
vegetable nonstick cooking spray
2 tablespoons shredded low-fat Cheddar cheese
2 tablespoons freshly grated Parmesan cheese

★ To make the salsa, preheat a broiler (griller). Place the tomatoes, onion slices, chili halves and bell pepper halves on a baking sheet and slip under the broiler. Broil (grill) until blackened and blistered, turning as needed. The timing will depend upon distance from heat source. Remove from the broiler and slip the bell and chili pepper halves in a paper bag or covered bowl and let stand until cool enough to handle. Then, using your fingertips and/or a small knife, peel off the skins.
★ Place the bell and chili peppers, tomatoes and onions in a food processor fitted with the metal blade or in a blender. Add the garlic, cilantro, lime juice and cumin and process until smooth. Set aside.
★ To make the crêpes, in a bowl, whisk the egg until blended and then whisk in 1 cup (8 fl oz/250 ml) of the milk until well mixed. Stir in the flour, cornmeal and *masa harina* until smooth. Whisk in additional milk until the batter is the consistency of thick cream.
★ Spray a small (8-in/20-cm) nonstick crêpe pan or frying pan with vegetable spray and warm over medium heat. Ladle in just enough batter to cover the bottom, about ¼ cup (2 fl oz/60 ml). Tilt and swirl the pan to spread the batter evenly. Cook until the surface looks dry, 1–2 minutes. Lift up one edge and carefully flip the crêpe over. Cook until lightly colored on the second side, about 30 seconds longer. Transfer to a flat surface and repeat with the remaining batter until all the batter has been used. You should have 8 crêpes in all.
★ To make the filling, in a large frying pan over medium heat, warm the olive oil. Add the mushrooms and sauté until golden, 2–3 minutes. Add the spinach, spray lightly with vegetable spray and sauté until wilted, 1–2 minutes longer. Transfer to a bowl and add the Cheddar and Parmesan cheeses. Mix well.
★ Spoon an equal amount of the spinach-mushroom mixture onto the center of each crêpe and roll up the crêpe. Place 2 crêpes, seam side down, on each of 4 individual plates. Spoon the salsa evenly over the tops and serve immediately.

SERVES 4

Spinach-Filled Corn Crêpes with Roasted Red Bell Pepper Salsa

HILL COUNTRY

HILL COUNTRY

Austin, the state capital and the most important city in the Texas Hill Country, is a place where people enjoy good food, and chefs from the many first-rate restaurants there are among the most innovative in the state. There are also new places opening all the time, nearly every one of them warranting a visit.

Austin, too, is home to the prestigious April Texas Hill Country Wine & Food Festival, where Austin's and San Antonio's finest chefs and wine makers show off their talents, and international culinary and wine stars come to exchange ideas with the best from Texas. Many events are sold out as soon as the schedule is published, for everyone is anxious to see what local chefs are doing, from the celebrated Janet Chaykin, who may be preparing her wonderful ancho cocoa crêpe with roast pork, mango and ginger salsa, to talented Jay McCarthy, who might whip up a sugar-cured beef tenderloin or a tempting cactus sauce.

Perhaps the most picturesque town in the Hill Country is Fredericksburg, the center of the peach industry and home to Oberhellmann's Bell Mountain Winery, an outpost of German-style wines. The German settlers claimed Fredericksburg as their second home in the 1800s, and today writers, artists and high-powered executives choose to live and work in the quaintly beautiful area. Nearby are Marble Falls, Johnson City and Horseshoe Bay, all of them worth a visit.

Previous pages: The classic barns and rolling pastures of the Hill Country evoke a timeless image of rural America. Left: The vaqueros, who drove the cattle that the Spanish brought to the New World in the 1500s, were the predecessors of the Texas cowboy.

To the south is Bandera, known as the Cowboy Capital of the World. It has many dude ranches and retreats that offer early Texas trails–type cooking over a campfire, turned out from a modern-day chuck wagon.

The Guadalupe River Ranch, a popular family and corporate retreat located in New Braunfels, is famous for gourmet cuisine prepared from organic produce grown in its many gardens and for its sausages and condiments. The restored lodge, built in 1929 and once the home of Olivia de Havilland, overlooks miles of the river. Wimberley is the location of several orchards, including Burnett Orchards, where apples and peaches are raised. Known for apple butters, peach jams and fruit toppings, this orchard is ideal for people who want to pick their own fruit. The trees are less than fifteen feet (four and one-half meters) tall, and the different varieties ripen over a period of several months.

About thirty miles (fifty kilometers) north of New Braunfels stands a town with the quaint, musical name of Dripping Springs. There you will find New Canaan Farms, whose line of products marries a variety of fresh ingredients into such tempting combinations as strawberry-almond jam; peach, amaretto and pecan jam; jalapeño jelly; and German and Polish mustards. Nearby, the Jardine Ranch, home of internationally acclaimed Jardine's Texas Foods, is known for a wide selection of genuine Texas specialty products. Begun in a home kitchen in 1979, the operation makes more than one hundred products that are in demand across the United States and in Canada, Europe and Japan. At Larsen Farms, a dozen varieties of delectable goat cheese are made, flavored with everything from pesto to peppers. Blanco, Comfort and Boerne, which all host local festivals, are home to a variety of small businesses that specialize in jams, jellies, salsas and condiments or grow outstanding herbs.

Tow is the site of Fall Creek Vineyards, one of the state's best-known wineries. Its vintages have been served at the tables of United States presidents and Texas governors and have won many medals in wine competitions.

The Lost Maples State Natural Area recalls a time when central Texas was less arid and covered with forests of maple trees.

Eleven premium wines are currently available under the Fall Creek label. Other award-winning Hill Country wineries include Sister Creek Vineyards, Slaughter Leftwich Vineyards, Grape Creek Vineyard, Stonewall Vineyard, Pedernales Vineyards and Hill Country Cellars.

Slaughter Leftwich planted the first Chardonnay vines in the state in 1982, and in 1984 the Chardonnay won a double gold medal at the San Francisco Fair. The 1988 and 1990 vintages took all the top awards in the *Dallas Morning News* World Wine Festival Competition, the only major wine competition in the Southwest open to wines produced throughout the world. The oldest winery in the state is Val Verde Winery, which is more than one hundred years old and is still run by the founding family.

The Y.O. Ranch, located in the heart of the Texas Hill Country about seventy miles (over one hundred kilometers) northwest of San Antonio, has been identified with the longhorn cattle industry since 1880, and is famous for its innovative ranching of exotic breeds and for its land management. Y.O. Ranch founder, Captain Charles Schreiner, was a Texas Ranger, a Confederate soldier, an entrepreneur and a born cattleman; it was his foresightedness that saved the nearly vanished longhorns.

In addition, the Schreiners pioneered exotic wildlife ranching. Black buck antelope and axis and silka deer from India and Africa romp with Texas whitetails and fallow deer, and crafty aoudad and mouflon sheep occupy the rocky crevices. Longhorns look over their shoulders at these exotic breeds and continue foraging the vast forty thousand acres (sixteen thousand hectares), undisturbed by them or the zebras and giraffes that regularly lope by. Other area ranches also boast herds of exotics: llamas, ostriches and emus are familiar sights in the fields.

The famous Y.O. Ranch, founded in 1880, maintains the largest herd of registered longhorn in the country.

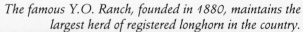

The State Capitol Building in Austin was completed in 1881 and, to the delight of Texans, was seven feet taller than the nation's capitol.

The occasional giraffe looks at home, for the land, which is similar to the African savannah grasslands, supports a variety of imported animals. The introduction of these beautiful animals to the Hill Country was an experiment to save them from near extinction. The program has been so successful that the ranchers are now exporting the animals to their native lands and assisting animal management programs to repopulate their diminished herds.

The ranch land in this part of the state is primarily scrub oak and juniper draws, with rolling hills of limestone and prickly pear flats. Much of the land, scruffy and aridly scrubby most of the year, is surprisingly beautiful in early spring, when the fruit trees are laden with blossoms and a sea of bluebonnets blankets the ground. The vista gradually changes, from cerulean and cobalt blue to myriad shades of yellow, orange and gold, to pink and white. Each spring, various wildflowers and emerald green grass offer an unequaled panorama of nature's splendid attire, and inviting streams and rivers sparkle in the sunshine. Even highways boast this colorful drama, thanks to Lady Bird Johnson, who has inspired countless volunteers and government agencies to join her in offering travelers views of the Lone Star State's many wildflowers.

SWEET CELEBRATIONS

Fruit often complements Texas desserts such as torte and sponge cake.

SWEET CELEBRATIONS

*K*uchen und nachspeirsen, *torte,* lebkuchen and similar desserts are an important part of the legacy handed down to Texans from their German, Alsatian and Czech ancestors. The Hill Country and Castroville are especially known for these delicious treats. A French influence is found throughout the state, however. La Madeleine is known for delicious French tarts and pastries that are the talk of Dallas, Austin and San Antonio. Austin's master baker, Alain Braux, and San Antonio's Swiss-born François Maeder turn out delectable continental confections that are the high point of any sweet celebration.

Mexican-inspired *sopaipillas,* flan, *buñuelos* and *bizcochitos,* a Christmas treat traditional in Hispanic families, are as popular as mom's apple pie—and some of the best apple pies you will ever find are made by Texas moms. Pralines (pronounced *praw-lene* if you are from the Deep South and *pray-lene* if you are from anyplace else), the ultimate melt-in-your-mouth taste sensation, are found in tiny cafes, at candy stands, at ball games, at roadside fairs and in fancy restaurants. Cajun cooks claim these as their own, as do Mexican cooks, and both groups will whip up a batch at the drop of the first fall harvest of the native pecans.

In the early days of the state, serving spirits of any kind was discouraged, but cooks soon overcame that obstacle and created some of the most delicious cakes and trifles imaginable—all with rum- or brandy-soaked raisins or other fruits. Mary Todd Lincoln's election cake, amply dotted with brandied raisins, was popular, as was sponge cake drenched in rum, slathered with mountains of rich whipped cream and topped with fresh berries. Fruitcakes always needed liquids to moisten them, and the most logical choice was a potent mixture designed to bring a glint to the eye. It is little wonder that fruitcake was so popular with our forebears and is still big business in the 1990s. Beverages such

Texans find creative ways to express their strong sense of regional pride.

Previous pages, left to right: Orange Sunburst with Orange Flower Water (recipe page 208), Papaya Bisque with Tequila-Pepper Ice (recipe page 208), Mango Cream with Mint Chocolate Leaves (recipe page 229)

206

Above: Local children enjoy plenty of refreshing summer fun at a watermelon festival in Austin. Left: Succulent peaches fill Hill Country markets during the summer.

as Roman punch were also popular. Comprised of lemon sherbet, rum and Champagne, this drink looked harmless but was as lethal as the rich, spiked eggnog popular at Christmas and New Year's.

Southern cooking traditions have endured in the state to this day in the form of pecan, apple, peach and buttermilk pies, bread pudding (again with a stiff bourbon, rum or brandy sauce) and fudge. Chocolate and coconut cakes and flambéed bananas Foster made from fruit shipped from Mexico and points south were found on the tables of aristocrats in the late 1800s. It was little wonder that desserts made from dozens of eggs and rich cream and butter were served generously, for farms produced these basic ingredients in great numbers even then. Mile-high meringues and deep-dish berry cobblers were the essence of indulgence in the hard-fought days of conquering the land, and today they are a just reward for working out and keeping fit.

Little change is taking place in Texas desserts other than to reduce portion sizes or to include two or three "sensible"

selections that feature fruit and a cookie or a sliver of torte or sponge cake. Small portions are displayed artfully and presented with panache on dessert carts, and fresh seasonal fruits, such as picture-perfect strawberries, are showcased. Specialty coffees have grown in popularity over the past few years and are predicted to remain strong, as they provide just the right note to end a meal.

The use of cinnamon and chocolate, found in many Mexican recipes as well as southern dishes, can be traced to precolonial days, when Montezuma and the Aztecs reigned supreme south of the Rio Grande. Early French explorers took chocolate back to France, where its popularity swept the nation. It was soon found in beautiful porcelain pots on the table of every upper-class household. The French added milk and sugar to the bitter concoction, which then was reintroduced to the Americas as the hot, comforting drink we know today.

The desserts included in this book are simple, and most are healthful. Whenever there appear to be too many calories, be assured that the sweet is well worth the indulgence. Texans enjoy adding a festive note to even the simplest desserts. They serve them on interesting handmade pottery or beautiful antique china on tea tables draped in organdy, or pack them in a basket and set a bountiful array of sweets on a blanket spread under a shade tree.

There is something about eating just the right dessert that makes people feel contented and happy, and Texans know that choosing the perfect dessert to serve is another way to show off the state's reputation for first-class hospitality.

E a s t   T e x a s

PECAN PIE

Serve this traditional Texas pie with a scoop of vanilla ice cream and a glass of ice-cold lemonade with violets frozen in the ice cubes.

unbaked 9-in (23-cm) pie shell (recipe pages 214–215)
3 eggs
2 tablespoons sugar
2 tablespoons all-purpose (plain) flour
2 cups (16 fl oz/500 ml) dark corn syrup
1 teaspoon vanilla extract (essence)
¼ teaspoon salt
1½ cups (6 oz/185 g) pecans
1 teaspoon butter, melted

★ Prepare the pie shell and set aside. Preheat an oven to 425°F (220°C).
★ In a bowl, using an electric mixer or a spoon, beat the eggs until light. In a small cup, stir together the sugar and flour and add to the eggs, beating to mix well. Add the corn syrup, vanilla, salt and pecans and stir until well mixed. Stir in the melted butter. Pour the mixture into the pie shell.
★ Bake for 10 minutes. Reduce the oven temperature to 325°F (165°C) and bake until the filling is set in the center and the crust is golden, about 45 minutes longer.
★ Transfer to a rack and let cool completely before serving.

SERVES 6–8

M e d i n a

APPLE-PECAN PIE

Farmers in the small community of Medina are particularly famous for their dwarf apple trees that produce varieties of full-sized fruits, from Crispin to Jonagold. In this recipe, the apple tree and the Texas state tree, the pecan, contribute to a true Texas dessert.

unbaked 9-in (23-cm) pie shell (recipe pages 214–215)

FOR THE CRUMB TOPPING:

¼ cup (2 oz/60 g) butter, chilled
⅓ cup (2 oz/60 g) all-purpose (plain) flour
½ cup (3 oz/90 g) lightly packed brown sugar
¼ cup (1 oz/30 g) pecans, chopped

FOR THE FILLING:

6 cups (1½ lb/750 g) sliced, peeled tart apples
¾ cup (6 oz/185 g) sugar
1 tablespoon all-purpose (plain) flour
½ teaspoon ground cinnamon
¼ teaspoon ground nutmeg
⅓ cup (1½ oz/45 g) pecans, chopped
2 tablespoons butter or margarine, cut into bits

★ Prepare the pie shell and set aside. Preheat an oven to 425°F (220°C).
★ To make the crumb topping, in a bowl, combine the butter, flour and brown sugar. Using a fork or a pastry blender, mix until crumbly. Stir in the pecans. Set aside.
★ To make the filling, in a large bowl, toss together the apples, granulated sugar, flour, cinnamon and nutmeg until well mixed. Spread the pecans evenly in the bottom of the pie shell. Spoon the apple mixture into the shell and dot the top with the butter or margarine. Cover evenly with the crumb topping.
★ Bake for 10 minutes. Reduce the oven temperature to 325°F (165°C) and bake until the filling is bubbly hot and the topping is golden brown, about 45 minutes longer. Remove to a rack and serve warm or at room temperature.

SERVES 6–8

R i o   G r a n d e   V a l l e y

ORANGE SUNBURST WITH ORANGE FLOWER WATER

The town of Mission in the Rio Grande Valley was founded by Oblate Fathers, who constructed a mission there in 1824. They are also credited with being the first to plant citrus in this region. This dessert allows the flavor of the orange to shine. The secret ingredient is orange flower water, which can be found in the specialty-food aisles of well-stocked markets or in health-food stores.

6 navel oranges
1½ teaspoons orange flower water
2 tablespoons confectioners' (icing) sugar
1 teaspoon ground cinnamon
fresh mint sprigs for garnish

★ Peel and thinly slice the oranges. Arrange in concentric circles on a large, round serving platter. Sprinkle with the orange flower water, confectioners' sugar and cinnamon. Cover and chill thoroughly before serving.
★ To serve, garnish with mint sprigs.

SERVES 4–6   *Photograph pages 204–205*

S o u t h   T e x a s

PAPAYA BISQUE WITH TEQUILA-PEPPER ICE

The contemporary Texan may order barbecue and beer for dinner and top it off with a dessert such as this.

FOR THE TEQUILA-PEPPER ICE:

2 cups (16 fl oz/500 ml) water
½ cup (4 fl oz/125 ml) gold tequila
juice of 4 limes
juice of 2 lemons
¾ cup (6 oz/185 g) sugar
1 teaspoon minced, seeded fresh serrano chili pepper
  (see glossary)

FOR THE PAPAYA BISQUE:

4 papayas, halved, seeded and peeled
3 cups (24 fl oz/750 ml) peach nectar
¾ cup (9 oz/280 g) honey, or to taste
3 tablespoons Triple Sec
3 tablespoons undiluted apple juice concentrate
½ cup (4 fl oz/125 ml) heavy (double) cream

★ To make the tequila-pepper ice, in a bowl, stir together all the ingredients until the sugar dissolves. Transfer to a shallow metal pan and place in the freezer until firm, 6–8 hours.
★ Break the ice into large pieces and place in a food processor fitted with the metal blade. Process until smooth. Return the mixture to the pan and refreeze until frozen solid.
★ To make the papaya bisque, in a food processor fitted with the metal blade or in a blender, combine the papayas and peach nectar and process until smooth. Add the honey, Triple Sec, apple juice concentrate and cream and process just until combined. Pour into a bowl, cover and refrigerate until well chilled, about 1½ hours.
★ To serve, taste the bisque and adjust with honey. Divide the bisque among 6–8 individual bowls and spoon the tequila-pepper ice in a mound in the center. Serve at once.

SERVES 6–8   *Photograph pages 204–205*

Top to bottom: Pecan Pie, Apple-Pecan Pie

South Texas

CRANBERRY-JALAPEÑO– TOPPED VANILLA ICE CREAM

East Texas and the Texas Hill Country provide an abundance of fresh blackberries in season. And here is a wonderful South Texas–inspired recipe to showcase these succulent fruits. The cranberry-jalapeño sauce adds sweet, sour and hot accents. If you are short of time, stir together equal amounts of cranberry sauce and pepper jelly for the cranberry-jalapeño jelly. For a true Texas presentation, serve the ice cream in crisp flour tortilla cups.

⅔ cup (6 oz/185 g) cranberry-jalapeño jelly (see glossary)
½ cup (5 oz/155 g) blackberry jam
cayenne pepper
zest and juice of ½ lemon
4½ teaspoons brandy
1–1½ qt (1–1½ l) vanilla ice cream
pesticide-free small peppermint geranium sprigs, black-
    berries and raspberries for garnish

★ In a small saucepan over low heat, combine the cranberry-jalapeño jelly, blackberry jam, cayenne pepper to taste, lemon zest and juice and brandy. Heat, stirring, until smooth.
★ Place scoops of ice cream in chilled parfait dishes and spoon about 2 tablespoons of the warm sauce over each serving. Garnish with geranium sprigs and berries and serve at once.

SERVES 8

*Top to bottom: Cranberry-Jalapeño–Topped Vanilla
Ice Cream, Peanut Brittle*

Del Rio

PEANUT BRITTLE

Peanuts, found growing in the central, northern and eastern areas of the state, are used in everything, from brownies to main dishes, but just about everybody's favorite is peanut brittle. The addition of pure ground red chili gives this brittle star status. To grind your own, toast dried ancho or pasilla chilies (see glossary) in a 300°F (150°C) oven until the skin is lightly crisped; do not allow to burn. Let cool, then remove the stems, seeds and ribs. Break into pieces and pulverize in a blender or a spice grinder. Store in the freezer.

1 cup (8 oz/250 g) sugar
½ cup (4 fl oz/125 ml) light corn syrup
1 cup (6 oz/185 g) salted, roasted peanuts
1½ teaspoons butter or margarine
1 tablespoon pure ground red chili, or to taste (see note)
1 teaspoon baking soda (bicarbonate of soda)

★ Butter a baking sheet and set aside.
★ To make the brittle in a microwave oven, in a 2½- to 3-qt (2½- to 3-l) microwave-safe dish, stir together the sugar and corn syrup. Microwave on high for 2 minutes. Stir and then microwave on high for 2 minutes longer. Stir in the peanuts and microwave on high, stirring every 1½ minutes, until the mixture is pale golden brown, 3–5 minutes.
★ Add the butter or margarine and ground chili and stir well. Microwave on high until the mixture is bubbly hot and fluid, 1–2 minutes longer. Stir in the baking soda and immediately pour onto the prepared baking sheet, spreading the caramel mixture about ⅛ in (3 mm) thick. Let cool until hardened, 20–30 minutes.
★ To make the brittle on the stove top, in a large, heavy saucepan over medium-high heat, stir together the sugar and corn syrup until the sugar dissolves and the mixture is bubbly. Stir in the peanuts and heat, stirring, until pale golden brown. Add the butter or margarine and ground chili and cook for 2–3 minutes longer. Stir in the baking soda, immediately pour onto the prepared baking sheet and proceed as directed.
★ Break the peanut brittle into pieces and store in an airtight container at room temperature or in the refrigerator for up to 1 month.

MAKES ABOUT 1 LB (500 G)

Rio Grande Valley

TEXAS RED GRAPEFRUIT– CHAMPAGNE SORBET WITH TORTILLA CINNAMON CRISPS

The Rio Grande Valley is famous for its bright red grapefruits. If you cannot find red grapefruits for making this sorbet, pink ones can be substituted. The crisp tortilla triangles sprinkled with a spicy cinnamon-and-clove-scented sugar are a delicious accompaniment.

5 cups (40 fl oz/1.1 l) Texas red grapefruit juice (about 6
    grapefruits)
1¼ cups (10 oz/315 g) sugar
¼ cup (2 fl oz/60 ml) light corn syrup
1 tablespoon grated grapefruit zest
¾ cup (6 fl oz/180 ml) Champagne or regular or pink
    sparkling wine

Top to bottom: Blackberry Cassis Sorbet with Rosemary Cookies (recipe page 212), Texas Red Grapefruit–Champagne Sorbet with Tortilla Cinnamon Crisps

FOR THE TORTILLA CINNAMON CRISPS:

4 flour tortillas
vegetable oil for deep-frying
¼ cup (2 oz/60 g) sugar
1 tablespoon ground cinnamon
1 teaspoon ground cloves

candied citrus peel

★ In a saucepan over medium heat, combine the grapefruit juice, sugar, corn syrup and grapefruit zest. Heat, stirring, until the sugar dissolves. Strain through a fine-mesh sieve into a bowl, then stir in the Champagne or sparkling wine. Cover and chill well.

★ To make the crisps, cut each tortilla into 8 triangles. In a deep frying pan over high heat, pour in oil to a depth of 1 in (2.5 cm). Heat to 360°F (182°C), or until bubbles form around a wooden skewer inserted into the oil. Working in batches, add the triangles to the hot oil and fry, turning once, until crisp and golden, 2–3 minutes total. Using a slotted spoon, transfer to paper towels to drain.

★ In a bowl, stir together the sugar, cinnamon and cloves and sprinkle over the triangles while they are still warm.

★ Transfer the chilled grapefruit juice mixture to an ice cream maker and freeze according to manufacturer's instructions. Scoop the sorbet into small chilled bowls. Garnish with candied citrus peel and the tortilla crisps.

SERVES 8–10

BLACKBERRY CASSIS SORBET WITH ROSEMARY COOKIES

Wild blackberries are found in the Texas Hill Country, as well as in the eastern and central parts of the state. They have a sweet yet tart flavor that is appreciated by those willing to brave the brambles. This vibrant purple sorbet partnered with rosemary cookies is a perfect ending to a spicy meal.

FOR THE ROSEMARY COOKIES:

1 cup (5 oz/155 g) all-purpose (plain) flour
½ cup (4 oz/125 g) unsalted butter or margarine, at room
    temperature
½ cup (4 oz/125 g) granulated sugar
1 egg yolk, beaten
½ teaspoon vanilla extract (essence)
2 tablespoons fresh rosemary or lemon thyme leaves, chopped
1¾ teaspoons grated lemon zest
pinch of salt
confectioners' (icing) sugar for sprinkling

FOR THE SORBET:

1 lb (500 g) blackberries
6 tablespoons (3 fl oz/90 ml) plus 1¼ cups (10 fl oz/310 ml)
    water
¾ cup (6 oz/185 g) sugar
2 teaspoons fresh lime or lemon juice

crème de cassis or blackberry-flavored liqueur
pesticide-free lavender flowers and fresh rosemary sprigs
    for garnish

★ To make the cookies, in a bowl, combine the flour and butter. Using a pastry blender or 2 knives, cut in the butter until the mixture resembles coarse crumbs. Add the sugar, mixing well with a fork. Add the egg yolk, vanilla, rosemary or lemon thyme, lemon zest and salt and stir until the mixture comes together to form a dough. Gather into a ball and divide into 2 equal portions. On a lightly floured work surface, using your palms, roll each portion into a log about 2 in (5 cm) in diameter. Wrap each log in waxed paper and refrigerate for 2–3 hours.
★ Preheat an oven to 350°F (180°C).
★ Cut each log crosswise into slices ¼ in (6 mm) thick and arrange 2 in (5 cm) apart on 2 ungreased baking sheets. Sprinkle with confectioners' sugar. Bake until light brown around the edges, about 10 minutes. Transfer to a rack to cool.
★ To make the sorbet, in a saucepan over medium-high heat, combine the blackberries and the 6 tablespoons water. Cover and simmer until quite soft, about 10 minutes. Uncover and raise the heat to high. Cook until the mixture thickens, 6–8 minutes. Place in a blender or in a food processor fitted with a metal blade and purée until smooth. Pass the purée through a fine-mesh sieve into a large measuring cup.
★ In a saucepan over high heat, combine the sugar and the 1¼ cups (10 fl oz/310 ml) water. Bring to a boil, stirring to dissolve the sugar. Boil until syrupy, about 10 minutes. Remove from the heat and let cool slightly, then stir in the lime or lemon juice. Add the syrup to the blackberries. Add enough water to the mixture to measure 3 cups (24 fl oz/750 ml) total.
★ Pour into a shallow metal pan and freeze until firm, about 3 hours. Remove and process in the blender or food processor until smooth. Refreeze and repeat until the desired consistency is achieved, usually 2 or 3 times.
★ To serve, spoon the sorbet into chilled wineglasses and drizzle with crème de cassis or blackberry liqueur. Top with lavender flowers. Arrange the cookies in a napkin-lined basket and tuck in a few rosemary sprigs. Serve at once. Store any leftover cookies in an airtight container at room temperature for up to 1 week.

SERVES 6   *Photograph page 211*

SHORTCAKES WITH MIXED BERRIES AND WHITE CHOCOLATE CREAM

There is something very genteel and southern about this delectable dessert. Garnish with crystallized rose petals or violets, if available. Serve with a good Riesling.

FOR THE SHORTCAKES:

1½ cups (7½ oz/235 g) all-purpose (plain) flour
1 cup (4 oz/125 g) sweetened shredded coconut
2 teaspoons baking powder
¼ teaspoon salt
1 cup (8 oz/250 g) sugar
¼ cup (2 oz/60 g) unsalted butter, at room temperature
2 eggs
1 teaspoon vanilla extract (essence)
½ cup (4 fl oz/125 ml) heavy (double) cream

FOR THE PEACH SAUCE:

3 cups (24 fl oz/750 ml) peach nectar
¼ cup (2 oz/60 g) sugar
1 teaspoon vanilla extract (essence)
¼ cup (2 oz/60 g) unsalted butter, at room temperature, cut
    into pieces

FOR THE CHOCOLATE CREAM:

6 oz (185 g) white chocolate
1 cup (8 fl oz/250 ml) heavy (double) cream, chilled

blueberries, blackberries, strawberries, freestone peach
    slices and toasted almond slices (flakes) for garnish

★ Preheat an oven to 325°F (165°C). Butter and flour a 9-in (23-cm) cake pan.
★ To make the shortcakes, in a food processor fitted with the metal blade, combine the flour, coconut, baking powder and salt. Use on-off pulses (about 12) to make coconut flour. In a mixing bowl, using an electric mixer, beat together the sugar and butter until smooth and fluffy. Beat in the eggs and vanilla until blended. Stir in the coconut flour alternately with the cream, in 3 additions each.
★ Spoon the batter into the prepared pan. Bake until a wooden toothpick inserted into the center comes out clean, 45–50 minutes. Remove to a rack and let cool in the pan for 10 minutes. Then invert onto the rack and let cool completely.
★ To make the peach sauce, in a saucepan over high heat, combine the peach nectar, sugar and vanilla, stirring to dissolve the sugar. Simmer until reduced to 1½ cups (12 fl oz/375 ml), 25–35 minutes. Whisk in the butter and remove from the heat. Let cool. (This may be prepared in advance and maintained at room temperature for up to 4 hours.)
★ To make the chocolate cream, in the top pan of a double boiler (or in a heatproof bowl) over gently simmering water, melt the white chocolate with ¼ cup (2 fl oz/65 ml) of the cream, stirring until smooth. Let cool to room temperature. In a chilled bowl, whip the remaining ¾ cup (6 fl oz/185 ml) cream until stiff peaks form. Using a rubber spatula, fold the chocolate mixture into the whipped cream, a little at a time. Cover and chill until firm.
★ Cut the cooled cake into 6 equal wedges. Spoon the peach sauce onto 6 dessert plates, dividing it evenly. Top with the cake wedges. Place a dollop of chocolate cream on each serving, then garnish with the berries, peach slices and almonds. Serve at once.

SERVES 6

Shortcakes with Mixed Berries and White
Chocolate Cream

J o h n s o n   C i t y

PEDERNALES PUMPKIN, GINGER AND PEACH ROULADE

Based on a recipe from one of the quaint bed-and-breakfasts in Johnson City, this lovely autumn treat combines pumpkin, spices, candied ginger and peaches. Decorate the serving plate with such seasonal items as acorns, pecans and autumn leaves. This is best served the same day it is made.

FOR THE CAKE:

3 eggs
1 cup (8 oz/250 g) granulated sugar
⅔ cup (5 oz/155 g) pumpkin purée
1 teaspoon fresh lemon juice
¾ cup (4 oz/125 g) all-purpose (plain) flour
2 teaspoons ground cinnamon
1 teaspoon baking powder
1 teaspoon ground ginger
½ teaspoon salt
½ teaspoon ground nutmeg
1 cup (4 oz/125 g) finely minced pecans
sifted confectioners' (icing) sugar

FOR THE FILLING:

1 cup (4 oz/125 g) confectioners' (icing) sugar
6 oz (185 g) cream cheese, at room temperature
¼ cup (2 oz/60 g) butter or margarine, at room
    temperature
zest of 1 small orange
3 tablespoons candied ginger, minced
3 tablespoons orange-flavored liqueur or amaretto

½ cup (5 oz/155 g) peach preserves
sifted confectioners' (icing) sugar
yellow chrysanthemums, autumn leaves, acorns and pecan
    halves for decoration

★ Preheat an oven to 375°F (190°C). Line a standard jelly-roll (Swiss-roll) pan with parchment (baking) or waxed paper and butter the paper.
★ To make the cake, in a large mixing bowl, using an electric mixer set on high speed, beat the eggs until light and fluffy, about 5 minutes. Gradually beat in the sugar until thoroughly blended. Stir in the pumpkin purée and lemon juice.
★ In a small bowl, stir together the flour, cinnamon, baking powder, ginger, salt and nutmeg. Fold the flour mixture into the pumpkin mixture until well blended. Spread the batter evenly in the prepared pan. Sprinkle the top with the pecans.
★ Bake until just firm in the center and a wooden toothpick inserted into the center comes out clean, about 15 minutes. Remove from the oven and immediately invert the cake onto a clean tea towel that has been sprinkled with confectioners' sugar. Peel off the paper. Starting from a long side, fold one edge up about 2 in (5 cm). Continue to roll up the cake in the towel, with the towel between the layers. Let stand until cool.
★ To make the filling, in a bowl, combine all the ingredients, beating until smooth.
★ Unroll the cake so that it lays flat. Spread evenly with the filling and then spread the peach preserves over the top. Reroll the cake, cover it tightly and chill for 4–6 hours.
★ Just before serving, uncover the cake, transfer it to a platter and sprinkle with confectioners' sugar. Surround with the chrysanthemums, leaves, acorns and pecans. To serve, cut into slices ¾ in (2 cm) thick.

SERVES 10–12

E a s t   T e x a s

VINEGAR PIE WITH GOLDEN RAISINS AND NUTS

My mother recalled my grandmother baking vinegar pie when fresh fruit was unavailable, a reflection of pioneer frugality. Enjoy an updated version of this deliciously addicting pie.

FOR THE PIE SHELL:

1½ cups (7½ oz/235 g) unbleached all-purpose (plain) flour
¾ teaspoon salt
½ cup (4 oz/125 g) vegetable shortening or unsalted butter
3 tablespoons ice water

FOR THE FILLING:

½ cup (4 oz/125 g) butter, melted and cooled

Clockwise from top left: Brazos Berry Cobbler (recipe page 217), Pedernales Pumpkin, Ginger and Peach Roulade, Five-Spice Gingerbread with Lemon Curd (recipe page 218), Vinegar Pie with Golden Raisins and Nuts

1½ cups (12 oz/375 g) sugar
2 tablespoons all-purpose (plain) flour
1½ teaspoons vanilla extract (essence), or to taste
3 tablespoons cider vinegar
3 eggs
⅓ cup (2 oz/60 g) golden raisins (sultanas)
⅓ cup (1½ oz/45 g) chopped pecans or sweetened
    shredded coconut

★ To make the pie shell, place all the ingredients in the refrigerator to chill for 1 hour. Then, in a bowl, stir together the flour and salt. Add the shortening or butter and, using a pastry blender or 2 knives, cut in until the mixture resembles small peas. Slowly add the ice water, 1 tablespoon at a time, stirring and tossing with a fork until the dough is evenly moistened and comes together. Gently pat the dough into a ball and flatten slightly into a disk.

★ On a lightly floured work surface, roll out the dough into a round 11 in (28 cm) in diameter and ⅛ in (3 mm) thick. Drape the dough round over the rolling pin and carefully transfer it to a 9-in (23-cm) pie plate. Gently press the round into the bottom and sides of the plate. Trim the overhang to about 1 in (2.5 cm) and fold the edges under. Flute the pastry with your fingers to form an attractive edge.
★ Preheat an oven to 300°F (150°C).
★ To make the filling, in a bowl, stir or whisk together the butter, sugar, flour, vanilla, vinegar and eggs until well mixed. Sprinkle the raisins and pecans or coconut evenly in the bottom of the pie shell. Carefully pour the vinegar mixture into the pie crust.
★ Bake until the crust is golden and the filling is just set in the center, 45–50 minutes. Transfer to a rack and let cool completely before serving.

SERVES 6–8

215

APPLE FRITTERS WITH CHOCOLATE-CARAMEL SAUCE

Texas Hill Country landowners, looking for ways to make their land more lucrative, have discovered apples. The area around Medina harvests more than 150,000 bushels of apples every year. This recipe for apple fritters dates back to 1930; it is updated with a chocolate-caramel sauce developed by San Antonio's premier French chef, Miguel Ardid.

FOR THE CHOCOLATE-CARAMEL SAUCE:

⅔ cup (3 oz/90 g) confectioners' (icing) sugar
⅓ cup (3 fl oz/80 ml) water
⅓ cup (3 fl oz/80 ml) chocolate-flavored liqueur

FOR THE FRITTERS:

1 cup (5 oz/155 g) all-purpose (plain) flour
1 teaspoon baking powder
1 teaspoon confectioners' (icing) sugar
¼ teaspoon salt
1 egg
¼ cup (2 fl oz/60 ml) milk
2 apples, unpeeled, cored and coarsely chopped
vegetable oil for deep-frying

moments of being dropped in the oil. Working in batches, drop the batter by heaping tablespoonfuls into the hot oil. Cook for about 1 minute. Turn the fritters over and cook until golden and tender when pierced, about 30 seconds longer. Using a slotted spoon, transfer to paper towels to drain briefly. Repeat with the remaining batter.

★ Arrange the hot fritters on a platter or individual plates and drizzle the warm chocolate-caramel sauce over the top. Serve immediately.

SERVES 4

Hill Country

BRAZOS BERRY COBBLER

This is an adaptation of a cobbler recipe that was judged the winner at the annual Medina Dutch Oven Cookoff. Prepared in a cast-iron dutch oven over a campfire, it is both romantic and rugged, and is a memorable treat from the past. Blackberries are found in the Hill Country, as well as in East Texas around Tyler. Or you can use dewberries, which grow wild in the eastern and central areas of the state, where they are gathered for home use and local sales in May and June.

FOR THE FILLING:

6 cups (1½ lb/750 g) blackberries
2½ cups (1¼ lb/625 g) sugar
2 cups (16 fl oz/500 ml) water
½ cup (2½ oz/75 g) all-purpose (plain) flour

FOR THE CRUST:

1½ cups (7½ oz/235 g) all-purpose (plain) flour
1½ teaspoons salt
⅔ cup (5 oz/155 g) vegetable shortening
1 egg yolk
2½ tablespoons water
1½ teaspoons distilled white vinegar

¼ cup (2 oz/60 g) butter, cut into bits

★ To make the filling, in a saucepan, combine the berries, sugar and 1 cup (8 fl oz/250 ml) of the water. Bring to a boil, then reduce the heat to low and cook, uncovered, until the berries are tender, 2–3 minutes. Remove from the heat. In a bowl, stir together the remaining 1 cup (8 fl oz/250 ml) water and the flour until well blended, then gradually stir into the berry mixture. Let cool to room temperature.

★ To make the crust, in a bowl, stir together the flour and salt. Add the shortening and, using a pastry blender or 2 knives, cut it in until the mixture resembles coarse meal. In another bowl, using a fork, whisk together the egg yolk, water and vinegar until well mixed. Stir the yolk mixture into the flour mixture until they come together into a dough. Transfer to a lightly floured work surface and knead lightly until smooth. Divide into 2 equal balls and flatten them slightly. (The dough can also be wrapped in plastic wrap and refrigerated for up to 24 hours or frozen for up to 3 months. Bring to room temperature before continuing.)

★ Preheat an oven to 350°F (180°C). Butter a shallow 3-qt (3-l) baking dish.

★ On a lightly floured work surface, roll out each ball into a round ⅛ in (3 mm) thick. Cut the pastry rounds into strips ¾ in (2 cm) wide.

★ Spoon the cooled filling into the prepared baking dish. Arrange the pastry strips in a lattice design over the top, pressing the ends firmly against the rim of the dish. Dot the top of the cobbler with the butter.

★ Bake until the pastry is lightly browned and the fruit filling is bubbly, about 1 hour. Serve hot, warm or chilled.

SERVES 6–8   *Photograph pages 214–215*

Apple Fritters with Chocolate-Caramel Sauce

★ To make the chocolate-caramel sauce, place the confectioners' sugar in a small saucepan. Cook over low heat, stirring, until the sugar caramelizes, 5–6 minutes. Carefully add the water and liqueur; do not add too quickly or it will splatter. Raise the heat to medium-high and continue cooking until the sauce thickens, about 5 minutes longer. Cover and keep warm over low heat (or reheat just before serving).

★ To make the fritters, in a bowl, stir together the flour, baking powder, confectioners' sugar and salt. In another bowl, whisk the egg until blended and then whisk in the milk. Add the egg mixture to the flour mixture, stirring until well combined. Fold in the chopped apples.

★ In a deep frying pan, pour in vegetable oil to a depth of 2½–3 in (6–7.5 cm). Heat to 360°F (182°C), or until a drop of the fritter batter sizzles and turns golden within

EMPANADITAS FILLED WITH MANGO AND CHEESE

Empanaditas are small pastry turnovers. They can be sweet or savory, and can be filled with pineapple, apricot, cinnamon-flavored applesauce, pumpkin purée sweetened with brown sugar, grated sweet chocolate, slivers of Monterey Jack cheese and green chilies, or refried beans (see glossary) and cheese. The fruit-filled version presented here is wonderful served with cinnamon-pecan ice cream (recipe page 229) or country vanilla and peach ice cream (recipe follows).

6 oz (185 g) cream cheese, at room temperature
1 cup (8 oz/250 g) butter, at room temperature
2 cups (10 oz/315 g) all-purpose (plain) flour

FOR THE FILLING:

1 large mango, pitted, peeled and thinly sliced
½ lb (250 g) *queso fresco* (see glossary) or cream cheese,
    at room temperature

★ In a bowl, using an electric mixer set on high, beat together the cream cheese and butter until light and fluffy. Reduce the speed to medium and gradually add the flour, beating until the mixture comes together in a rough mass. Form into a ball, wrap in plastic wrap and refrigerate for 1–2 hours or as long as overnight.
★ Preheat an oven to 375°F (190°C).
★ On a lightly floured work surface, roll out the dough ¼ in (6 mm) thick. Using a round cookie cutter about 3 in (7.5 cm) in diameter, cut out rounds. For the filling, place a piece of mango slice on one-half of a round and top with a small spoonful of the cheese. Dampen the edges of the round with water, fold over and seal by pressing around the edges with floured fork tines. Place on a baking sheet. Repeat with the remaining filling and dough rounds.
★ Bake until golden brown, 15–20 minutes. Serve warm or at room temperature.

MAKES ABOUT 36 PASTRIES

FIVE-SPICE GINGERBREAD WITH LEMON CURD

Warm gingerbread is delicious served with butter melting over the top and a dusting of sugar, or with sweetened whipped cream and a sprinkling of cinnamon. But you might also enjoy it, as my mother used to, with lemon curd. For an attractive garnish, tuck lemon thyme sprigs and blossoms and candied lemon curls on the dessert plates. As a variation, sprinkle the top of the gingerbread evenly with ½ cup (3 oz/90 g) raisins and ½ cup (2 oz/60 g) pecans before it goes into the oven.

FOR THE LEMON CURD:

2 lemons
1 cup (8 oz/250 g) sugar
dash of salt
3 eggs
½ cup (4 oz/125 g) butter, at room temperature, cut
    into pieces

FOR THE FIVE-SPICE GINGERBREAD:

2 cups (10 oz/315 g) all-purpose (plain) flour
1 cup (7 oz/220 g) firmly packed dark brown sugar
7 tablespoons (3½ oz/105 g) butter, at room temperature

¾ cup (6 fl oz/180 ml) water
¾ cup (6 fl oz/180 ml) dark molasses
3 eggs
1½ teaspoons baking soda (bicarbonate of soda)
1½ teaspoons ground cinnamon
2 teaspoons ground ginger
1½ teaspoons ground cloves
½ teaspoon ground nutmeg
½ teaspoon ground allspice
3 tablespoons finely chopped crystallized ginger (optional)

★ To make the lemon curd, using a vegetable peeler, remove the zest from the lemons in strips and place in a food processor fitted with the metal blade. Add the sugar and process until the zest is finely chopped. Juice the lemons and add the juice to the food processor, along with the salt, eggs and butter. Process until well combined. Pour the mixture into a small saucepan and place over medium heat. Cook, stirring constantly with a whisk, just until the mixture thickens and coats the back of a spoon, 5–7 minutes; do not allow to boil. Remove from the heat and let cool to room temperature. Cover and refrigerate until needed. You should have about 2 cups (16 fl oz/500 ml).
★ Preheat an oven to 325°F (165°C). Butter and flour a 9-in (23-cm) square baking pan.
★ To make the gingerbread, in a large bowl, combine all the ingredients. Using an electric mixer set on medium speed, beat until well mixed, 1–2 minutes, scraping the bowl often. Pour into the prepared pan.
★ Bake until a wooden toothpick inserted into the center comes out clean, 45–50 minutes. Transfer to a rack and let cool for 15 minutes in the pan.
★ To serve, cut into squares and serve warm with lemon curd spooned over the top. Store any remaining lemon curd in the refrigerator for up to 2 weeks.

SERVES 8–10   *Photograph pages 214–215*

COUNTRY VANILLA AND PEACH ICE CREAM WITH STRAWBERRY DAIQUIRI SAUCE

The Blue Bell Creamery in Brenham has been making ice cream since 1911, when it was packed in wooden tubs and delivered by horse-drawn wagons. Today, the creamery treats Texans to such fresh-fruit flavors as peach, strawberry and apple. Stonewall, whose main claim to fame is as the site of the LBJ ranch, is also known as the capital of the Texas peach industry. Farm-fresh fruit is sold at roadside stands throughout the area in summer.

FOR THE STRAWBERRY DAIQUIRI SAUCE:

5 cups (1¼ lb/625 g) strawberries, stems removed
2 teaspoons sugar
⅓ cup (3½ oz/105 g) strawberry preserves
¼ cup (2 fl oz/60 ml) light rum
2 tablespoons strawberry-flavored liqueur or brandy
4 teaspoons fresh lime juice

FOR THE ICE CREAM:

4 or 5 peaches
4 eggs
1¾ cups (14 oz/440 g) sugar
1 cup (8 fl oz/250 ml) milk
4 cups (32 fl oz/1 l) heavy (double) cream
1 teaspoon vanilla extract (essence)
½ teaspoon salt

Top to bottom: Country Vanilla and Peach Ice Cream with Strawberry Daiquiri Sauce, Empanaditas Filled with Mango and Cheese

★ To make the strawberry daiquiri sauce, in a bowl, toss the strawberries with the sugar. Let stand at room temperature for 1 hour. In a food processor fitted with the metal blade or in a blender, combine the strawberry mixture and the preserves and purée until smooth. Add the rum, liqueur or brandy and lime juice and stir to mix well. Cover and chill for 3 hours. (The sauce will keep in the refrigerator for 2–3 days.)

★ To make the ice cream, bring a saucepan three-fourths full of water to a boil. Drop the peaches into the boiling water for 20–30 seconds. Using a slotted spoon, transfer the peaches to a bowl of cold water and, when cool enough to handle, slip off the skins. Pit and coarsely chop. Set aside.

★ In a bowl, using an electric mixer, beat the eggs until blended. Gradually add the sugar, continuing to beat until the mixture is thickened and quite stiff, 5–6 minutes. Add the peaches, milk, cream, vanilla and salt, mixing thoroughly.

★ Pour into a 4-qt (4-l) ice cream freezer and freeze according to the manufacturer's instructions.

★ Spoon into bowls and pour the sauce over the top.

MAKES 3 QT (3 L) ICE CREAM, 5 CUPS (40 FL OZ/1.25 L) SAUCE

W e s t   T e x a s

SHEET CAKE WITH CHOCOLATE-CINNAMON FROSTING

No ranch-style barbecue or wild-game cookout is complete without this addicting chocolate-, coffee- and cinnamon-flavored cake. Every good Texas cook has a variation on this cake, but this is one of the most popular.

FOR THE SHEET CAKE:

½ cup (4 oz/125 g) butter or margarine
¼ cup (¾ oz/20 g) unsweetened cocoa powder
1 cup (8 fl oz/250 ml) water
2 cups (10 oz/315 g) all-purpose (plain) flour
2 cups (1 lb/500 g) sugar
½ cup (4 fl oz/125 ml) buttermilk
2 eggs, lightly beaten
1 teaspoon baking soda (bicarbonate of soda)
1 teaspoon vanilla extract (essence)
1 teaspoon ground cinnamon
1 teaspoon instant coffee granules
½ teaspoon salt
¾ cup (4½ oz/140 g) pecan pieces

FOR THE CHOCOLATE-CINNAMON FROSTING:

4 cups (1 lb/500 g) confectioners' (icing) sugar
½ cup (4 oz/125 g) butter, melted and cooled
1 cup (3 oz/90 g) unsweetened cocoa powder
⅓ cup (3 fl oz/80 ml) milk
1 teaspoon vanilla extract (essence)
1 teaspoon instant coffee granules
1 teaspoon ground cinnamon

whipped cream and ground cinnamon for garnish (optional)

★ Preheat an oven to 400°F (200°C). Butter and flour a 15-by-10-by-2-in (37-by-25-by-5-cm) baking pan.
★ To make the cake, in a saucepan, combine the butter or margarine, cocoa and water. Bring to a boil, stirring to dissolve the cocoa. Remove from the heat and set aside.
★ In a large bowl, stir together the flour and sugar. Add the cocoa mixture and, using an electric mixer or a spoon, beat until well blended. Continue to beat while adding the buttermilk, eggs, baking soda, vanilla, cinnamon, instant coffee granules and salt. When the mixture is well blended, stir in the pecans.
★ Pour the batter into the prepared pan. Bake until a wooden toothpick inserted into the center comes out clean, about 20 minutes. Transfer to a rack and let cool for 15 minutes.
★ Meanwhile, to make the chocolate-cinnamon frosting, in a bowl, using an electric mixer or a spoon, beat together the confectioners' sugar, butter, cocoa and milk until well blended. Stir in the vanilla, instant coffee granules and cinnamon until thoroughly combined.
★ When the cake has cooled for 15 minutes, spread the frosting over the still-warm cake.
★ Cut into squares and serve warm or at room temperature. If you like, garnish with a dollop of whipped cream dusted with cinnamon.

SERVES 20–24

F r e d e r i c k s b u r g

APPLE STRUDEL BAKLAVA

Apples are now being grown in the fertile soil around the historic German community of Fredericksburg, where Cynthia Pedregon created this luscious dessert for the Peach Tree Tea Room.

FOR THE BAKLAVA:

1 cup (8 oz/250 g) butter
2 cups (8 oz/250 g) coarsely chopped, peeled apples
2 cups (8 oz/250 g) pecans or walnuts, toasted
⅔ cup (5 oz/155 g) sugar
¼ cup (1½ oz/45 g) golden raisins (sultanas)
1 teaspoon grated lemon zest
3 tablespoons fresh lemon juice
2 teaspoons ground cinnamon
½ lb (250 g) filo sheets, each about 14 by 18 in (35 by 50 cm)

FOR THE SYRUP:

1¼ cups (10 oz/315 g) sugar
1¼ cups (10 fl oz/310 ml) water
½ cup (6 oz/185 g) honey
½ teaspoon ground cinnamon
2 or 3 whole cloves
1 tablespoon fresh lemon juice

Left to right: Apple Strudel Baklava, Sheet Cake with Chocolate-Cinnamon Frosting

★ To make the baklava, in a small frying pan or saucepan over low heat, melt the butter. Remove from the heat and let stand for a few minutes, then skim off and discard the white foam that rises to the top. Pour off the clear yellow liquid into a small bowl, leaving the milky residue in the bottom of the pan. (This is clarified butter.) Set aside.

★ In a bowl, combine the apples, nuts, sugar, raisins, lemon zest and juice and cinnamon; toss to mix thoroughly. Set aside.

★ Preheat an oven to 350°F (180°C).

★ Carefully unroll the filo sheets onto a clean work surface. Cut the stack in half lengthwise to form 2 stacks each about 9 by 14 in (23 by 35 cm). Cover the filo sheets with plastic wrap and top with a damp towel to prevent drying.

★ Brush the bottom and sides of a 9-by-13-in (23-by-32.5-cm) baking dish with some of the melted butter. Lay 1 filo sheet in the dish and brush with butter. Repeat with 5 more sheets, brushing each one with butter. Spread half of the apple filling over the pastry. Top with 4 more filo sheets, buttering each sheet well. Spread with the remaining apple mixture. Top

with the remaining filo sheets, again buttering each sheet before topping it with the next sheet. When all of the sheets are in the dish, brush the top with melted butter. Using a very sharp knife, cut into diamonds about 1½ by 2 in (4 by 5 cm). Alternatively, cut into squares of about the same size.

★ Bake until golden, about 45 minutes. Transfer the dish to a wire rack and let cool completely.

★ While the baklava is baking, make the syrup. In a saucepan over medium-high heat, combine all the ingredients and bring to a boil, stirring to dissolve the sugar. Reduce the heat to low and simmer until a syrup consistency forms, about 10 minutes. Remove from the heat and remove and discard the cloves. Let the syrup cool completely.

★ Pour the cooled syrup evenly over the top of the baklava. As the baklava sets, the syrup is absorbed. Run a sharp knife along the previously made cuts and carefully lift out the baklava pieces. Serve on small plates. Leftovers can be wrapped well and frozen for up to 1 month.

MAKES ABOUT 40 PIECES

221

STRAWBERRY AND CREAM SUNFLOWERS

In springtime, Texans follow the wildflower trail to Poteet, fifteen miles (twenty-five kilometers) south of San Antonio, where the strawberries are sweet and juicy. San Antonio chef Paul Cameron created this recipe to celebrate April in Texas, with its abundance of bluebonnets and Indian paintbrush.

½ cup (4 oz/125 g) sugar
¼ teaspoon ground cinnamon
vegetable oil for deep-frying
12 flour tortillas
1½ cups (12 fl oz/375 ml) heavy (double) cream
1 cup (6 oz/185 g) sliced banana
1 cup (4 oz/125 g) strawberries, stems removed and sliced
toasted pecan pieces and fresh mint sprigs for garnish

★ In a small bowl, stir together the sugar and cinnamon. Set aside.
★ In a deep frying pan, pour in oil to a depth of 1½–2 in (4–5 cm). Heat to 360°F (182°C), or until bubbles form around a wooden skewer inserted into the oil. Add the tortillas, one at a time, and fry, turning once, until crisp, 1½–2 minutes total. Using tongs, transfer to paper towels to drain. Sprinkle on both sides with some of the cinnamon-sugar mixture.
★ In a chilled bowl, using an electric mixer, whip the cream until stiff peaks form. Place a tortilla on each of 6 plates. Spoon a layer of some of the whipped cream over each tortilla and top with the banana slices and strawberries, reserving a few fruit pieces for use later.
★ For each serving, break a second tortilla into fragments. Wedge some of these fragments at a 45-degree angle into the layer of strawberries, bananas and whipped cream. Spoon more whipped cream in the middle of each tortilla and top with the reserved fruit. Sprinkle with the remaining cinnamon-sugar mixture and garnish with the pecans and mint sprigs. Serve immediately.

SERVES 6

1 teaspoon vanilla extract (essence)
2 teaspoons light rum
½ cup (4 fl oz/125 ml) peach brandy
15 fresh lemon verbena leaves, washed and dried
fresh lemon verbena sprigs and pesticide-free begonia
    blossoms for garnish

★ Preheat an oven to 325°F (165°C). Butter and flour a 10-in (25-cm) bundt pan.
★ In a large bowl, using an electric mixer, beat the butter and sugar until light and fluffy. Add the eggs, one at a time, beating well after each addition. In another bowl, stir together the flour and salt. Beat in the flour mixture alternately with the sour cream, in 3 additions each. Stir in the orange, almond, lemon and vanilla extracts, then add the rum and peach brandy.
★ Place the lemon verbena leaves on the bottom of the prepared pan, with the underside of the leaves facing up. Carefully spoon the batter into the pan, being careful not to dislodge the sprigs. Bake until a wooden toothpick inserted into the center comes out clean, about 1¼ hours.
★ Transfer to a rack to cool for 10 minutes in the pan, then invert onto the rack and let cool completely. Place on a serving plate and garnish the plate with lemon verbena sprigs and begonias. Cut into wedges to serve.

SERVES 8

East Texas

BLUEBERRY CRÈME BRÛLÉE WITH ROSE GERANIUM

San Antonio chef Kim Swendson-Cameron created this delightful way to use wonderful East Texas blueberries. In an unusual touch, she tucks delicately scented rose geranium leaves beneath the caramelized crust. There are many different varieties of scented geraniums available, from lemon, rose, lime, apple and peppermint to the more exotic apricot, peach and nutmeg. If you grow your own geraniums, be sure to pick the leaves early in the morning for maximum flavor.

5 egg yolks
⅔ cup (5 oz/150 g) sugar
2 cups (16 fl oz/500 ml) heavy (double) cream
2 pesticide-free rose geranium leaves, plus rose geranium
    leaves for garnish
¾ cup (3 oz/90 g) blueberries
boiling water

★ Preheat an oven to 325°F (165°C).
★ In a bowl, whisk together the egg yolks and ⅓ cup (2½ oz/75 g) of the sugar until the sugar dissolves and the mixture is a light lemon color. In a saucepan over medium heat, combine the cream and the 2 rose geranium leaves and heat gently to just under a boil. Remove from the heat and discard the leaves. Whisk 1–2 tablespoons of the cream into the egg mixture, then gradually whisk the egg mixture into the cream.
★ Place 2 tablespoons of the blueberries in the bottom of each of six 4–5-fl oz (125–150-ml) ramekins. Set them in a baking pan. Divide the custard evenly among the ramekins. Pour boiling water into the baking pan to reach halfway up the sides of the ramekins. Bake until the custard is set, about 25 minutes. Let cool in the water bath, then remove from the water bath, cover and refrigerate until thoroughly chilled, at least 4 hours or as long as 2 days.
★ Just before serving, preheat a broiler (griller). Evenly dust the tops of the custards with the remaining ⅓ cup (2½ oz/75 g) of the sugar. Place under the broiler until the sugar caramelizes, 1–3 minutes. Remove from the broiler, let cool slightly, garnish with rose geranium leaves and serve at once.

SERVES 6

Clockwise from bottom left: Blueberry Crème Brûlée with Rose Geranium, Peach Brandy Pound Cake with Lemon Verbena, Strawberry and Cream Sunflowers

Texas

PEACH BRANDY POUND CAKE WITH LEMON VERBENA

Lemon verbena, an herb with narrow, pointed green leaves and an intense lemon scent, covers the bottom of the cake pan so that when the cake is inverted the leaves are on top. Lemon geranium, lemon thyme, lemon balm or rose geranium would be equally fragrant and would also make lovely garnishes for the cake plate.

1 cup (8 oz/250 g) butter, at room temperature
3 cups (1½ lb/750 g) sugar
6 eggs, at room temperature
3 cups (15 oz/470 g) all-purpose (plain) flour
¼ teaspoon salt
1 cup (8 fl oz/250 ml) sour cream
1 teaspoon orange extract (essence)
¼ teaspoon almond extract (essence)
½ teaspoon lemon extract (essence)

Fredericksburg

PEPPERMINT BROWNIES

The Fredericksburg Herb Farm serves iced or hot herbal teas and these delicious brownies.

FOR THE BROWNIES:

1⅓ cups (11 oz/340 g) margarine, at room temperature
2 cups (1 lb/500 g) sugar
4 eggs
2 teaspoons vanilla extract (essence)
2 tablespoons honey
1½ cups (6 oz/185 g) all-purpose (plain) flour
⅞ cup (3 oz/90 g) instant hot cocoa mix
1 teaspoon salt
1 teaspoon baking powder
2 cups (8 oz/250 g) coarsely chopped toasted pecans

FOR THE FROSTING:

2 cups (8 oz/250 g) confectioners' (icing) sugar
6 tablespoons (3 oz/90 g) unsalted butter, at room temperature
2 tablespoons milk
1½ teaspoons finely minced fresh peppermint leaves or
   1 teaspoon peppermint extract (essence)
3 drops green food coloring (optional)

FOR THE GLAZE:

3 oz (90 g) unsweetened chocolate
1 tablespoon unsalted butter

fresh peppermint sprigs and edible flowers for garnish

★ Preheat an oven to 350°F (180°C). Butter and flour a standard jelly-roll (Swiss-roll) pan.
★ To make the brownies, in a bowl, using an electric mixer, beat together the margarine and sugar until light and fluffy. Add the eggs, one at a time, beating well after each addition. Then beat in the vanilla and honey until the mixture is blended.
★ In another bowl, sift together the flour, cocoa mix, salt and baking powder. With the mixer set at low speed, gradually beat the flour mixture into the egg mixture. Fold in the nuts.
★ Spread the batter in the prepared pan. Bake until only a moist crumb adheres to a wooden toothpick inserted into the center, about 30 minutes. Transfer to a rack and let cool completely in the pan.
★ To make the frosting, in a bowl, using an electric mixer set on medium speed, beat together the confectioners' sugar and the butter until smooth. Beat in the milk, the minced peppermint or peppermint extract and the food coloring, if using.
★ Spread the frosting over the cooled brownies. Place in the freezer for 20 minutes.
★ Meanwhile, to make the glaze, in the top pan of a double boiler (or in a heatproof bowl) over gently simmering water, melt together the chocolate and butter. Stir until blended, remove from the heat and let cool.
★ Drizzle the cooled glaze over the frosting.
★ Cut into 2-in (5-cm) squares and serve. Store any leftovers in an airtight container at room temperature for up to 5 days.

MAKES ABOUT 3 DOZEN

Peppermint Brownies

Chocolate-Raspberry Cream Puffs with Almond Praline Powder

CHOCOLATE-RASPBERRY CREAM PUFFS WITH ALMOND PRALINE POWDER

The chocolate-raspberry cream filling makes these light puffs a rich and elegant dessert.

FOR THE CREAM PUFFS:

1 cup (8 fl oz/250 ml) water
½ cup (4 oz/125 g) butter
1 cup (5 oz/155 g) all-purpose (plain) flour
4 eggs

FOR THE CHOCOLATE-RASPBERRY CREAM:

1 cup (6 oz/185 g) semisweet chocolate chips
6 oz (185 g) cream cheese, at room temperature
½ cup (2 oz/60 g) confectioners' (icing) sugar
1 tablespoon raspberry-flavored liqueur
½ cup (4 fl oz/125 ml) heavy (double) cream

FOR THE PRALINE POWDER:

½ cup (4 oz/125 g) sugar
½ cup (2 oz/60 g) almonds or macadamia nuts, lightly toasted

1½ cups (6 oz/185 g) fresh raspberries or 1 package (6 oz/ 185 g) frozen raspberries, puréed and sieved
fresh raspberries and blueberries for garnish

★ Preheat an oven to 400°F (200°C).
★ To make the cream puffs, in a saucepan over low heat, combine the water and butter. Bring to a boil and remove from the heat. Add the flour all at once and stir vigorously until the mixture forms a ball and leaves a film on the sides of the pan. Allow to cool slightly, 3–4 minutes. Add the eggs, one at a time, beating well after each addition.
★ To form each cream puff, drop 2 rounded tablespoonfuls of dough onto an ungreased baking sheet, forming mounds spaced about 2 in (5 cm) apart.
★ Bake until puffed and golden, 35–40 minutes. Let cool completely on the baking sheet.
★ To make the chocolate-raspberry cream, in the top pan of a double boiler (or a heatproof bowl) over gently simmering water, melt the chocolate; stir until smooth. Set aside. In a bowl, combine the cream cheese, confectioners' sugar and liqueur; beat with an electric mixer or a spoon until creamy. Gradually add the melted chocolate, beating well. In another bowl, beat the cream until stiff peaks form. Fold the cream into the chocolate mixture just until blended. Cover and refrigerate until needed.
★ To make the praline powder, in a heavy frying pan over medium-low heat, melt the sugar, stirring constantly. Alternatively, melt in a 350°F (180°C) oven. When the sugar has turned to liquid and is light brown, stir in the almonds or macadamias. Pour the nuts onto a large buttered plate and let stand until cool. When cool, break into pieces and place in a food processor fitted with the metal blade. Process until crumbly.
★ To assemble the cream puffs, slice the cream puffs in half horizontally. Fill the bottoms with the cream filling, using a pastry (piping) bag if desired. Replace the tops.
★ Ladle the raspberry purée onto individual plates and set the puffs on the purée. Drizzle the cream puffs with any remaining cream filling and sprinkle liberally with the praline powder. Garnish each plate with raspberries and blueberries and serve at once.

MAKES 20 CREAM PUFFS; SERVES 10

Texas

CARAMEL-BRANDY FLAN WITH STRAWBERRY PURÉE

A hint of brandy and some luscious puréed strawberries dress up this flan. If you like, substitute a coffee-flavored liqueur for the brandy and add ¼ teaspoon ground cinnamon.

1¼ cups (10 oz/310 g) sugar
4 eggs
1 can (12 fl oz/375 g) evaporated milk
1¼ cups (10 fl oz/310 ml) cold water
¼ cup (2 fl oz/60 ml) brandy
boiling water, as needed
1 cup (4 oz/125 g) strawberries, puréed
whole strawberries and toasted almond slices (flakes)
   for garnish

★ Preheat an oven to 350°F (180°C).
★ Spread ½ cup (4 oz/125 g) of the sugar evenly over the bottom of a round 1½ qt (1.5 l) baking dish 8 in (20 cm) in diameter. Heat in the oven, checking frequently and turning as needed to ensure even heating, until the sugar is completely melted to a golden brown syrup, 35–45 minutes. Do not allow to burn. Transfer to a rack and let cool for 10 minutes.
★ In a bowl, beat the eggs until well blended. Add the remaining ¾ cup (6 oz/185 g) sugar and the evaporated milk, cold water and brandy, stirring until the sugar dissolves.
★ Place the prepared dish in a shallow baking pan and pour the egg mixture into the dish. Pour boiling water into the baking pan to a depth of about 1 in (2.5 cm). Bake until a knife inserted into the center of the custard comes out clean, 1¼–1½ hours. Remove the pan from the oven and lift the baking dish from the water bath. Place the flan on a rack to cool for 30 minutes, then cover and refrigerate for at least 4 hours or for as long as overnight.
★ To unmold, run a knife blade around the edge of the flan to loosen it. Invert a shallow serving dish with a small lip over the flan, then, holding the containers firmly together, invert them. Lift off the flan dish. Spoon the puréed strawberries around the flan and garnish with whole strawberries and almonds. Cut into wedges to serve.

SERVES 6–8

San Antonio

BUÑUELOS WITH PINEAPPLE-BRANDY SAUCE

At Christmas and New Year's in San Antonio, these thin, round, crisp pastries are traditionally served with a mug of piping-hot Mexican chocolate. If you will not be serving all of the buñuelos, store the pastries and sauce separately in airtight containers at room temperature for up to 3 days. A spicy Moscato goes well with this dessert.

FOR THE BUÑUELOS:

3⅓ cups (17 oz/530 g) all-purpose (plain) flour
1 teaspoon salt
1 teaspoon baking powder
4½ teaspoons sugar
¼ cup (2 oz/60 g) butter, chilled
2 eggs
½ cup (4 fl oz/125 ml) milk
vegetable oil for deep-frying

FOR THE PINEAPPLE-BRANDY SAUCE:

1 cup (10 oz/315 g) pineapple preserves
3 tablespoons brandy

FOR THE CINNAMON SUGAR:

1 teaspoon ground cinnamon
1 cup (8 oz/250 g) sugar

★ To make the *buñuelos,* in a bowl, stir together the flour, salt, baking powder and sugar. Add the butter and, using a pastry blender or 2 knives, cut it in until the mixture resembles coarse meal. In another bowl, whisk the eggs until blended, then whisk in the milk. Add to the flour mixture, stirring until a dough forms. Transfer to a lightly floured work surface and knead gently until smooth, about 2 minutes.
★ Cut the dough into pieces the size of large marbles and, rolling them between your palms, form into balls. Place on the work surface, cover with a kitchen towel and let rest for 15 minutes.
★ On the lightly floured work surface, roll out each ball into a very thin pancake about 4 in (10 cm) in diameter. Cut a hole in the center of each round with a tiny round cutter the size of a thimble.
★ In a deep frying pan, pour in vegetable oil to a depth of 2 in (5 cm). Heat to 360°–365°F (182°–185°C), or until a tiny piece of dough turns golden within a few seconds of being dropped in the oil.
★ While the oil is heating, make the pineapple-brandy sauce. In a small saucepan over low heat, combine the preserves and brandy and heat gently until blended and warm, stirring occasionally. Keep warm.
★ To make the cinnamon sugar, in a bowl, stir the cinnamon into the sugar until evenly distributed. Set aside.
★ Working in batches, add the dough rounds to the oil and fry, turning once, until puffed and golden brown, about 35 seconds on each side. Using a slotted spoon, transfer to paper towels to drain briefly.
★ Transfer the warm pastries to a platter and sprinkle the cinnamon sugar over the top. Spoon the sauce over the *buñuelos* and serve.

MAKES ABOUT 5 DOZEN

South Texas

TACOS FILLED WITH FRUIT AND CHOCOLATE MOUSSE

These lacy cookies can also be formed into basket shapes (using an inverted glass or bottle and flaring the edges slightly to form a lip) to showcase summer ice creams, fruits or sorbets. During the holidays, thread the cookies on thin ribbon or gold cord and hang from the Christmas tree.

FOR THE COOKIES:

¼ cup (2 fl oz/60 ml) light corn syrup
2 tablespoons butter
2 tablespoons vegetable shortening
⅓ cup (2½ oz/75 g) firmly packed brown sugar
½ cup (2½ oz/75 g) all-purpose (plain) flour
½ cup (2 oz/60 g) chopped pecans or almonds

FOR THE CHOCOLATE MOUSSE:

1¼ cups (8 oz/250 g) semisweet chocolate chips
¼ cup (1 oz/30 g) confectioners' (icing) sugar
½ cup (4 oz/125 g) unsalted butter, at room temperature, cut into small pieces
6 eggs, separated

Clockwise from left: Tacos Filled with Fruit and Chocolate Mousse, Buñuelos with Pineapple-Brandy Sauce, Caramel-Brandy Flan with Strawberry Purée, Churros with Cinnamon-Pecan Ice Cream (recipe page 229)

1 tablespoon dark rum
1 tablespoon coffee-flavored liqueur
½ teaspoon vanilla extract (essence)
2 tablespoons granulated sugar

about 4 cups (1 lb/500 g) finely diced strawberries, pineapple and kiwifruits, in roughly equal amounts
finely shredded fresh mint leaves

★ Preheat an oven to 350°F (180°C). Grease 2 baking sheets with butter.

★ To make the cookies, in a heavy saucepan, combine the corn syrup, butter, shortening and brown sugar. Bring to a boil, stirring to dissolve the sugar. Immediately remove from the heat and add the flour alternately with the nuts, in 2 additions each; mix thoroughly.

★ Drop the mixture by ½ teaspoonfuls onto the prepared baking sheets, spacing them 4 in (10 cm) apart. The cookies will spread to 2½ in (6 cm) in diameter when baked. Bake until lightly browned, 8–10 minutes. Let cool on the baking sheets for 2–3 minutes, then carefully place the still-warm cookies

over a wooden dowel (or the handle of a wooden spoon) about ½ in (12 mm) in diameter to form the shape of a taco shell. Transfer to a rack to cool completely.

★ To make the mousse, in the top pan of a double boiler (or in a heatproof bowl) over gently simmering water, melt the chocolate. When it has melted, stir in the confectioners' sugar. Then add the butter, bit by bit, stirring until melted. Remove from the heat.

★ In a bowl, using an electric mixer set on medium-high to high speed, beat the egg yolks until thick and lemon colored. Using a rubber spatula, fold in the chocolate. Stir in the rum, liqueur and vanilla until well combined.

★ In a clean bowl, using clean beaters, beat the egg whites until foamy. Add the granulated sugar and beat until stiff peaks form. Using the spatula, gently fold the egg whites into the chocolate mixture just until mixed. Cover and chill.

★ To serve, spoon about 1 tablespoon chilled mousse into each shell. Top with a spoonful of the fruits and garnish with mint. Serve immediately.

MAKES ABOUT 8 DOZEN

*Left to right: Peach and Blackberry Clafouti, Rose-Scented
Ice Cream in Chocolate Seashells*

Tyler

ROSE-SCENTED ICE CREAM IN CHOCOLATE SEASHELLS

*The Municipal Rose Garden of the city of Tyler covers more than
twenty-seven acres (sixty-seven hectares) and boasts thirty-eight
thousand bushes in four hundred different hues. In the twenty-mile
(thirty-kilometer) area surrounding the city, more than half of
America's commercial roses are grown. It is no wonder, then, that
Tyler has been designated the Rose Capital of the World. This
delicately scented vanilla ice cream, garnished with rosebuds,
candied violets or rose petals is the perfect ending to a lovely East
Texas meal.*

1 qt (1 l) vanilla ice cream with vanilla bean flecks, softened
    at room temperature for about 30 minutes
rose water

FOR THE CHOCOLATE SEASHELLS:

1½ lb (750 g) semisweet chocolate chips
2 tablespoons vegetable oil

pesticide-free rose petals, baby rosebuds or miniature roses
    or candied violets for garnish

★ Place the ice cream in a bowl and, using a large spoon or
an electric mixer, beat in rose water to taste, starting with
2–3 teaspoons. The ice cream should be delicately flavored,
not overwhelming. Repack the ice cream into its container
and refreeze.

★ To make the chocolate seashells, cover the inside of six to
eight 4- to 5-in (10- to 13-cm) scallop shells tightly with
aluminum foil. Make certain to press the foil down to retain
the shell shape. In the top pan of a double boiler (or in a
heatproof bowl) placed over gently simmering water, melt the
chocolate chips with the vegetable oil. Let cool slightly.

Using a flat brush, spread the chocolate evenly over the foil, forming a smooth, thick coating. Place on waxed paper–lined baking sheets and chill until firm, 30–45 minutes.

★ Carefully loosen and remove the chocolate shells and then peel away the foil.

★ Reheat any remaining chocolate and use to repair any cracks and to paint the inside of each chocolate shell. Use the shells immediately or store in a cool place until needed.

★ To serve, place the shells on individual plates. Scoop out the ice cream and arrange in the shells. Garnish with the rose petals, buds or blossoms or candied violets. Serve at once.

SERVES 6–8

Texas

Mango Cream with Mint Chocolate Leaves

The flavor of mango is much like that of peach, but a bit more floral. Fresh or canned mangoes or even peaches can be used here. To make the mint chocolate leaves for garnishing the cream, using tweezers, dip fresh mint leaves into cooled melted chocolate and set aside on waxed paper to dry in a cool, dry place for about 2 hours.

1 can (14 oz/440 g) mangoes, drained, or 2 fresh mangoes, about 1½ lb (750 g), peeled and pitted
1 teaspoon grated lime zest
2 tablespoons fresh lime juice
1 cup (8 fl oz/250 ml) heavy (double) cream, well chilled
mint chocolate leaves (see note) and raspberries, blackberries or blueberries for garnish

★ In a food processor fitted with the metal blade or in a blender, combine the mangoes and lime zest and juice. Purée until smooth. Transfer to a bowl.

★ In a chilled bowl, beat the cream until it forms stiff peaks. Using a rubber spatula, gently fold the cream into the purée.

★ Spoon the mango mixture into chilled wineglasses. Garnish with the mint chocolate leaves and berries. Serve at once.

SERVES 6   *Photograph pages 204–205*

Houston

Peach and Blackberry Clafouti

You will enjoy a taste of France in this year-round dessert that is equally good when made with pitted black cherries, pitted prunes or sliced tart apples. Add ¼ cup (1½ oz/45 g) chopped, drained pineapple to the black cherries for an interesting variation. Accompany with whipped cream or with vanilla ice cream lightly flavored with finely minced candied ginger.

2 cups (12 oz/375 g) sliced peaches
¾ cup (3 oz/90 g) blackberries
2 tablespoons kirsch, brandy or bourbon or ½ teaspoon vanilla extract (essence)
⅓ cup (2 oz/60 g) all-purpose (plain) flour
dash of salt
⅓ cup (3 oz/90 g) granulated sugar
3 eggs
1 cup (8 fl oz/250 ml) milk
3 tablespoons butter, melted
confectioners' (icing) sugar for sprinkling

★ Butter a 9-in (23-cm) pie plate. Spread the peach slices and blackberries evenly in the plate. Sprinkle with the liquor or

vanilla and let stand for 10 minutes.

★ Preheat an oven to 350°F (180°C).

★ In a bowl, whisk together the flour, salt, sugar, eggs, milk and melted butter until the mixture has the consistency of pancake batter. Pour the mixture evenly over the fruit; do not stir.

★ Bake until lightly browned and puffed and a wooden toothpick inserted into the center comes out clean, 45–60 minutes. The timing will depend upon the juiciness of the fruit.

★ Sprinkle with confectioners' sugar and serve warm.

SERVES 4

South Texas

Churros with Cinnamon-Pecan Ice Cream

These light, flavorful, crispy pastries are also delightful for breakfast sprinkled with cinnamon sugar or confectioners' (icing) sugar and served with Mexican-style hot chocolate flavored with cinnamon.

FOR THE CINNAMON-PECAN ICE CREAM:

1 qt (1 l) vanilla ice cream, softened at room temperature for about 30 minutes
1 teaspoon ground cinnamon
1 cup (4 oz/125 g) pecans, lightly toasted
3–4 tablespoons applejack brandy
3 tablespoons dried cranberries, soaked in hot water until softened and drained

FOR THE *CHURROS:*

1 cup (8 fl oz/250 ml) water
½ cup (4 oz/125 g) butter
¼ teaspoon salt
1 cup (5 oz/155 g) all-purpose (plain) flour
1 tablespoon unsweetened cocoa powder (optional)
3 eggs
vegetable oil for deep-frying
¼ cup (2 oz/60 g) sugar
¼ teaspoon ground cinnamon

★ To make the cinnamon-pecan ice cream, place the vanilla ice cream in a large bowl. Using a large spoon or an electric mixer set on medium speed, beat in the cinnamon, pecans, brandy to taste and cranberries. Repack the ice cream into its container and refreeze.

★ To make the *churros,* in a heavy-bottomed saucepan, over low heat, combine the water, butter and salt. When the butter melts, bring to a boil. Add the flour and the cocoa, if using, all at once and stir vigorously until the mixture forms a ball. Remove from the heat and add the eggs, one at a time, beating well after each addition until smooth.

★ In a large frying pan, pour in oil to a depth of about 2 in (5 cm). Heat to 360°F (182°C), or until a drop of the *churro* mixture sizzles almost immediately upon contact with the oil. In a small bowl, stir together the sugar and cinnamon and set aside.

★ Spoon the *churro* mixture into a pastry (piping) bag fitted with a ½-in (12-mm) plain or star tip. Squeeze the bag over the hot oil, pushing out a rope of paste about 4 in (10 cm) long. Then cut it off with a sharp knife, letting it fall gently into the oil. Rapidly form about 3 more ropes in the same way. Turn them frequently in the oil until they are golden, about 2 minutes. Using a slotted spoon, transfer to paper towels to drain. Repeat with the remaining *churro* mixture.

★ While the *churros* are still warm, sprinkle them evenly with the cinnamon-sugar mixture. To serve, spoon the ice cream into dishes and serve the *churros* hot, warm or at room temperature alongside.

SERVES 8   *Photograph page 227*

GLOSSARY

Note: Some recipes in this book call for raw or lightly cooked eggs, which in some areas have been known to be the source of salmonella bacteria. If this is a concern, when appropriate, use an egg substitute.

ACHIOTE SEED
The dried brick-red seed of the annatto tree lends a bright orange-yellow color to food. The seeds have a subtle, earthy flavor and are most often ground into a paste. Before grinding the seeds, soak them overnight in water to cover and then drain, or bring to a simmer in water to cover, remove from the heat and allow to stand for 1 hour, then drain. Look for achiote seeds in Latin American markets and specialty-food stores.

ANAHEIM CHILI PEPPER
See *chili peppers, fresh and dried.*

ANCHO CHILI PEPPER
See *chili peppers, fresh and dried.*

ANEJO CHEESE
This firm, white Mexican cheese has a dry texture and is usually quite salty. If it is unavailable, a dry feta can be used in its place, although the feta will be more crumbly. Sold in Latin American markets and specialty-food stores.

ASADERO CHEESE
A mild, soft Mexican cheese that melts easily. Mozzarella can be substituted.

ASIAN SESAME OIL
A highly fragrant oil pressed from roasted sesame seeds, most often used as a flavoring. Cold-pressed sesame oil, sold in health-food stores, is mild and is thus not a good substitute. Available in Asian stores and well-stocked food stores.

AVOCADO CREAM
Cut 1 large ripe avocado in half and remove and discard the pit. Scoop the flesh from the skin into a bowl. Using the back of a fork, mash the avocado, then stir in ⅓ cup (3 fl oz/80 ml) sour cream; 2 tablespoons fresh lime juice; 3 green (spring) onions, minced; 1 clove garlic, minced; and ¼ teaspoon ground cumin. Season to taste with salt and freshly ground pepper. Serve the avocado cream as an accompaniment to heated flour tortillas, as a garnish or for dipping vegetables.

BEANS, DRIED
Black beans, pinto beans and black-eyed peas are among the many dried beans used in the Texas kitchen. To cook dried beans, pick over the beans and discard any misshapen ones, small stones or other impurities. Rinse well and place in a large bowl with water to cover by 2 in (5 cm). Let the beans stand for at least 3 hours or as long as overnight to rehydrate them, which will reduce the cooking time and improve digestibility. (Alternatively, place the beans in a saucepan with water to cover, bring to a boil, boil for 1 minute and remove from the heat; let stand for 1 hour before continuing.) Drain the beans and place in a saucepan. Add 1 small yellow or white onion, cut up, if desired, and water to cover by about 2 in (5 cm). Bring to a boil, reduce the heat to low, cover and barely simmer until tender but not soft.

Make sure that the beans are always well covered with water; add more hot water as needed. Cooking times will depend upon the variety of bean, but most dried beans will be ready in 1–2 hours. Season as desired at the end of cooking. See also *refried beans.*

BEEF STOCK
If you have time, making your own beef stock is well worth the effort, as commercial beef stocks are often quite salty. To make beef stock, in a large pot, combine 3–4 lb (1.5–2 kg) beef knuckle bones, cut up; 2 yellow onions, cut in half; 2 celery stalks, cut in half; 3 or 4 cloves garlic; 2 bay leaves; 10–12 fresh parsley stems; 12 peppercorns, lightly crushed; and water to cover by 2 in (5 cm). Bring to a boil, skim off any scum that forms on the surface and reduce the heat to medium-low. Cover partially and simmer for 2–4 hours, or until desired concentration of flavor is achieved; skim off additional scum as necessary. (For a richer stock, brown the bones and vegetables in a 450°F/230°C oven for 30 minutes before placing them in the pot.) Strain through a sieve lined with cheesecloth (muslin) into a clean container, cover and refrigerate for up to 3 days; remove the fat that has solidified on top before using. The stock may also be frozen for up to 2 months; remove the solidified fat before freezing. Makes 2–3 qt (2–3 l).

BLACKENED SEASONING MIX
Popularized by Creole and Cajun chefs, this packaged mix of black pepper, cayenne pepper, salt and other herbs and spices is used for coating fish before charring it in a searing-hot cast-iron frying pan.

BLUE CORNMEAL
A meal ground from the dried kernels of blue corn. The kernels, which are actually dark gray, are treated with alkaline substances to give them their unusual bluish hue. Blue cornmeal has a stronger flavor than either yellow or white cornmeal and is sold in well-stocked food stores and in specialty-food shops.

BLUE CORN TORTILLAS
Corn tortillas made from *masa harina* (see separate entry) ground from blue corn kernels. Chips made from these colorful tortillas are sold in well-stocked food stores and in specialty-food shops.

BUTTERFLY

To halve foods—shrimp (prawns), pork tenderloins, fowl—horizontally without cutting all the way through. This technique allows the food to be laid flat for cooking or for stuffing and then cooking.

CACTUS PADDLES

The succulent, flat pads of the *nopal* cactus, also known as the prickly pear cactus. Most commonly eaten as a vegetable, in salads or stirred into scrambled eggs, the deep green pads, also known as *nopales,* can be purchased fresh with or without the spines removed. If purchasing with the spines intact, hold the paddles with a heavy kitchen towel or while wearing thick gloves and, using a sharp knife or vegetable peeler, pare off the bumps that conceal the tiny thorns. Do not peel away all of the green skin that covers the paddle. Then cut the paddles into strips or slices as directed and cook in boiling water to cover until tender, about 10 minutes, drain, rinse well with cool water and drain again before adding to dishes. Cactus pieces are also sold in jars and cans. See also *pickled nopalitos* and *prickly pear*.

CHALUPA SHELL

Crisply fried boat-shaped corn tortilla that is thicker than a conventional tortilla. The shells are generally filled with chicken or pork, tomatoes, onion, salsa and sometimes beans. They take their name and shape from a small Mexican canoe.

CHICKEN STOCK

Commercial chicken stock is a great convenience, but home-made stock has a superior flavor and is worth the effort when time permits. To make chicken stock, in a large pot, combine 4 lb (2 kg) chicken backs, wings and necks; 2 yellow onions, cut in half; 2 carrots, cut in half; 2 celery stalks, cut in half; 1 bay leaf; 6 fresh parsley stems; 6 peppercorns, lightly crushed; and water to cover by 2 in (5 cm). Bring to a boil, skim off any scum that forms on the surface and reduce the heat to medium-low. Cover partially and simmer for 1–1½ hours, or until the desired concentration of flavor is achieved; skim off additional scum as necessary. Strain through a sieve lined with cheesecloth (muslin) into a clean container, cover and refrigerate for up to 3 days; remove the fat that has solidified on top before using. The stock may also be frozen for up to 2 months; remove the solidified fat before freezing. Makes 2–3 qt (2–3 l).

CHIFFONADE

This French term refers to the cutting of lettuces and other leafy greens and herbs into narrow ribbons. To prepare, trim and discard any stems from the leaves and stack them. Roll the leaves into a tight cylinder and then thinly cut crosswise to form fine strips.

CHIHUAHUA CHEESE

A Mexican cheese with a slightly tangy flavor and a high fat content that ensures it will melt easily. A mild longhorn Cheddar, mozzarella or Monterey Jack may be substituted.

CHILI FLOWERS

Chili flowers make an attractive garnish for a variety of dishes. To make the flowers, select fresh jalapeño, serrano, anaheim and poblano chili peppers, alone or in any combination. Wearing rubber gloves and working from the blossom end of each pepper, make 4–6 lengthwise slits at regular intervals, stopping within ½–1 in (12 mm–2.5 cm) of the end. Scrape out the seeds and ribs. Place the chilies in a bowl of ice water to cover and refrigerate until the chilies curl and "blossom," at least 1 hour.

CHILI PEPPERS, FRESH AND DRIED

There are many varieties of fresh and dried chilies, of different colors, flavors and intensities of heat. Purchase shiny, unblemished fresh chilies and store them in the refrigerator. Select dried chilies that are not brittle and store them in airtight containers at room temperature. Look for chilies in Latin American and some Asian markets and in well-stocked food stores. Chilies, especially fresh chilies, must be handled with care, as they contain capsaicin, which can irritate the skin. Wear rubber gloves when working with chilies and be careful not to rub your eyes. As soon as you have finished working with the chilies, wash your hands and any utensils you have used with warm soapy water.

To rehydrate dried chilies, toast them in a dry frying pan over medium heat until flexible and fragrant, 2–3 minutes. Watch them closely; they burn easily, which results in a bitter taste. Transfer to a bowl of hot water to cover and let stand until soft, 20–30 minutes. To purée the soaked chilies for use in a sauce, place them and some of their soaking water in a blender or a food processor fitted with the metal blade and purée until smooth. Strain off any remaining solids if necessary.

To roast fresh chilies, see *roasting peppers*.

ANAHEIM CHILI PEPPER: A light green, mild chili that is widely sold fresh in markets. Also known as the California or long green chili, the anaheim averages 6 in (15 cm) long and is commonly used for stuffing. Red, ripe anaheims are only rarely found.

ANCHO CHILI PEPPER: Ranging in color from deep red to dark brown, the ancho is the dried form of the poblano chili pepper. It measures about 4 in (10 cm) long and 3 in (7.5 cm) wide and has a fruity, sweet flavor. Check any anchos carefully before purchase, as pasilla chilies (see separate entry) are sometimes mislabeled anchos.

CHIPOTLE CHILIES IN *ADOBO*: Chipotle chilies sold in cans in *adobo,* a red sauce containing ground chilies, vinegar, herbs and spices.

CHIPOTLE CHILI PEPPER: Mature red jalapeño chili peppers that are smoked and dried.

HABANERO CHILI PEPPER: Ranging in color from deep green to bright red and usually about 1½ in (4 cm) in diameter, the round, fresh habanero pepper, also known as the Scotch bonnet, is considered the most incendiary of all chili peppers. Dried habanero peppers and bottled habanero hot sauce are also available.

JALAPEÑO CHILI PEPPER: Thick-walled, tapered hot chili pepper usually about 2 in (5 cm) long and ¾–1 in (2–2.5 cm) wide. This popular chili is generally sold while still green; red, ripe jalapeños are much rarer. Both red and green jalapeños are also sold pickled in cans and jars.

PASILLA CHILI PEPPER: A tapered, purple-black dried chili about 5 in (15 cm) long and 1 in (2.5 cm) wide. The pasilla has an intense smoky flavor and is used in the preparation of traditional moles.

POBLANO CHILI PEPPER: A shiny, dark green, wedge-shaped fresh chili about 4 in (10 cm) long and ranging in heat from mild to very hot. It has a rich flavor and is used in a wide variety of dishes, including soups and chilis; it is also sometimes used for making *chiles rellenos*.

RED PEPPER FLAKES: Dried chilies sold already crushed for use in salsas, sauces, salad dressings and so on. Sold in jars in the spice section of food stores.

SERRANO CHILI PEPPERS: A small, thick-walled fresh chili pepper 1–2 in (2.5–5 cm) long and about ½ in (12 mm) in diameter. Sold in colors ranging from deep green to bright red, serranos are somewhat hotter than jalapeños and are frequent additions to salsas.

CHILI POWDER
A blend of ground dried red chilies, paprika, garlic, oregano, cumin and other spices and herbs. It is used to season chili con carne, stews and other dishes. Do not confuse chili powder with ground dried chili, which is the ground form of a single chili pepper variety.

CHIPOTLE CHILIES IN *ADOBO*
See chilies peppers, fresh and dried.

CHIPOTLE CHILI PEPPER
See *chili peppers, fresh and dried.*

CHORIZO
A highly seasoned pork sausage flavored with garlic, vinegar, chili powder and other spices, chorizo is used in Mexican and Spanish cooking. It is most useful in bulk form, but can be easily removed from its casing if available only in links. Chorizo can be found in most well-stocked supermarkets.

CILANTRO
Widely used in Texas cooking, cilantro resembles flat-leaf (Italian) parsley but has a more aromatic, sweet flavor. Look for crisp, green, unwilted leaves; store in the refrigerator with the stems in a glass of water and a plastic bag covering the leaves. Also known as fresh coriander and Chinese parsley.

CILANTRO PESTO
In a food processor fitted with the metal blade or in a blender, combine ¼ cup (1 oz/30 g) pumpkin seeds, sunflower seeds or pine nuts; 2 cups (2 oz/60 g) fresh cilantro (fresh coriander) leaves; 2 cloves garlic, cut up; and ½ cup (2 oz/60 g) freshly grated Parmesan cheese. Process until minced. With the motor running, pour in ½ cup (4 fl oz/125 ml) olive oil, processing until a smooth paste forms. Stir in 1 tablespoon fresh lime juice and transfer to a jar with a tight-fitting lid. Makes about 1 cup (8 fl oz/250 ml). Use on freshly cooked corn on the cob or grilled fish, chicken, pork or vegetables; as a garnish for soups; tossed with pasta; or mixed with an equal amount of mayonnaise and served as a dip for cooked shrimp or raw vegetables.

CORN HUSKS
The leaves that cover ears (cobs) of corn are dried for use as wrappers for tamales and in other Southwest and Mexican dishes. Before use, the husks must be soaked in hot water to cover for 30 minutes to soften them sufficiently for wrapping. Drain, shake well and then pat dry with a kitchen towel to remove any excess moisture. Dried corn husks are sold by weight or in packages in Latin American markets and well-stocked food stores.

CORNMEAL
A meal ground from dried yellow, white or blue corn kernels. Nondegerminated cornmeal (with the bran and germ intact), sold in health-food stores, contains more nutrition than the degerminated cornmeal commonly sold in food stores. Stone-ground cornmeal has a slightly gritty texture that appeals to many cooks.

CORN TORTILLAS
In many towns and cities in Texas and in other areas with Mexican communities, freshly made tortillas are readily available. If you do not have access to a supply of fresh tortillas, they can be easily made at home. To make corn tortillas, in a large bowl, place 2 cups (10 oz/ 315 g) *masa harina* (see separate entry). Add about 1½ cups (12 fl oz/ 375 ml) warm water (115°F/46°C) to the bowl and, using a fork, work it into the *masa* until a pliable dough forms. The dough should be soft but not dry, crumbly or sticky. If it is too dry, add additional water, 1 tablespoon at a time, until the correct consistency is achieved. Knead the dough in the bowl until it comes together into a ball. Pinch off pieces of the dough and roll between your palms into balls about 1½ in (4 cm) in diameter. As the balls are formed, cover them with a lightly dampened kitchen towel. Let stand for about 10 minutes.

To form the tortillas, place a ball between two sheets of waxed paper and roll out into a round 5–6 in (13–15 cm) in diameter. Alternatively, cover the lower half of a tortilla press with a sheet of plastic wrap, place the ball in the center, cover with a second sheet of plastic wrap and close the press to flatten the tortilla. Open the press, peel off the top piece of plastic wrap, then peel the tortilla off the bottom sheet. Repeat with the remaining balls.

To cook the tortillas, heat a dry griddle or frying pan over medium-high heat. Place the tortillas on the hot pan and cook until the edges begin to dry out, about 1 minute. Flip the tortillas over and cook briefly on the second side until browned. Transfer to a towel-lined basket, cover lightly and serve warm. Makes 16–18 tortillas. To reheat cooked tortillas, wrap in aluminum foil and place in a 350°F (180°C) oven for 5–6 minutes.

CRANBERRY-JALAPEÑO JELLY

In a food processor fitted with the metal blade or in a blender, combine 1 cup (5 oz/155 g) chopped fresh jalapeño chili peppers and ½ cup (4 fl oz/125 ml) cranberry juice. Process until the chilies are very finely chopped. Transfer the mixture to a large nonreactive saucepan. Add 2½ cups (20 fl oz/625 ml) cranberry juice and 7 cups (3½ lb/1.75 kg) sugar and stir well. Bring to a rolling boil over high heat and boil vigorously for 1 minute, stirring constantly. Remove from the heat and stir in 1 cup (8 fl oz/250 ml) cider vinegar and 1 bottle (6 fl oz/180 ml) liquid fruit pectin. Quickly ladle into hot, sterilized jelly jars and seal with paraffin (see *paraffin seal*). Store in a cool, dark place. Makes 6 or 7 small jelly jars. Serve as an accompaniment to lamb, game or even fried wontons. It can also be served with cream cheese as an appetizer or melted and spooned over ice cream as a dessert.

CRAYFISH

This freshwater crustacean, also known as a crawfish or crawdad, is usually 3–4 in (7.5–10 cm) long and is sought out primarily for its tail meat. Crayfish, which are farmed in Texas, can be purchased live or cooked in high-quality fish markets and sometimes directly from the grower.

CREMA

A Mexican cultured cream with a slightly sour taste that is reminiscent of French crème fraîche (see separate entry). It is used as a topping for enchiladas and other dishes and can be purchased in Latin American markets and well-stocked food stores. To make your own, in a jar, stir together ¼ cup (2 fl oz/60 ml) buttermilk and 2 cups (16 fl oz/500 ml) heavy (double) cream; cover and let stand in a warm, draft-free place until the mixture begins to set, 4–6 hours. Then cover and refrigerate overnight until thickened. Use within 2 days. Makes about 2 cups (16 fl oz/500 ml).

CRÈME FRAÎCHE

A French cultured cream with a tangy flavor. It is sold in specialty-food shops and well-stocked food stores. To make a quick version at home, in a bowl, stir together ⅓ cup (3 fl oz/80 ml) heavy (double) cream and ⅔ cup (5 fl oz/150 ml) sour cream. Use the mixture immediately or cover and refrigerate and use within 2 days. Makes 1 cup (8 fl oz/250 ml).

CURED LEMONS

Scrub 6–8 lemons with cool, clear water, quarter them lengthwise and place in a 1-qt (1-l) jar. Add fresh lemon juice to cover and ¾ cup (6 oz/185 g) kosher salt. Cover

tightly and leave at room temperature for 7 days, turning or shaking once or twice daily. Drain off the liquid and add olive oil to cover the lemons fully. Cover and refrigerate; the lemons will be ready to use in 2 weeks and will keep indefinitely. Always keep the lemons submerged in olive oil to avoid spoilage. The lemons may also be sliced and layered in the jar with dried chilies, fresh oregano sprigs and bay leaves; limes may be substituted for the lemons. Cured lemons can be slivered or diced and added to salads, julienned for stir-fry dishes or stuffed into the cavity of a chicken before roasting.

DIRECT-HEAT FIRE FOR GRILLING

This method of grilling is used for foods that cook quickly, such as fish fillets, vegetables and kabobs. Ignite the charcoal briquettes in the normal way. When they are covered by a light gray ash, spread them out to a form a single layer. If using a grill with a cover, cover the food as it cooks.

EPAZOTE

An herb that grows wild in the United States and Mexico, epazote has pointed leaves and a distinctive pungent flavor. It is often used to flavor dried beans as they cook, and is believed to decrease the digestive discomfort some bean eaters experience. Also known as wormseed, Mexican tea and stinkweed, it propagates easily and can spread quickly if not controlled.

FILO

Large paper-thin pastry sheets used in Greek and Middle Eastern cooking. They are sold frozen in boxes in Middle Eastern shops and the frozen food section of well-stocked food stores; thaw in the refrigerator. Filo can be used in German recipes calling for strudel dough. The sheets dry out easily and can become quite brittle; open the package only after you have readied all the other ingredients for the recipe and then keep the sheets well covered with waxed paper or plastic wrap topped with a damp kitchen towel until just before using.

FLOUR TORTILLAS

In addition to the many conventional culinary uses for flour tortillas, Texans use them in a variety of innovative ways: for wrapping German sausages, as pizza crusts, as manicotti wrappers. To make flour tortillas, in a large bowl, combine 3 cups (15 oz/470 g) all-purpose (plain) flour, 1 tablespoon baking powder, 1 teaspoon salt and ¼ cup (2 fl oz/125 ml) vegetable oil. Using a fork, work the mixture together until crumbly. Slowly add 1 cup (8 fl oz/250 ml) warm water (115°F/46°C), stirring with a fork until blended. Knead the mixture in the bowl until a soft dough forms and then shape into a ball. Turn out onto a lightly floured work surface and knead until soft and no longer sticky, about 3 minutes. Cover with a kitchen towel and let rest for 30–60 minutes. Pinch off pieces of the dough and roll between your palms into balls about 1½ in (4 cm) in diameter. As the balls are formed, cover them with a lightly dampened kitchen towel. On a floured work surface, roll out each ball into a round about 6 in (15 cm) in diameter and ⅛ in (3 mm) thick, adding flour as need to prevent sticking. To cook the tortillas, heat a dry griddle or frying pan over medium-high heat. Place the tortillas on the hot pan and cook, turning 3 or 4 times, until lightly browned on both sides, about 1 minute. Transfer to a towel-lined basket, cover lightly and serve warm. Makes 16–18 tortillas. To reheat cooked tortillas, wrap in aluminum foil and place in a 250°F (120°C) oven for 5–6 minutes.

FOUR-PEPPER JELLY

This jelly, the creation of chef Jay McCarthy, is delicious with cream cheese on crackers, is good served as a glaze for hot fried Camembert cheese, can be heated with sautéed shallots and a little brandy and poured over seared peppered steaks, or can be melted and served plain over grilled fresh fruits (apples, peaches, pears, pineapple, mangoes). To make the jelly, stem, discarding the seeds, then cut up ⅓ lb (155 g) fresh jalapeño chili peppers, 1⅛ lb (560 g) fresh serrano chili peppers, ⅔ lb (315 g) fresh anaheim chili peppers and ⅔ lb (315 g) red bell peppers (capsicums). Place in a food processor fitted with the metal blade and add 2 cloves garlic, cut up. Process until finely chopped; do not purée. Transfer to a large, heavy nonreactive pot and add ⅔ cup (5 fl oz/150 ml) cider vinegar, 4 lb (2 kg) sugar and 1 tablespoon minced, peeled fresh ginger (optional). Bring to a boil, stirring constantly. Cook, stirring occasionally, until the mixture begins to thicken, 20–30 minutes. Using a slotted spoon skim off any scum that forms on the surface during cooking. Remove from the heat and stir in 1 bottle (6 fl oz/180 ml) liquid fruit pectin. Return to high heat and cook, stirring occasionally, for 5 minutes. Remove from the heat, quickly ladle into hot, sterilized jelly jars and seal with paraffin (see *paraffin seal*). Store in a cool, dark place. Makes about 6 large jelly jars.

FRESH TOMATO SALSA

In a bowl, stir together 4 ripe tomatoes, finely chopped; 1 small white onion, finely chopped; 4 fresh jalapeño or serrano chili peppers, or more to taste, seeded and finely chopped; 2–3 teaspoons fresh lime or lemon juice; 2–3 tablespoons finely chopped fresh cilantro (fresh coriander); and salt to taste. Let stand for 1–2 hours before serving. Makes about 2 cups (16 fl oz/500 ml). Serve as a condiment to grilled meats, poultry or seafood, enchiladas or tacos, or offer as a dip for tortilla chips.

GUACAMOLE

Every Texas cook has a recipe for guacamole; here is a simple one that is excellent with nearly any dish or can be served as a dip. Hass avocados are the best choice for guacamole, as they have a flavor superior to that of the other common variety, the Fuerte. Cut 1 large ripe avocado in half. Remove and discard the pit and scoop the avocado flesh from the skin into a bowl. Using the back of a fork, mash the avocado and stir in ¼ small white onion, finely chopped; 1–1½ fresh serrano chili peppers, seeded and finely chopped; 1 tablespoon fresh lime juice; and 1 or 2 fresh cilantro (fresh coriander) sprigs, finely chopped. The mixture should be almost smooth. Peel, seed and chop 1 large ripe tomato and add to the guacamole mixture, stirring just until combined. Season to taste with salt. Makes about 1½ cups (12 oz/375 g).

HABANERO CHILI PEPPER
See *chili peppers, fresh and dried*.

HOT-WATER BATH PROCESS
Use this method to kill any microorganisms present in jams, chutneys and other preserves that may cause spoilage and to ensure a good seal. The preserves can then be stored unrefrigerated. To process the preserves, ladle them into sterilized jars to within ½ in (12 mm) of the jar rims, wipe the rims clean, cover with sterilized lids and place on a canning rack or other low rack in a large, deep pan. Add water to cover the jars by several inches and bring the water to a boil. Start timing from when the water is at a full rolling boil and boil for the time indicated in individual recipes, usually 10–20 minutes. Remove the jars from the pan and let cool for 12 hours, then check for a good seal; the lids should be slightly concave. Store in a cool, dark place.

INDIRECT-HEAT FIRE FOR GRILLING
To grill foods, such as chickens, turkeys, briskets and so on, by indirect heat, ignite the charcoal briquettes in the normal way in a kettle grill. Then, when the briquettes are covered with pale gray ash, push them into a pile on either side of the kettle and place a large disposable aluminum pan between the piles. Set the food to be grilled on the grill rack over the pan to catch any drippings, cover the kettle with a lid and adjust the vents and grill as directed. If using a gas grill, preheat all the burners, then turn off the center burner before adding the food to be grilled.

JALAPEÑO CHILI PEPPER
See *chili peppers, fresh and dried*.

JULIENNE
To cut foods—vegetables, cheeses, fruits, meats—into small, thin, uniform strips for use in salads, stir-fries and other dishes and as a garnish.

MASA HARINA
Treated and ground dried corn that, when combined with water, is used for making tamales and tortillas. *Masa harina* is sold in bags in Mexican markets and well-stocked food stores.

MEXICAN MARIGOLD MINT
The flavor of this herb is similar to that of tarragon, but with a subtle anise accent. Both the blossoms and the leaves are

edible. Look for this distinctive mint in Mexican markets, or substitute regular mint.

MEXICAN OREGANO
Small, highly aromatic leaves that are used primarily for seasoning soups and sauces. Use fresh leaves or whole dried ones for the best flavor. Mexican oregano is more pungent than Mediterranean varieties; marjoram can be substituted.

OLIVE TAPENADE
In a food processor fitted with the metal blade, combine 1 cup (5 oz/155 g) pitted, sharply flavored black olives, 1 cup (5 oz/155 g) pitted, sharply flavored green olives, 1 tablespoon finely chopped pickled jalapeños (see separate entry), 1 tablespoon finely chopped garlic, 2 tablespoons well-drained capers, 2 tablespoons balsamic vinegar and 2 tablespoons dried oregano. Process until finely chopped. With the motor running, add 4–6 tablespoons (2–3 fl oz/60–90 ml) olive oil in a thin, steady stream and process until thick. Add only as much oil as needed to form a thick paste; do not overprocess, as a little texture is desirable. Season with freshly ground pepper and store in a covered jar in the refrigerator for 1–2 weeks. Makes about 2½ cups (20 fl oz/625 ml). Use the tapenade as a sandwich spread, on toasts as an hors d'oeuvre, in dips and as a stuffing beneath the skin of chicken breasts.

PARAFFIN SEAL
This method of sealing is used for ensuring a good seal on straight-sided jars filled with hot jelly. Ladle the hot jelly into hot, sterilized jars to within ¼ in (6 mm) of the jar rims, wipe the rims clean and let the jelly cool. Melt household paraffin in a heatproof glass pitcher placed over boiling water. Pour a layer of paraffin ⅛ in (3 mm) thick over the surface of the jelly and tilt and rotate the jar so that the paraffin forms a tight seal against the jar sides. Allow the paraffin to set, then pour on a second layer of the same thickness and allow it to set. Store in a cool, dark place.

PARBOIL
To cook foods partially in boiling water or other liquid. Usually foods are about half-cooked and then are finished later by another cooking method, such as stir-frying or sautéing.

PASILLA CHILI PEPPER
See *chili peppers, fresh and dried.*

PEPPER JACK CHEESE
Monterey Jack or *asadero* (see separate entry) cheese to which minced jalapeño chili peppers have been added. Available in most food stores.

PICKLED *NOPALITOS*
Nopales (see *cactus paddles*) that have been diced or cut into strips and packed in vinegar in jars. Sold in Mexican markets and well-stocked food stores.

PICO DE GALLO
This popular mixture, which translates as "beak of the rooster," is regularly found on Texas tables. It is spooned over everything from eggs to steak and is an excellent dip for tortilla chips. In El Paso, guero (yellow) chili peppers are used in place of the serranos or jalapeños. To make *pico de gallo,* in a bowl, combine 1 white onion, chopped; 2 ripe tomatoes, chopped; 2–3 fresh serrano or jalapeño chili peppers, seeded, if desired, and chopped; finely chopped fresh cilantro (fresh coriander) to taste; and a dash of fresh lemon or lime juice. Stir the mixture well. Makes about 2 cups (16 fl oz/500 ml).

PINK PEPPERBERRIES
Pungent rose-colored berries that resemble peppercorns but are unrelated. Sold in jars in specialty-food stores.

POBLANO CHILI PEPPER
See *chili peppers, fresh and dried.*

POLENTA
The term for ground Italian cornmeal, which is cooked in water or other liquid to make a thick mush of the same name. The more available yellow cornmeal (see separate entry) can be substituted.

PRICKLY PEAR
The red, pear-shaped fruit of the prickly pear *(nopal)* cactus has a rich, sweet flavor. Also known as cactus pears and *tunas*, the fruits are always peeled and seeded before eating. The flesh may also be puréed and then strained of its seeds before using as a sauce. See also *cactus paddles.*

PUMPKIN SEEDS
Dark green seeds from the heart of the pumpkin. They are most commonly sold hulled; when toasted and salted, they make a tasty snack. The seeds are also a good addition to salads and other dishes and are often ground for adding to sauces. Sold in Latin American markets and well-stocked food stores.

QUESO FRESCO
Also sometimes called *ranchero seco,* this Mexican cheese is similar to farmer's cheese but slightly saltier. White Cheddar or feta cheese may be substituted.

RED CORN TORTILLAS
Tortillas that have red food coloring added to the dough. They are especially popular during Christmastime. See also *corn tortillas.*

RED PEPPER FLAKES
See *chili peppers, fresh and dried.*

REFRIED BEANS
These mildly flavored beans make a good accompaniment to spicy Tex-Mex dishes. You may also spice up the beans themselves by adding chopped fresh jalapeño chili peppers to taste. To make refried beans *(frijoles refritos),* in a large cast-iron frying pan over medium heat, melt 6 tablespoons

(3 oz/90 g) bacon drippings, lard or butter. Add 6 cups (2⅔ lb/1.4 kg) drained, cooked pinto beans (see *beans, dried*) and, using a fork or potato masher, mash the beans to form a coarse purée; continue to cook until heated through, adding liquid from cooking the beans as needed to form a slightly creamy consistency. Transfer to a warmed serving dish and top with ¼ cup crumbled *queso fresco* (see separate entry), if desired. Serve at once. Serves 6.

ROASTED GARLIC
Preheat an oven to 425°F (220°C). Using a sharp knife, cut off the top one-third of each whole garlic head and remove the loose papery skins; do not separate the cloves and be sure to leave the tight-fitting skins intact. Wrap tightly in aluminum foil and place in a small baking dish. Bake until the garlic is soft when pierced with the tip of a knife, about 45 minutes. Remove from the oven and discard the foil. To use, squeeze the soft garlic pulp free of the skins.

ROASTING PEPPERS
Many recipes call for roasting chili peppers or bell peppers (capsicums) in order to remove their skins and to heighten their flavors. To roast peppers, place them on a baking sheet and slip under a preheated broiler (griller), place on a grill rack over a charcoal fire or spear them, one at a time, on a fork and hold over an open flame. Turn the peppers as needed to blacken and blister the skins evenly on all sides, then enclose in a paper or plastic bag or cover with a kitchen towel and let sweat until cool enough to handle, about 10 minutes. Using your fingertips or a small knife, peel off the blackened skin. Remove the stem and seeds and cut as directed in individual recipes. Peeled, roasted peppers can be refrigerated for up to 3 days.

SERRANO CHILI PEPPERS
See *chili peppers, fresh and dried.*

SOUTH TEXAS CRAB GRASS
Preheat an oven to 325°F (165°C). In a small ovenproof dish, stir together 2 tablespoons chili powder and 1 teaspoon ground cumin and place in the oven. Heat, stirring occasionally, until toasted, about 5 minutes. Remove from the oven and set aside. Reduce the oven temperature to 250°F (120°C). Cut 12-day-old corn tortillas into strips ¼ in (6 mm) wide. Pour vegetable oil into a deep-fat fryer or deep frying pan to a depth of 1½–2 in (4–5 cm) and heat to 360°F (185°C), or until a tiny piece of tortilla begins to brown within moments of being dropped in the oil. Working in batches, add the tortilla strips and fry until crisp and golden, 30–60 seconds. Using a slotted spoon, transfer to paper towels to drain. When all of the strips have been fried, spread them on a baking sheet and sprinkle with the chili powder mixture and cayenne pepper and salt to taste. Place

in the oven and bake until very crisp, about 5 minutes. Let cool completely and store in an airtight container at room temperature for up to 3 days. Use the strips as a garnish for soups, as a "nest" for stir-fried vegetables or stuffed chilies, or as an accompaniment to steak. The strips may also be prepared without any seasoning.

TEXAS 1015 SUPERSWEET ONIONS
Large, white onion with a very sweet flavor. This Texas variety is excellent roasted whole or sliced and used for onion rings.

TEX'S ANCHO PASTE
Stem and discard the seeds of ½ lb (250 g) dried ancho chili peppers and 2 small dried red chili peppers. Place the chilies in a large saucepan and add 5 ripe tomatoes, seeded and chopped; 1 large yellow onion, chopped; 3 or 4 cloves garlic; 8 cups (64 fl oz/2 l) water; and 1 tablespoon salt. Bring to a boil over high heat, reduce the heat to low and simmer, uncovered, until the chilies are very soft, 1½–2 hours. Remove from the heat and let cool. Transfer to a blender or to a food processor fitted with the metal blade and process until smooth. If the purée is thin, transfer to a saucepan over low heat and cook, uncovered, until thickened. Makes about 3 cups (24 fl oz/750 ml). Cover and store in the refrigerator for up to 3 weeks. Use as a substitute for chili powder in chili con carne, to flavor enchiladas and soups and as a basting sauce for grilled chicken breasts.

TOASTING NUTS
To toast pecans, walnuts, almonds or pine nuts, place them in a heavy, dry frying pan over medium-low heat. Stir and toss gently until lightly browned and fragrant. The pine nuts burn easily, so watch them closely. Alternatively, place on a baking sheet in a 350°F (180°C) oven and toast, stirring occasionally, until browned and fragrant, 8–10 minutes.

TOMATILLOS
A member of the gooseberry family, the tomatillo resembles a small green tomato encased in a papery, light brown husk. To use, peel away the husks and rinse well to remove any stickiness. Available fresh and canned, tomatillos can be used raw or cooked and are common additions to sauces, enchiladas and other dishes. Look for them in Latin American markets and well-stocked food stores.

TORTILLA CHIPS
These small triangles, made from corn tortillas, are used for dipping and as a garnish. To make tortilla chips, cut each corn tortilla into 6 wedges, or cut out shapes—cacti, arrows, stars—as desired. In a deep frying pan, pour in corn oil or other vegetable oil to a depth of 1½–2 in (4–5 cm) and heat to 360°F (185°C), or until a tiny piece of tortilla begins to brown within moments of being dropped in the oil. Working in batches, add the tortilla pieces and fry until crisp and golden, 30–60 seconds. Using a slotted spoon, transfer to paper towels to drain. Sprinkle with salt, if desired, and store in an airtight container at room temperature for up to 2–3 days.

ILLUSTRATION GUIDE

WHOOPING CRANE

Each fall, small flocks of whooping cranes head south from their nesting grounds in Canada, trumpeting their character-  istic call—*ker-loo ker-lee-loo*. The cranes migrate over 2,500 miles (4,000 kilometers) to their primary wintering grounds at the Aransas National Wildlife Refuge on the central Gulf Coast of Texas. Standing over 5 feet (150 centimeters) high, the crane is the tallest North American bird. The whooping crane population, once so low that the species was close to extinction, has grown slowly from fourteen cranes in the late 1940s to over one hundred fifty migrating and nonmigrating cranes today. Despite this improvement, the species is still classified as endangered. (See half title.)

BLACK-TAILED JACKRABBIT

The hares known as jackrabbits were originally called jackass rabbits after their very long ears, from 3 to 5 inches (7.5 to 12.5 centimeters) tall. This particular jackrabbit, the most abundant in the western United States, has a tail  topped by a black stripe extending slightly onto the animal's mottled buff-gray body. The black-tailed jackrabbit jumps 5 to 10 feet (150 to 300 centimeters) with each hop. A fleeing jackrabbit will stop to thump the ground with a hind foot to warn other jacks of the presence of a coyote or other potential threat. (See page 13.)

WESTERN DIAMONDBACK RATTLESNAKE

 Like all rattlers, the western diamondback vibrates its rattle to warn intruders and is often heard before it is seen. The rattle consists of interlocking scaly segments unique to this family of serpents. A new segment is added to the rattle when the snake sheds its skin. From 30 to over 80 inches (75 to over 200 centimeters) in length, the western diamondback is the longest rattler in the western United States and is found throughout the western part of Texas from the plains to the mountains. The name of the snake refers to the diamond or hexagonal pattern on its gray, brown or pinkish back. (See page 27.)

BLUE MARLIN

One of the most prized game fishes in North America, the blue marlin of the Atlantic inhabits the warm waters of the Gulf of Mex  ico. Fully grown marlin average 11 feet (330 centimeters) in length, and large marlin reach 14 feet (420 centimeters) and 1,800 pounds (820 kilograms). Named for the bluish bars on its sides, the blue marlin belongs to the billfish family, which are among the fastest-swimming fishes in the world. It can rapidly descend beneath the ocean surface, but customarily feeds at the surface on smaller fish and crustaceans. (See page 61.)

TEXAS HORNED LIZARD

Legends about this Texas native abound—that it is the creation of the devil, that it spits blood from its eyes, that  killing a horned lizard brings bad luck. One of the sources of these beliefs was the sharp spines, including two prominent horns, crowning the back of its head. The horned lizard, now found only in western Texas, lives in open, arid terrain and emerges from its hiding places to feed on ants, beetles and grasshoppers. Once abundant, the 4-inch (10-centimeter) horned lizard is classified by the state of Texas as a threatened species. (See page 97.)

TEXAS LONGHORN

Inextricably linked to the ranching heritage of the Lone Star State, the Texas longhorn descended from a breed of cattle that originated in the Old World.  As the imported stock adapted to its new environment, it became a distinctive breed and in the mid-1800s was given the name Texas longhorn. Over the years, the longhorn developed characteristics that made the breed desirable. They can walk great distances, go a long time without water and fend off predators. After the Civil War, the longhorn became the keystone of the recovering Texas economy. As a result of this vigorous trade, the breed neared extinction in the early 1900s. Reintroduced to Texas and Oklahoma, the longhorn made a successful recovery, and hundreds of thousands now thrive throughout the state. (See page 131.)

RED SWAMP CRAYFISH

 The most common crayfish in Texas and other Gulf Coast states, the red swamp crayfish ambles along the bottom of rivers, bayous and other sources of fresh water. Reaching up to 6 inches (15 centimeters) in length, the crayfish varies in color depending on the environment it inhabits. Where the soil is a red clay, crayfish are a reddish gray. In areas with soils of a different mineral content, they may be grayish tan. When alarmed, the red swamp crayfish rapidly swims backward and hides itself in the aquatic vegetation. (See page 177.)

NINE-BANDED ARMADILLO

The conquistadors, struck by the appearance of this unusual mammal, chose the Spanish word *armado,* meaning "armed," as the root for its name. The armadillo is the only  mammal in North America that wears an armor of thick, bony plates. These scalelike plates cover the animal's head, body and tail. Nine narrow bands, sometimes fewer, in the midsection of the nine-banded armadillo give it enough flexibility so it can curl up in a defensive posture to protect its vulnerable belly. These curious mammals, 24 to 30 inches (60 to 75 centimeters) long, are found throughout Texas in arid or semiarid areas. They live in deep underground tunnels, which they spend most of their waking hours digging and maintaining. (See page 201.)

PHOTOGRAPHY CREDITS

The Publishers would like to thank the following photographers and organizations for permission to reproduce their photographs:

(Abbreviations: t = top, b = bottom)

Reagan Bradshaw 68, 69(t)
Willard Clay 24–25, 28(t), 64, 99, 102(t), 178, 198–99
Bob Daemmrich Photography 20, 35(t), 69(b), 132(t), 207(t)
Lynn Hermann 202(t)
Zigy Kaluzny 23, 132(b), 137
David Muench 21, 63, 176–177, 179
Earl Nottingham 34
Laurence Parent jacket, 22, 26–27, 30–31, 35(b), 58–59, 94–95, 96–97, 203
Robert Parvin 19, 65(b), 136(b)
Photo 20-20/Richard Reynolds 2–3, Photo 20-20/Richard Reynolds 6–7, Photo 20-20/Richard Reynolds 10–11, Photo 20-20/Richard Reynolds 16, Photo 20-20/Richard Reynolds 29, Photo 20-20/Richard Reynolds 65(t), Photo 20-20/Richard Reynolds 98, Photo 20-20/Richard Reynolds 103, Photo 20-20/Richard Reynolds 133, Photo 20-20/Richard Reynolds 174–175, Photo 20-20/Richard Reynolds 206(b)
Stock Market/Gabe Palmer endpapers
Tony Stone Images/Keith Wood 28(b)
Harald Sund 17, 60–61, 62, 102(b), 128–129, 130–131, 136(t), 182, 183(t), 183(b), 200–201, 202(b), 206(t), 207(b)
West Light/Mauritius-E. Gebhardt 14–15

ACKNOWLEDGMENTS

Patsy Swendson acknowledges the following: My deepest love and most sincere gratitude go, with enormous pride, to my daughter Kim Swendson-Cameron for her encouragement, faith, talent and assistance. Thanks also to Anne Dickerson from Weldon Owen Inc. for her patience and perseverance and to E. J. Armstrong for bringing the book so beautifully to life. My appreciation extends to my unwavering support system: Debra Baker, Lin Gee Way Bessey, Katrina Beyer, Michael Bomberg, Paul Cameron, Karen Haram, Carolyn Hatton-Nield, June Hayes, Dottie Hunter, W. Park Kerr, Carolyn Lummus, Fernando de Luna, Jay McCarthy, Sonia Morton, Jim Peyton, Robert Pope, Stephen Pyles and Sandra Sanner. And finally my indebtedness to the many Texans, both native and transplanted, who have been and will always be my constant inspiration.

June Hayes acknowledges the following: My thanks go to my mother Carmen B. Wood, my daughter Janet and her sons and husband for their support and encouragement. My gratitude also extends to the Texas Department of Agriculture and its Taste of Texas participants, wine makers and food critic friends who responded to requests for industry updates and trends; to Naomi Shihab Nye, award-winning poet, for permission to include a passage from "At the Seven-Mile Ranch, Comstock, Texas"; and to the editors who guided this project to its beautiful completion.

Weldon Owen thanks the following: Jane Fraser, Dawn Low, Richard VanOosterhout, Angela Williams, John Bull, Jonette Banzon, Keith Wong, Mick Bagnato, Annalise Ophelian, Anne Greensall, Wendely Harvey, Tori Ritchie, Patty Hill, Claire Sanchez, Carlos Rojas, Sigrid Chase, Laurie Wertz, Janique Gascoine, Jim Obata, Jennifer Hauser, Jennifer Mullins and Stephani Grant.

INDEX